Praise for the First Edition

"I sure wish I had this book ten years ago. Some might think that I don't need any Java books, but I need this one."

—James Gosling, fellow and vice president, Sun Microsystems, Inc., and inventor of the Java programming language

"An excellent book, crammed with good advice on using the Java programming language and object-oriented programming in general."

—Gilad Bracha, distinguished engineer, Cadence Design Systems, and coauthor of *The Java™ Language Specification, Third Edition* (Addison-Wesley, 2005)

"10/10—anyone aspiring to write good Java code that others will appreciate reading and maintaining should be required to own a copy of this book. This is one of those rare books where the information won't become obsolete with subsequent releases of the JDK library."

—Peter Tran, bartender, JavaRanch.com

"The best Java book yet written.... Really great; very readable and eminently useful. I can't say enough good things about this book. At JavaOne 2001, James Gosling said, 'Go buy this book!' I'm glad I did, and I couldn't agree more."

—Keith Edwards, senior member of research staff, Computer Science Lab at the Palo Alto Research Center (PARC), and author of *Core JINI* (Prentice Hall, 2000)

"This is a truly excellent book done by the guy who designed several of the better recent Java platform APIs (including the Collections API)."

—James Clark, technical lead of the XML Working Group during the creation of the XML 1.0 Recommendation; editor of the XPath and XSLT Recommendations

"Great content. Analogous to Scott Meyers's classic *Effective C++*. If you know the basics of Java, this has to be your next book."

—Gary K. Evans, OO mentor and consultant, Evanetics, Inc.

"In my estimation, no more than one good programming book appears per year (and there are certainly many years that saw none): Knuth's trilogy, the K&R White Book, Kernighan and Plauger's *Software Tools*... Bloch's book fits in well with this august company. Get it."

—Andrew Binstock, *Software Development Times*, August 15, 2001

"This is a superb book. It clearly covers many of the language/platform subtleties and trickery you need to learn to become a real Java master."

—Victor Wiewiorowski, vice president development and code quality manager, ValueCommerce Co., Tokyo, Japan

"I like books that under-promise in their titles and over-deliver in their contents. This book has 57 items of programming advice that are well chosen. Each item reveals a clear, deep grasp of the language. Each one illustrates in simple, practical terms the limits of programming on intuition alone, or taking the most direct path to a solution without fully understanding what the language offers."

—Michael Ernest, Inkling Research, Inc.

"Every bit of this book is essential for Java designers. Reading this book before you start delivering products can easily repay its cost thousands of times."

—Richard Mateosian, IEEE micro, July/August 2002 (vol. 22, no. 4)

"Great how-to resource for the experienced developer."

—John Zukowski, author of numerous Java books

"I picked this book up two weeks ago and can safely say I learned more about the Java language in three days of reading than I did in three months of study! An excellent book and a welcome addition to my Java library."

—Jane Griscti, I/T advisory specialist

Effective Java™

Second Edition

Effective Java™

Second Edition

Joshua Bloch

✦Addison-Wesley

Upper Saddle River, NJ • Boston • Indianapolis • San Francisco
New York • Toronto • Montreal London • Munich • Paris • Madrid
Capetown • Sydney • Tokyo • Singapore • Mexico City

The publisher offers excellent discounts on this book when ordered in quantity for bulk purchases or special sales, which may include electronic versions and/or custom covers and content particular to your business, training goals, marketing focus, and branding interests. For more information, please contact:

U.S. Corporate and Government Sales
(800) 382-3419
corpsales@pearsontechgroup.com

For sales outside the United States please contact:

International Sales
international@pearsoned.com

 This Book Is Safari Enabled

The Safari® Enabled icon on the cover of your favorite technology book means the book is available through Safari Bookshelf. When you buy this book, you get free access to the online edition for 45 days.

Safari Bookshelf is an electronic reference library that lets you easily search thousands of technical books, find code samples, download chapters, and access technical information whenever and wherever you need it.

To gain 45-day Safari Enabled access to this book:
- Go to www.informit.com/onlineedition
- Complete the brief registration form
- Enter the coupon code I1DV-B4HC-5AP3-6WCL-R4MC

If you have difficulty registering on Safari Bookshelf or accessing the online edition, please e-mail customer-service@safaribooksonline.com.

Visit us on the Web: informit.com/aw

Library of Congress Control Number: 2008926278

Copyright © 2008 Sun Microsystems, Inc.
4150 Network Circle,
Santa Clara, California 95054 U.S.A.

All rights reserved. Printed in the United States of America. This publication is protected by copyright, and permission must be obtained from the publisher prior to any prohibited reproduction, storage in a retrieval system, or transmission in any form or by any means, electronic, mechanical, photocopying, recording, or likewise. For information regarding permissions, write to:

Pearson Education, Inc.
Rights and Contracts Department
501 Boylston Street, Suite 900
Boston, MA 02116
Fax: (617) 671-3447

ISBN-13: 978-0-321-35668-0
ISBN-10: 0-321-35668-3

Text printed in the United States on recycled paper at Courier in Westford, Massachusetts.
Eleventh printing, March 2012

To my family: Cindy, Tim, and Matt

Contents

Foreword

$\mathbf{I}$F a colleague were to say to you, "Spouse of me this night today manufactures the unusual meal in a home. You will join?" three things would likely cross your mind: third, that you had been invited to dinner; second, that English was not your colleague's first language; and first, a good deal of puzzlement.

If you have ever studied a second language yourself and then tried to use it outside the classroom, you know that there are three things you must master: how the language is structured (grammar), how to name things you want to talk about (vocabulary), and the customary and effective ways to say everyday things (usage). Too often only the first two are covered in the classroom, and you find native speakers constantly suppressing their laughter as you try to make yourself understood.

It is much the same with a programming language. You need to understand the core language: is it algorithmic, functional, object-oriented? You need to know the vocabulary: what data structures, operations, and facilities are provided by the standard libraries? And you need to be familiar with the customary and effective ways to structure your code. Books about programming languages often cover only the first two, or discuss usage only spottily. Maybe that's because the first two are in some ways easier to write about. Grammar and vocabulary are properties of the language alone, but usage is characteristic of a community that uses it.

The Java programming language, for example, is object-oriented with single inheritance and supports an imperative (statement-oriented) coding style within each method. The libraries address graphic display support, networking, distributed computing, and security. But how is the language best put to use in practice?

There is another point. Programs, unlike spoken sentences and unlike most books and magazines, are likely to be changed over time. It's typically not enough to produce code that operates effectively and is readily understood by other persons; one must also organize the code so that it is easy to modify. There may be ten ways to write code for some task T. Of those ten ways, seven will be awkward, inefficient, or puzzling. Of the other three, which is most likely to be similar to the code needed for the task T' in next year's software release?

There are numerous books from which you can learn the grammar of the Java Programming Language, including *The Java™ Programming Language* by Arnold, Gosling, and Holmes [Arnold05] or *The Java™ Language Specification* by Gosling, Joy, yours truly, and Bracha [JLS]. Likewise, there are dozens of books on the libraries and APIs associated with the Java programming language.

This book addresses your third need: customary and effective usage. Joshua Bloch has spent years extending, implementing, and using the Java programming language at Sun Microsystems; he has also read a lot of other people's code, including mine. Here he offers good advice, systematically organized, on how to structure your code so that it works well, so that other people can understand it, so that future modifications and improvements are less likely to cause headaches—perhaps, even, so that your programs will be pleasant, elegant, and graceful.

Guy L. Steele Jr.
Burlington, Massachusetts
April 2001

Preface

Preface to the Second Edition

A lot has happened to the Java platform since I wrote the first edition of this book in 2001, and it's high time for a second edition. The most significant set of changes was the addition of generics, enum types, annotations, autoboxing, and the for-each loop in Java 5. A close second was the addition of the new concurrency library, `java.util.concurrent`, also released in Java 5. With Gilad Bracha, I had the good fortune to lead the teams that designed the new language features. I also had the good fortune to serve on the team that designed and developed the concurrency library, which was led by Doug Lea.

The other big change in the platform is the widespread adoption of modern Integrated Development Environments (IDEs), such as Eclipse, IntelliJ IDEA, and NetBeans, and of static analysis tools, such as FindBugs. While I have not been involved in these efforts, I've benefited from them immensely and learned how they affect the Java development experience.

In 2004, I moved from Sun to Google, but I've continued my involvement in the development of the Java platform over the past four years, contributing to the concurrency and collections APIs through the good offices of Google and the Java Community Process. I've also had the pleasure of using the Java platform to develop libraries for use within Google. Now I know what it feels like to be a user.

As was the case in 2001 when I wrote the first edition, my primary goal is to share my experience with you so that you can imitate my successes while avoiding my failures. The new material continues to make liberal use of real-world examples from the Java platform libraries.

The first edition succeeded beyond my wildest expectations, and I've done my best to stay true to its spirit while covering all of the new material that was required to bring the book up to date. It was inevitable that the book would grow, and grow it did, from fifty-seven items to seventy-eight. Not only did I add twenty-three items, but I thoroughly revised all the original material and retired a few items whose better days had passed. In the Appendix, you can see how the material in this edition relates to the material in the first edition.

In the Preface to the First Edition, I wrote that the Java programming language and its libraries were immensely conducive to quality and productivity, and a joy to work with. The changes in releases 5 and 6 have taken a good thing and made it better. The platform is much bigger now than it was in 2001 and more complex, but once you learn the patterns and idioms for using the new features, they make your programs better and your life easier. I hope this edition captures my continued enthusiasm for the platform and helps make your use of the platform and its new features more effective and enjoyable.

San Jose, California
April 2008

Preface to the First Edition

In 1996 I pulled up stakes and headed west to work for JavaSoft, as it was then known, because it was clear that that was where the action was. In the intervening five years I've served as Java platform libraries architect. I've designed, implemented, and maintained many of the libraries and served as a consultant for many others. Presiding over these libraries as the Java platform matured was a once-in-a-lifetime opportunity. It is no exaggeration to say that I had the privilege to work with some of the great software engineers of our generation. In the process, I learned a lot about the Java programming language—what works, what doesn't, and how to use the language and its libraries to best effect.

This book is my attempt to share my experience with you so that you can imitate my successes while avoiding my failures. I borrowed the format from Scott Meyers's *Effective C++* [Meyers98], which consists of fifty items, each conveying one specific rule for improving your programs and designs. I found the format to be singularly effective, and I hope you do too.

In many cases, I took the liberty of illustrating the items with real-world examples from the Java platform libraries. When describing something that could have been done better, I tried to pick on code that I wrote myself, but occasionally I pick on something written by a colleague. I sincerely apologize if, despite my best efforts, I've offended anyone. Negative examples are cited not to cast blame but in the spirit of cooperation, so that all of us can benefit from the experience of those who've gone before.

While this book is not targeted solely at developers of reusable components, it is inevitably colored by my experience writing such components over the past two decades. I naturally think in terms of exported APIs (Application Programming Interfaces), and I encourage you to do likewise. Even if you aren't developing reusable components, thinking in these terms tends to improve the quality of the software you write. Furthermore, it's not uncommon to write a reusable component without knowing it: You write something useful, share it with your buddy across the hall, and before long you have half a dozen users. At this point, you no longer have the flexibility to change the API at will and are thankful for all the effort that you put into designing the API when you first wrote the software.

My focus on API design may seem a bit unnatural to devotees of the new lightweight software development methodologies, such as *Extreme Programming* [Beck99]. These methodologies emphasize writing the simplest program that could possibly work. If you're using one of these methodologies, you'll find that a focus on API design serves you well in the *refactoring* process. The fundamental goals of refactoring are the improvement of system structure and the avoidance of code duplication. These goals are impossible to achieve in the absence of well-designed APIs for the components of the system.

No language is perfect, but some are excellent. I have found the Java programming language and its libraries to be immensely conducive to quality and productivity, and a joy to work with. I hope this book captures my enthusiasm and helps make your use of the language more effective and enjoyable.

Cupertino, California
April 2001

Acknowledgments

Acknowledgments for the Second Edition

I thank the readers of the first edition of this book for giving it such a kind and enthusiastic reception, for taking its ideas to heart, and for letting me know what a positive influence it had on them and their work. I thank the many professors who used the book in their courses, and the many engineering teams that adopted it.

I thank the whole team at Addison-Wesley for their kindness, professionalism, patience, and grace under pressure. Through it all, my editor Greg Doench remained unflappable: a fine editor and a perfect gentleman. My production manager, Julie Nahil, was everything that a production manager should be: diligent, prompt, organized, and friendly. My copy editor, Barbara Wood, was meticulous and tasteful.

I have once again been blessed with the best team of reviewers imaginable, and I give my sincerest thanks to each of them. The core team, who reviewed every chapter, consisted of Lexi Baugher, Cindy Bloch, Beth Bottos, Joe Bowbeer, Brian Goetz, Tim Halloran, Brian Kernighan, Rob Konigsberg, Tim Peierls, Bill Pugh, Yoshiki Shibata, Peter Stout, Peter Weinberger, and Frank Yellin. Other reviewers included Pablo Bellver, Dan Bloch, Dan Bornstein, Kevin Bourrillion, Martin Buchholz, Joe Darcy, Neal Gafter, Laurence Gonsalves, Aaron Greenhouse, Barry Hayes, Peter Jones, Angelika Langer, Doug Lea, Bob Lee, Jeremy Manson, Tom May, Mike McCloskey, Andriy Tereshchenko, and Paul Tyma. Again, these reviewers made numerous suggestions that led to great improvements in this book and saved me from many embarrassments. And again, any remaining embarrassments are my responsibility.

I give special thanks to Doug Lea and Tim Peierls, who served as sounding boards for many of the ideas in this book. Doug and Tim were unfailingly generous with their time and knowledge.

I thank my manager at Google, Prabha Krishna, for her continued support and encouragement.

Finally, I thank my wife, Cindy Bloch, for encouraging me to write, for reading each item in raw form, for helping me with Framemaker, for writing the index, and for putting up with me while I wrote.

Acknowledgments for the First Edition

I thank Patrick Chan for suggesting that I write this book and for pitching the idea to Lisa Friendly, the series managing editor; Tim Lindholm, the series technical editor; and Mike Hendrickson, executive editor of Addison-Wesley. I thank Lisa, Tim, and Mike for encouraging me to pursue the project and for their superhuman patience and unyielding faith that I would someday write this book.

I thank James Gosling and his original team for giving me something great to write about, and I thank the many Java platform engineers who followed in James's footsteps. In particular, I thank my colleagues in Sun's Java Platform Tools and Libraries Group for their insights, their encouragement, and their support. The team consists of Andrew Bennett, Joe Darcy, Neal Gafter, Iris Garcia, Konstantin Kladko, Ian Little, Mike McCloskey, and Mark Reinhold. Former members include Zhenghua Li, Bill Maddox, and Naveen Sanjeeva.

I thank my manager, Andrew Bennett, and my director, Larry Abrahams, for lending their full and enthusiastic support to this project. I thank Rich Green, the VP of Engineering at Java Software, for providing an environment where engineers are free to think creatively and to publish their work.

I have been blessed with the best team of reviewers imaginable, and I give my sincerest thanks to each of them: Andrew Bennett, Cindy Bloch, Dan Bloch, Beth Bottos, Joe Bowbeer, Gilad Bracha, Mary Campione, Joe Darcy, David Eckhardt, Joe Fialli, Lisa Friendly, James Gosling, Peter Haggar, David Holmes, Brian Kernighan, Konstantin Kladko, Doug Lea, Zhenghua Li, Tim Lindholm, Mike McCloskey, Tim Peierls, Mark Reinhold, Ken Russell, Bill Shannon, Peter Stout, Phil Wadler, and two anonymous reviewers. They made numerous suggestions that led to great improvements in this book and saved me from many embarrassments. Any remaining embarrassments are my responsibility.

Numerous colleagues, inside and outside Sun, participated in technical discussions that improved the quality of this book. Among others, Ben Gomes, Steffen Grarup, Peter Kessler, Richard Roda, John Rose, and David Stoutamire contributed useful insights. A special thanks is due Doug Lea, who served as a sounding board for many of the ideas in this book. Doug has been unfailingly generous with his time and his knowledge.

I thank Julie Dinicola, Jacqui Doucette, Mike Hendrickson, Heather Olszyk, Tracy Russ, and the whole team at Addison-Wesley for their support and professionalism. Even under an impossibly tight schedule, they were always friendly and accommodating.

I thank Guy Steele for writing the Foreword. I am honored that he chose to participate in this project.

Finally, I thank my wife, Cindy Bloch, for encouraging and occasionally threatening me to write this book, for reading each item in its raw form, for helping me with Framemaker, for writing the index, and for putting up with me while I wrote.

CHAPTER 1

Introduction

THIS book is designed to help you make the most effective use of the Java™ programming language and its fundamental libraries, java.lang, java.util, and, to a lesser extent, java.util.concurrent and java.io. The book discusses other libraries from time to time, but it does not cover graphical user interface programming, enterprise APIs, or mobile devices.

This book consists of seventy-eight items, each of which conveys one rule. The rules capture practices generally held to be beneficial by the best and most experienced programmers. The items are loosely grouped into ten chapters, each concerning one broad aspect of software design. The book is not intended to be read from cover to cover: each item stands on its own, more or less. The items are heavily cross-referenced so you can easily plot your own course through the book.

Many new features were added to the platform in Java 5 (release 1.5). Most of the items in this book use these features in some way. The following table shows you where to go for primary coverage of these features:

Feature	Chapter or Item
Generics	Chapter 5
Enums	Items 30–34
Annotations	Items 35–37
For-each loop	Item 46
Autoboxing	Items 40, 49
Varargs	Item 42
Static import	Item 19
java.util.concurrent	Items 68, 69

Most items are illustrated with program examples. A key feature of this book is that it contains code examples illustrating many design patterns and idioms. Where appropriate, they are cross-referenced to the standard reference work in this area [Gamma95].

Many items contain one or more program examples illustrating some practice to be avoided. Such examples, sometimes known as *antipatterns,* are clearly labeled with a comment such as "`// Never do this!`" In each case, the item explains why the example is bad and suggests an alternative approach.

This book is not for beginners: it assumes that you are already comfortable with the Java programming language. If you are not, consider one of the many fine introductory texts [Arnold05, Sestoft05]. While the book is designed to be accessible to anyone with a working knowledge of the language, it should provide food for thought even for advanced programmers.

Most of the rules in this book derive from a few fundamental principles. Clarity and simplicity are of paramount importance. The user of a module should never be surprised by its behavior. Modules should be as small as possible but no smaller. (As used in this book, the term *module* refers to any reusable software component, from an individual method to a complex system consisting of multiple packages.) Code should be reused rather than copied. The dependencies between modules should be kept to a minimum. Errors should be detected as soon as possible after they are made, ideally at compile time.

While the rules in this book do not apply 100 percent of the time, they do characterize best programming practices in the great majority of cases. You should not slavishly follow these rules, but violate them only occasionally and with good reason. Learning the art of programming, like most other disciplines, consists of first learning the rules and then learning when to break them.

For the most part, this book is not about performance. It is about writing programs that are clear, correct, usable, robust, flexible, and maintainable. If you can do that, it's usually a relatively simple matter to get the performance you need (Item 55). Some items do discuss performance concerns, and a few of these items provide performance numbers. These numbers, which are introduced with the phrase "On my machine," should be regarded as approximate at best.

For what it's worth, my machine is an aging homebuilt 2.2 GHz dual-core AMD Opteron™ 170 with 2 gigabytes of RAM, running Sun's 1.6_05 release of the Java SE Development Kit (JDK) atop Microsoft Windows® XP Professional SP2. This JDK has two virtual machines, the Java HotSpot™ Client and Server VMs. Performance numbers were measured on the Server VM.

When discussing features of the Java programming language and its libraries, it is sometimes necessary to refer to specific releases. For brevity, this book uses "engineering version numbers" in preference to official release names. This table shows the mapping between release names and engineering version numbers.

Official Release Name	Engineering Version Number
JDK 1.1.x / JRE 1.1.x	1.1
Java 2 Platform, Standard Edition, v 1.2	1.2
Java 2 Platform, Standard Edition, v 1.3	1.3
Java 2 Platform, Standard Edition, v 1.4	1.4
Java 2 Platform, Standard Edition, v 5.0	1.5
Java Platform, Standard Edition 6	1.6

The examples are reasonably complete, but they favor readability over completeness. They freely use classes from the packages `java.util` and `java.io`. In order to compile the examples, you may have to add one or more of these import statements:

```
import java.util.*;
import java.util.concurrent.*;
import java.io.*;
```

Other boilerplate is similarly omitted. The book's Web site, `http://java.sun.com/docs/books/effective`, contains an expanded version of each example, which you can compile and run.

For the most part, this book uses technical terms as they are defined in *The Java Language Specification, Third Edition* [JLS]. A few terms deserve special mention. The language supports four kinds of types: *interfaces* (including *annotations*), *classes* (including *enums*), *arrays*, and *primitives*. The first three are known as *reference types*. Class instances and arrays are *objects*; primitive values are not. A class's *members* consist of its *fields*, *methods*, *member classes*, and *member interfaces*. A method's *signature* consists of its name and the types of its formal parameters; the signature does *not* include the method's return type.

This book uses a few terms differently from the *The Java Language Specification*. Unlike *The Java Language Specification*, this book uses *inheritance* as a synonym for *subclassing*. Instead of using the term inheritance for interfaces, this book simply states that a class *implements* an interface or that one interface *extends* another. To describe the access level that applies when none is specified, this book uses the descriptive term *package-private* instead of the technically correct term *default access* [JLS, 6.6.1].

This book uses a few technical terms that are not defined in *The Java Language Specification*. The term *exported API*, or simply *API*, refers to the classes, interfaces, constructors, members, and serialized forms by which a programmer accesses a class, interface, or package. (The term *API*, which is short for *application programming interface*, is used in preference to the otherwise preferable term *interface* to avoid confusion with the language construct of that name.) A programmer who writes a program that uses an API is referred to as a *user* of the API. A class whose implementation uses an API is a *client* of the API.

Classes, interfaces, constructors, members, and serialized forms are collectively known as *API elements*. An exported API consists of the API elements that are accessible outside of the package that defines the API. These are the API elements that any client can use and the author of the API commits to support. Not coincidentally, they are also the elements for which the Javadoc utility generates documentation in its default mode of operation. Loosely speaking, the exported API of a package consists of the public and protected members and constructors of every public class or interface in the package.

CHAPTER 2

Creating and Destroying Objects

THIS chapter concerns creating and destroying objects: when and how to create them, when and how to avoid creating them, how to ensure they are destroyed in a timely manner, and how to manage any cleanup actions that must precede their destruction.

Item 1: Consider static factory methods instead of constructors

The normal way for a class to allow a client to obtain an instance of itself is to provide a public constructor. There is another technique that should be a part of every programmer's toolkit. A class can provide a public *static factory method*, which is simply a static method that returns an instance of the class. Here's a simple example from Boolean (the boxed primitive class for the primitive type boolean). This method translates a boolean primitive value into a Boolean object reference:

```
public static Boolean valueOf(boolean b) {
    return b ? Boolean.TRUE : Boolean.FALSE;
}
```

Note that a static factory method is not the same as the *Factory Method* pattern from *Design Patterns* [Gamma95, p. 107]. The static factory method described in this item has no direct equivalent in *Design Patterns*.

A class can provide its clients with static factory methods instead of, or in addition to, constructors. Providing a static factory method instead of a public constructor has both advantages and disadvantages.

One advantage of static factory methods is that, unlike constructors, they have names. If the parameters to a constructor do not, in and of themselves, describe the object being returned, a static factory with a well-chosen name is easier to use and the resulting client code easier to read. For example, the constructor

BigInteger(int, int, Random), which returns a BigInteger that is probably prime, would have been better expressed as a static factory method named BigInteger.probablePrime. (This method was eventually added in release 1.4.)

A class can have only a single constructor with a given signature. Programmers have been known to get around this restriction by providing two constructors whose parameter lists differ only in the order of their parameter types. This is a really bad idea. The user of such an API will never be able to remember which constructor is which and will end up calling the wrong one by mistake. People reading code that uses these constructors will not know what the code does without referring to the class documentation.

Because they have names, static factory methods don't share the restriction discussed in the previous paragraph. In cases where a class seems to require multiple constructors with the same signature, replace the constructors with static factory methods and carefully chosen names to highlight their differences.

A second advantage of static factory methods is that, unlike constructors, they are not required to create a new object each time they're invoked. This allows immutable classes (Item 15) to use preconstructed instances, or to cache instances as they're constructed, and dispense them repeatedly to avoid creating unnecessary duplicate objects. The Boolean.valueOf(boolean) method illustrates this technique: it never creates an object. This technique is similar to the *Flyweight* pattern [Gamma95, p. 195]. It can greatly improve performance if equivalent objects are requested often, especially if they are expensive to create.

The ability of static factory methods to return the same object from repeated invocations allows classes to maintain strict control over what instances exist at any time. Classes that do this are said to be *instance-controlled.* There are several reasons to write instance-controlled classes. Instance control allows a class to guarantee that it is a singleton (Item 3) or noninstantiable (Item 4). Also, it allows an immutable class (Item 15) to make the guarantee that no two equal instances exist: a.equals(b) if and only if a==b. If a class makes this guarantee, then its clients can use the == operator instead of the equals(Object) method, which may result in improved performance. Enum types (Item 30) provide this guarantee.

A third advantage of static factory methods is that, unlike constructors, they can return an object of any subtype of their return type. This gives you great flexibility in choosing the class of the returned object.

One application of this flexibility is that an API can return objects without making their classes public. Hiding implementation classes in this fashion leads to a very compact API. This technique lends itself to *interface-based frameworks* (Item 18), where interfaces provide natural return types for static factory methods.

Interfaces can't have static methods, so by convention, static factory methods for an interface named *Type* are put in a noninstantiable class (Item 4) named *Types*.

For example, the Java Collections Framework has thirty-two convenience implementations of its collection interfaces, providing unmodifiable collections, synchronized collections, and the like. Nearly all of these implementations are exported via static factory methods in one noninstantiable class (`java.util.Collections`). The classes of the returned objects are all nonpublic.

The Collections Framework API is much smaller than it would have been had it exported thirty-two separate public classes, one for each convenience implementation. It is not just the bulk of the API that is reduced, but the *conceptual weight*. The user knows that the returned object has precisely the API specified by its interface, so there is no need to read additional class documentation for the implementation classes. Furthermore, using such a static factory method requires the client to refer to the returned object by its interface rather than its implementation class, which is generally good practice (Item 52).

Not only can the class of an object returned by a public static factory method be nonpublic, but the class can vary from invocation to invocation depending on the values of the parameters to the static factory. Any class that is a subtype of the declared return type is permissible. The class of the returned object can also vary from release to release for enhanced software maintainability and performance.

The class `java.util.EnumSet` (Item 32), introduced in release 1.5, has no public constructors, only static factories. They return one of two implementations, depending on the size of the underlying enum type: if it has sixty-four or fewer elements, as most enum types do, the static factories return a `RegularEnumSet` instance, which is backed by a single `long`; if the enum type has sixty-five or more elements, the factories return a `JumboEnumSet` instance, backed by a `long` array.

The existence of these two implementation classes is invisible to clients. If `RegularEnumSet` ceased to offer performance advantages for small enum types, it could be eliminated from a future release with no ill effects. Similarly, a future release could add a third or fourth implementation of `EnumSet` if it proved beneficial for performance. Clients neither know nor care about the class of the object they get back from the factory; they care only that it is some subclass of `EnumSet`.

The class of the object returned by a static factory method need not even exist at the time the class containing the method is written. Such flexible static factory methods form the basis of *service provider frameworks*, such as the Java Database Connectivity API (JDBC). A service provider framework is a system in which multiple service providers implement a service, and the system makes the implementations available to its clients, decoupling them from the implementations.

There are three essential components of a service provider framework: a *service interface*, which providers implement; a *provider registration API*, which the system uses to register implementations, giving clients access to them; and a *service access API*, which clients use to obtain an instance of the service. The service access API typically allows but does not require the client to specify some criteria for choosing a provider. In the absence of such a specification, the API returns an instance of a default implementation. The service access API is the "flexible static factory" that forms the basis of the service provider framework.

An optional fourth component of a service provider framework is a *service provider interface*, which providers implement to create instances of their service implementation. In the absence of a service provider interface, implementations are registered by class name and instantiated reflectively (Item 53). In the case of JDBC, Connection plays the part of the service interface, DriverManager.registerDriver is the provider registration API, DriverManager.getConnection is the service access API, and Driver is the service provider interface.

There are numerous variants of the service provider framework pattern. For example, the service access API can return a richer service interface than the one required of the provider, using the Adapter pattern [Gamma95, p. 139]. Here is a simple implementation with a service provider interface and a default provider:

```
// Service provider framework sketch

// Service interface
public interface Service {
    ... // Service-specific methods go here
}

// Service provider interface
public interface Provider {
    Service newService();
}

// Noninstantiable class for service registration and access
public class Services {
    private Services() { }  // Prevents instantiation (Item 4)

    // Maps service names to services
    private static final Map<String, Provider> providers =
        new ConcurrentHashMap<String, Provider>();
    public static final String DEFAULT_PROVIDER_NAME = "<def>";
```

```java
// Provider registration API
public static void registerDefaultProvider(Provider p) {
    registerProvider(DEFAULT_PROVIDER_NAME, p);
}
public static void registerProvider(String name, Provider p){
    providers.put(name, p);
}

// Service access API
public static Service newInstance() {
    return newInstance(DEFAULT_PROVIDER_NAME);
}
public static Service newInstance(String name) {
    Provider p = providers.get(name);
    if (p == null)
        throw new IllegalArgumentException(
            "No provider registered with name: " + name);
    return p.newService();
}
}
```

A fourth advantage of static factory methods is that they reduce the verbosity of creating parameterized type instances. Unfortunately, you must specify the type parameters when you invoke the constructor of a parameterized class even if they're obvious from context. This typically requires you to provide the type parameters twice in quick succession:

```java
Map<String, List<String>> m =
    new HashMap<String, List<String>>();
```

This redundant specification quickly becomes painful as the length and complexity of the type parameters increase. With static factories, however, the compiler can figure out the type parameters for you. This is known as *type inference*. For example, suppose that HashMap provided this *generic static factory* (Item 27):

```java
public static <K, V> HashMap<K, V> newInstance() {
    return new HashMap<K, V>();
}
```

Then you could replace the wordy declaration above with this succinct alternative:

```java
Map<String, List<String>> m = HashMap.newInstance();
```

Someday the language may perform this sort of type inference on constructor invocations as well as method invocations, but as of release 1.6, it does not.

Unfortunately, the standard collection implementations such as HashMap do not have factory methods as of release 1.6, but you can put these methods in your own utility class. More importantly, you can provide such static factories in your own parameterized classes.

The main disadvantage of providing only static factory methods is that classes without public or protected constructors cannot be subclassed. The same is true for nonpublic classes returned by public static factories. For example, it is impossible to subclass any of the convenience implementation classes in the Collections Framework. Arguably this can be a blessing in disguise, as it encourages programmers to use composition instead of inheritance (Item 16).

A second disadvantage of static factory methods is that they are not readily distinguishable from other static methods. They do not stand out in API documentation in the way that constructors do, so it can be difficult to figure out how to instantiate a class that provides static factory methods instead of constructors. The Javadoc tool may someday draw attention to static factory methods. In the meantime, you can reduce this disadvantage by drawing attention to static factories in class or interface comments, and by adhering to common naming conventions. Here are some common names for static factory methods:

- valueOf—Returns an instance that has, loosely speaking, the same value as its parameters. Such static factories are effectively type-conversion methods.

- of—A concise alternative to valueOf, popularized by EnumSet (Item 32).

- getInstance—Returns an instance that is described by the parameters but cannot be said to have the same value. In the case of a singleton, getInstance takes no parameters and returns the sole instance.

- newInstance—Like getInstance, except that newInstance guarantees that each instance returned is distinct from all others.

- get*Type*—Like getInstance, but used when the factory method is in a different class. *Type* indicates the type of object returned by the factory method.

- new*Type*—Like newInstance, but used when the factory method is in a different class. *Type* indicates the type of object returned by the factory method.

In summary, static factory methods and public constructors both have their uses, and it pays to understand their relative merits. Often static factories are preferable, so avoid the reflex to provide public constructors without first considering static factories.

Item 2:   Consider a builder when faced with many constructor parameters

Static factories and constructors share a limitation: they do not scale well to large numbers of optional parameters. Consider the case of a class representing the Nutrition Facts label that appears on packaged foods. These labels have a few required fields—serving size, servings per container, and calories per serving—and over twenty optional fields—total fat, saturated fat, trans fat, cholesterol, sodium, and so on. Most products have nonzero values for only a few of these optional fields.

What sort of constructors or static factories should you write for such a class? Traditionally, programmers have used the *telescoping constructor* pattern, in which you provide a constructor with only the required parameters, another with a single optional parameter, a third with two optional parameters, and so on, culminating in a constructor with all the optional parameters. Here's how it looks in practice. For brevity's sake, only four optional fields are shown:

```java
// Telescoping constructor pattern - does not scale well!
public class NutritionFacts {
    private final int servingSize;  // (mL)            required
    private final int servings;     // (per container) required
    private final int calories;     //                 optional
    private final int fat;          // (g)             optional
    private final int sodium;       // (mg)            optional
    private final int carbohydrate; // (g)             optional

    public NutritionFacts(int servingSize, int servings) {
        this(servingSize, servings, 0);
    }

    public NutritionFacts(int servingSize, int servings,
            int calories) {
        this(servingSize, servings, calories, 0);
    }

    public NutritionFacts(int servingSize, int servings,
            int calories, int fat) {
        this(servingSize, servings, calories, fat, 0);
    }

    public NutritionFacts(int servingSize, int servings,
            int calories, int fat, int sodium) {
        this(servingSize, servings, calories, fat, sodium, 0);
    }
```

```
    public NutritionFacts(int servingSize, int servings,
            int calories, int fat, int sodium, int carbohydrate) {
        this.servingSize  = servingSize;
        this.servings     = servings;
        this.calories     = calories;
        this.fat          = fat;
        this.sodium       = sodium;
        this.carbohydrate = carbohydrate;
    }
}
```

When you want to create an instance, you use the constructor with the shortest parameter list containing all the parameters you want to set:

```
NutritionFacts cocaCola =
    new NutritionFacts(240, 8, 100, 0, 35, 27);
```

Typically this constructor invocation will require many parameters that you don't want to set, but you're forced to pass a value for them anyway. In this case, we passed a value of 0 for fat. With "only" six parameters this may not seem so bad, but it quickly gets out of hand as the number of parameters increases.

In short, **the telescoping constructor pattern works, but it is hard to write client code when there are many parameters, and harder still to read it.** The reader is left wondering what all those values mean and must carefully count parameters to find out. Long sequences of identically typed parameters can cause subtle bugs. If the client accidentally reverses two such parameters, the compiler won't complain, but the program will misbehave at runtime (Item 40).

A second alternative when you are faced with many constructor parameters is the *JavaBeans* pattern, in which you call a parameterless constructor to create the object and then call setter methods to set each required parameter and each optional parameter of interest:

```
// JavaBeans Pattern - allows inconsistency, mandates mutability
public class NutritionFacts {
    // Parameters initialized to default values (if any)
    private int servingSize  = -1; // Required; no default value
    private int servings     = -1; //    "        "      "        "
    private int calories     = 0;
    private int fat          = 0;
    private int sodium       = 0;
    private int carbohydrate = 0;

    public NutritionFacts() { }
```

```
    // Setters
    public void setServingSize(int val)   { servingSize = val; }
    public void setServings(int val)      { servings = val; }
    public void setCalories(int val)      { calories = val; }
    public void setFat(int val)           { fat = val; }
    public void setSodium(int val)        { sodium = val; }
    public void setCarbohydrate(int val) { carbohydrate = val; }
}
```

This pattern has none of the disadvantages of the telescoping constructor pattern. It is easy, if a bit wordy, to create instances, and easy to read the resulting code:

```
NutritionFacts cocaCola = new NutritionFacts();
cocaCola.setServingSize(240);
cocaCola.setServings(8);
cocaCola.setCalories(100);
cocaCola.setSodium(35);
cocaCola.setCarbohydrate(27);
```

Unfortunately, the JavaBeans pattern has serious disadvantages of its own. Because construction is split across multiple calls, **a JavaBean may be in an inconsistent state partway through its construction.** The class does not have the option of enforcing consistency merely by checking the validity of the constructor parameters. Attempting to use an object when it's in an inconsistent state may cause failures that are far removed from the code containing the bug, hence difficult to debug. A related disadvantage is that **the JavaBeans pattern precludes the possibility of making a class immutable** (Item 15), and requires added effort on the part of the programmer to ensure thread safety.

It is possible to reduce these disadvantages by manually "freezing" the object when its construction is complete and not allowing it to be used until frozen, but this variant is unwieldy and rarely used in practice. Moreover, it can cause errors at runtime, as the compiler cannot ensure that the programmer calls the freeze method on an object before using it.

Luckily, there is a third alternative that combines the safety of the telescoping constructor pattern with the readability of the JavaBeans pattern. It is a form of the *Builder* pattern [Gamma95, p. 97]. Instead of making the desired object directly, the client calls a constructor (or static factory) with all of the required parameters and gets a *builder object*. Then the client calls setter-like methods on the builder object to set each optional parameter of interest. Finally, the client calls a parameterless build method to generate the object, which is immutable. The builder is a static member class (Item 22) of the class it builds. Here's how it looks in practice:

```java
// Builder Pattern
public class NutritionFacts {
    private final int servingSize;
    private final int servings;
    private final int calories;
    private final int fat;
    private final int sodium;
    private final int carbohydrate;

    public static class Builder {
        // Required parameters
        private final int servingSize;
        private final int servings;

        // Optional parameters - initialized to default values
        private int calories      = 0;
        private int fat           = 0;
        private int carbohydrate  = 0;
        private int sodium        = 0;

        public Builder(int servingSize, int servings) {
            this.servingSize = servingSize;
            this.servings    = servings;
        }

        public Builder calories(int val)
            { calories = val;      return this; }
        public Builder fat(int val)
            { fat = val;           return this; }
        public Builder carbohydrate(int val)
            { carbohydrate = val;  return this; }
        public Builder sodium(int val)
            { sodium = val;        return this; }

        public NutritionFacts build() {
            return new NutritionFacts(this);
        }
    }

    private NutritionFacts(Builder builder) {
        servingSize  = builder.servingSize;
        servings     = builder.servings;
        calories     = builder.calories;
        fat          = builder.fat;
        sodium       = builder.sodium;
        carbohydrate = builder.carbohydrate;
    }
}
```

Note that `NutritionFacts` is immutable, and that all parameter default values are in a single location. The builder's setter methods return the builder itself so that invocations can be chained. Here's how the client code looks:

```
NutritionFacts cocaCola = new NutritionFacts.Builder(240, 8).
    calories(100).sodium(35).carbohydrate(27).build();
```

This client code is easy to write and, more importantly, to read. **The Builder pattern simulates named optional parameters** as found in Ada and Python.

Like a constructor, a builder can impose invariants on its parameters. The `build` method can check these invariants. It is critical that they be checked after copying the parameters from the builder to the object, and that they be checked on the object fields rather than the builder fields (Item 39). If any invariants are violated, the `build` method should throw an `IllegalStateException` (Item 60). The exception's detail message should indicate which invariant is violated (Item 63).

Another way to impose invariants involving multiple parameters is to have setter methods take entire groups of parameters on which some invariant must hold. If the invariant isn't satisfied, the setter method throws an `IllegalArgumentException`. This has the advantage of detecting the invariant failure as soon as the invalid parameters are passed, instead of waiting for `build` to be invoked.

A minor advantage of builders over constructors is that builders can have multiple varargs parameters. Constructors, like methods, can have only one varargs parameter. Because builders use separate methods to set each parameter, they can have as many varargs parameters as you like, up to one per setter method.

The Builder pattern is flexible. A single builder can be used to build multiple objects. The parameters of the builder can be tweaked between object creations to vary the objects. The builder can fill in some fields automatically, such as a serial number that automatically increases each time an object is created.

A builder whose parameters have been set makes a fine *Abstract Factory* [Gamma95, p. 87]. In other words, a client can pass such a builder to a method to enable the method to create one or more objects for the client. To enable this usage, you need a type to represent the builder. If you are using release 1.5 or a later release, a single generic type (Item 26) suffices for *all* builders, no matter what type of object they're building:

```
// A builder for objects of type T
public interface Builder<T> {
    public T build();
}
```

Note that our `NutritionFacts.Builder` class could be declared to implement `Builder<NutritionFacts>`.

Methods that take a `Builder` instance would typically constrain the builder's type parameter using a *bounded wildcard type* (Item 28). For example, here is a method that builds a tree using a client-provided `Builder` instance to build each node:

```
Tree buildTree(Builder<? extends Node> nodeBuilder) { ... }
```

The traditional Abstract Factory implementation in Java has been the `Class` object, with the `newInstance` method playing the part of the `build` method. This usage is fraught with problems. The `newInstance` method always attempts to invoke the class's parameterless constructor, which may not even exist. You don't get a compile-time error if the class has no accessible parameterless constructor. Instead, the client code must cope with `InstantiationException` or `IllegalAc-cessException` at runtime, which is ugly and inconvenient. Also, the `newIn-stance` method propagates any exceptions thrown by the parameterless constructor, even though `newInstance` lacks the corresponding `throws` clauses. In other words, **`Class.newInstance` breaks compile-time exception checking.** The `Builder` interface, shown above, corrects these deficiencies.

The Builder pattern does have disadvantages of its own. In order to create an object, you must first create its builder. While the cost of creating the builder is unlikely to be noticeable in practice, it could be a problem in some performance-critical situations. Also, the Builder pattern is more verbose than the telescoping constructor pattern, so it should be used only if there are enough parameters, say, four or more. But keep in mind that you may want to add parameters in the future. If you start out with constructors or static factories, and add a builder when the class evolves to the point where the number of parameters starts to get out of hand, the obsolete constructors or static factories will stick out like a sore thumb. Therefore, it's often better to start with a builder in the first place.

In summary, **the Builder pattern is a good choice when designing classes whose constructors or static factories would have more than a handful of parameters**, especially if most of those parameters are optional. Client code is much easier to read and write with builders than with the traditional telescoping constructor pattern, and builders are much safer than JavaBeans.

Item 3:   Enforce the singleton property with a private constructor or an enum type

A *singleton* is simply a class that is instantiated exactly once [Gamma95, p. 127]. Singletons typically represent a system component that is intrinsically unique, such as the window manager or file system. **Making a class a singleton can make it difficult to test its clients,** as it's impossible to substitute a mock implementation for a singleton unless it implements an interface that serves as its type.

Before release 1.5, there were two ways to implement singletons. Both are based on keeping the constructor private and exporting a public static member to provide access to the sole instance. In one approach, the member is a final field:

```
// Singleton with public final field
public class Elvis {
    public static final Elvis INSTANCE = new Elvis();
    private Elvis() { ... }

    public void leaveTheBuilding() { ... }
}
```

The private constructor is called only once, to initialize the public static final field `Elvis.INSTANCE`. The lack of a public or protected constructor *guarantees* a "monoelvistic" universe: exactly one `Elvis` instance will exist once the `Elvis` class is initialized—no more, no less. Nothing that a client does can change this, with one caveat: a privileged client can invoke the private constructor reflectively (Item 53) with the aid of the `AccessibleObject.setAccessible` method. If you need to defend against this attack, modify the constructor to make it throw an exception if it's asked to create a second instance.

In the second approach to implementing singletons, the public member is a static factory method:

```
// Singleton with static factory
public class Elvis {
    private static final Elvis INSTANCE = new Elvis();
    private Elvis() { ... }
    public static Elvis getInstance() { return INSTANCE; }

    public void leaveTheBuilding() { ... }
}
```

All calls to `Elvis.getInstance` return the same object reference, and no other `Elvis` instance will ever be created (with the same caveat mentioned above).

The main advantage of the public field approach is that the declarations make it clear that the class is a singleton: the public static field is final, so it will always contain the same object reference. There is no longer any performance advantage to the public field approach: modern Java virtual machine (JVM) implementations are almost certain to inline the call to the static factory method.

One advantage of the factory-method approach is that it gives you the flexibility to change your mind about whether the class should be a singleton without changing its API. The factory method returns the sole instance but could easily be modified to return, say, a unique instance for each thread that invokes it. A second advantage, concerning generic types, is discussed in Item 27. Often neither of these advantages is relevant, and the public field approach is simpler.

To make a singleton class that is implemented using either of the previous approaches *serializable* (Chapter 11), it is not sufficient merely to add `implements Serializable` to its declaration. To maintain the singleton guarantee, you have to declare all instance fields `transient` and provide a `readResolve` method (Item 77). Otherwise, each time a serialized instance is deserialized, a new instance will be created, leading, in the case of our example, to spurious Elvis sightings. To prevent this, add this `readResolve` method to the Elvis class:

```
// readResolve method to preserve singleton property
private Object readResolve() {
    // Return the one true Elvis and let the garbage collector
    // take care of the Elvis impersonator.
    return INSTANCE;
}
```

As of release 1.5, there is a third approach to implementing singletons. Simply make an enum type with one element:

```
// Enum singleton - the preferred approach
public enum Elvis {
    INSTANCE;

    public void leaveTheBuilding() { ... }
}
```

This approach is functionally equivalent to the public field approach, except that it is more concise, provides the serialization machinery for free, and provides an ironclad guarantee against multiple instantiation, even in the face of sophisticated serialization or reflection attacks. While this approach has yet to be widely adopted, **a single-element enum type is the best way to implement a singleton**.

Item 4:   Enforce noninstantiability with a private constructor

Occasionally you'll want to write a class that is just a grouping of static methods and static fields. Such classes have acquired a bad reputation because some people abuse them to avoid thinking in terms of objects, but they do have valid uses. They can be used to group related methods on primitive values or arrays, in the manner of java.lang.Math or java.util.Arrays. They can also be used to group static methods, including factory methods (Item 1), for objects that implement a particular interface, in the manner of java.util.Collections. Lastly, they can be used to group methods on a final class, instead of extending the class.

Such *utility classes* were not designed to be instantiated: an instance would be nonsensical. In the absence of explicit constructors, however, the compiler provides a public, parameterless *default constructor*. To a user, this constructor is indistinguishable from any other. It is not uncommon to see unintentionally instantiable classes in published APIs.

Attempting to enforce noninstantiability by making a class abstract does not work. The class can be subclassed and the subclass instantiated. Furthermore, it misleads the user into thinking the class was designed for inheritance (Item 17). There is, however, a simple idiom to ensure noninstantiability. A default constructor is generated only if a class contains no explicit constructors, so **a class can be made noninstantiable by including a private constructor**:

```
// Noninstantiable utility class
public class UtilityClass {
    // Suppress default constructor for noninstantiability
    private UtilityClass() {
        throw new AssertionError();
    }
    ...  // Remainder omitted
}
```

Because the explicit constructor is private, it is inaccessible outside of the class. The AssertionError isn't strictly required, but it provides insurance in case the constructor is accidentally invoked from within the class. It guarantees that the class will never be instantiated under any circumstances. This idiom is mildly counterintuitive, as the constructor is provided expressly so that it cannot be invoked. It is therefore wise to include a comment, as shown above.

As a side effect, this idiom also prevents the class from being subclassed. All constructors must invoke a superclass constructor, explicitly or implicitly, and a subclass would have no accessible superclass constructor to invoke.

Item 5:   Avoid creating unnecessary objects

It is often appropriate to reuse a single object instead of creating a new functionally equivalent object each time it is needed. Reuse can be both faster and more stylish. An object can always be reused if it is *immutable* (Item 15).

As an extreme example of what not to do, consider this statement:

```
String s = new String("stringette");  // DON'T DO THIS!
```

The statement creates a new `String` instance each time it is executed, and none of those object creations is necessary. The argument to the `String` constructor ("stringette") is itself a `String` instance, functionally identical to all of the objects created by the constructor. If this usage occurs in a loop or in a frequently invoked method, millions of `String` instances can be created needlessly.

The improved version is simply the following:

```
 String s = "stringette";
```

This version uses a single `String` instance, rather than creating a new one each time it is executed. Furthermore, it is guaranteed that the object will be reused by any other code running in the same virtual machine that happens to contain the same string literal [JLS, 3.10.5].

You can often avoid creating unnecessary objects by using *static factory methods* (Item 1) in preference to constructors on immutable classes that provide both. For example, the static factory method `Boolean.valueOf(String)` is almost always preferable to the constructor `Boolean(String)`. The constructor creates a new object each time it's called, while the static factory method is never required to do so and won't in practice.

In addition to reusing immutable objects, you can also reuse mutable objects if you know they won't be modified. Here is a slightly more subtle, and much more common, example of what not to do. It involves mutable `Date` objects that are never modified once their values have been computed. This class models a person and has an `isBabyBoomer` method that tells whether the person is a "baby boomer," in other words, whether the person was born between 1946 and 1964:

```
public class Person {
    private final Date birthDate;

    // Other fields, methods, and constructor omitted
```

```java
// DON'T DO THIS!
public boolean isBabyBoomer() {
    // Unnecessary allocation of expensive object
    Calendar gmtCal =
        Calendar.getInstance(TimeZone.getTimeZone("GMT"));
    gmtCal.set(1946, Calendar.JANUARY, 1, 0, 0, 0);
    Date boomStart = gmtCal.getTime();
    gmtCal.set(1965, Calendar.JANUARY, 1, 0, 0, 0);
    Date boomEnd = gmtCal.getTime();
    return birthDate.compareTo(boomStart) >= 0 &&
            birthDate.compareTo(boomEnd)    < 0;
    }
}
```

The isBabyBoomer method unnecessarily creates a new Calendar, TimeZone, and two Date instances each time it is invoked. The version that follows avoids this inefficiency with a static initializer:

```java
public class Person {
    private final Date birthDate;
    // Other fields, methods, and constructor omitted

    /**
     * The starting and ending dates of the baby boom.
     */
    private static final Date BOOM_START;
    private static final Date BOOM_END;

    static {
        Calendar gmtCal =
            Calendar.getInstance(TimeZone.getTimeZone("GMT"));
        gmtCal.set(1946, Calendar.JANUARY, 1, 0, 0, 0);
        BOOM_START = gmtCal.getTime();
        gmtCal.set(1965, Calendar.JANUARY, 1, 0, 0, 0);
        BOOM_END = gmtCal.getTime();
    }

    public boolean isBabyBoomer() {
        return birthDate.compareTo(BOOM_START) >= 0 &&
                birthDate.compareTo(BOOM_END)    < 0;
    }
}
```

The improved version of the Person class creates Calendar, TimeZone, and Date instances only once, when it is initialized, instead of creating them every time isBabyBoomer is invoked. This results in significant performance gains if the method is invoked frequently. On my machine, the original version takes 32,000 ms for 10 million invocations, while the improved version takes 130 ms, which is about 250 times faster. Not only is performance improved, but so is clarity. Changing boomStart and boomEnd from local variables to static final fields makes it clear that these dates are treated as constants, making the code more understandable. In the interest of full disclosure, the savings from this sort of optimization will not always be this dramatic, as Calendar instances are particularly expensive to create.

If the improved version of the Person class is initialized but its isBabyBoomer method is never invoked, the BOOM_START and BOOM_END fields will be initialized unnecessarily. It would be possible to eliminate the unnecessary initializations by *lazily initializing* these fields (Item 71) the first time the isBabyBoomer method is invoked, but it is not recommended. As is often the case with lazy initialization, it would complicate the implementation and would be unlikely to result in a noticeable performance improvement beyond what we've already achieved (Item 55).

In the previous examples in this item, it was obvious that the objects in question could be reused because they were not modified after initialization. There are other situations where it is less obvious. Consider the case of *adapters* [Gamma95, p. 139], also known as *views*. An adapter is an object that delegates to a backing object, providing an alternative interface to the backing object. Because an adapter has no state beyond that of its backing object, there's no need to create more than one instance of a given adapter to a given object.

For example, the keySet method of the Map interface returns a Set view of the Map object, consisting of all the keys in the map. Naively, it would seem that every call to keySet would have to create a new Set instance, but every call to keySet on a given Map object may return the same Set instance. Although the returned Set instance is typically mutable, all of the returned objects are functionally identical: when one of the returned objects changes, so do all the others because they're all backed by the same Map instance. While it is harmless to create multiple instances of the keySet view object, it is also unnecessary.

There's a new way to create unnecessary objects in release 1.5. It is called *autoboxing*, and it allows the programmer to mix primitive and boxed primitive types, boxing and unboxing automatically as needed. Autoboxing blurs but does not erase the distinction between primitive and boxed primitive types. There are subtle semantic distinctions, and not-so-subtle performance differences (Item 49). Consider the following program, which calculates the sum of all the positive int values. To do this, the program has to use `long` arithmetic, because an `int` is not big enough to hold the sum of all the positive `int` values:

```
// Hideously slow program! Can you spot the object creation?
public static void main(String[] args) {
    Long sum = 0L;
    for (long i = 0; i <= Integer.MAX_VALUE; i++) {
        sum += i;
    }
    System.out.println(sum);
}
```

This program gets the right answer, but it is *much* slower than it should be, due to a one-character typographical error. The variable `sum` is declared as a `Long` instead of a `long`, which means that the program constructs about 2^{31} unnecessary `Long` instances (roughly one for each time the `long i` is added to the `Long sum`). Changing the declaration of `sum` from `Long` to `long` reduces the runtime from 43 seconds to 6.8 seconds on my machine. The lesson is clear: **prefer primitives to boxed primitives, and watch out for unintentional autoboxing.**

This item should not be misconstrued to imply that object creation is expensive and should be avoided. On the contrary, the creation and reclamation of small objects whose constructors do little explicit work is cheap, especially on modern JVM implementations. Creating additional objects to enhance the clarity, simplicity, or power of a program is generally a good thing.

Conversely, avoiding object creation by maintaining your own *object pool* is a bad idea unless the objects in the pool are extremely heavyweight. The classic example of an object that *does* justify an object pool is a database connection. The cost of establishing the connection is sufficiently high that it makes sense to reuse these objects. Also, your database license may limit you to a fixed number of connections. Generally speaking, however, maintaining your own object pools clutters your code, increases memory footprint, and harms performance. Modern JVM implementations have highly optimized garbage collectors that easily outperform such object pools on lightweight objects.

The counterpoint to this item is Item 39 on *defensive copying*. Item 5 says, "Don't create a new object when you should reuse an existing one," while Item 39 says, "Don't reuse an existing object when you should create a new one." Note that the penalty for reusing an object when defensive copying is called for is far greater than the penalty for needlessly creating a duplicate object. Failing to make defensive copies where required can lead to insidious bugs and security holes; creating objects unnecessarily merely affects style and performance.

Item 6:   Eliminate obsolete object references

When you switch from a language with manual memory management, such as C or C++, to a garbage-collected language, your job as a programmer is made much easier by the fact that your objects are automatically reclaimed when you're through with them. It seems almost like magic when you first experience it. It can easily lead to the impression that you don't have to think about memory management, but this isn't quite true.

Consider the following simple stack implementation:

```
// Can you spot the "memory leak"?
public class Stack {
    private Object[] elements;
    private int size = 0;
    private static final int DEFAULT_INITIAL_CAPACITY = 16;

    public Stack() {
        elements = new Object[DEFAULT_INITIAL_CAPACITY];
    }

    public void push(Object e) {
        ensureCapacity();
        elements[size++] = e;
    }

    public Object pop() {
        if (size == 0)
            throw new EmptyStackException();
        return elements[--size];
    }

    /**
     * Ensure space for at least one more element, roughly
     * doubling the capacity each time the array needs to grow.
     */
    private void ensureCapacity() {
        if (elements.length == size)
            elements = Arrays.copyOf(elements, 2 * size + 1);
    }
}
```

There's nothing obviously wrong with this program (but see Item 26 for a generic version). You could test it exhaustively, and it would pass every test with flying colors, but there's a problem lurking. Loosely speaking, the program has a "memory leak," which can silently manifest itself as reduced performance due to increased garbage collector activity or increased memory footprint. In extreme cases, such memory leaks can cause disk paging and even program failure with an OutOfMemoryError, but such failures are relatively rare.

So where is the memory leak? If a stack grows and then shrinks, the objects that were popped off the stack will not be garbage collected, even if the program using the stack has no more references to them. This is because the stack maintains *obsolete references* to these objects. An obsolete reference is simply a reference that will never be dereferenced again. In this case, any references outside of the "active portion" of the element array are obsolete. The active portion consists of the elements whose index is less than size.

Memory leaks in garbage-collected languages (more properly known as *unintentional object retentions*) are insidious. If an object reference is unintentionally retained, not only is that object excluded from garbage collection, but so too are any objects referenced by that object, and so on. Even if only a few object references are unintentionally retained, many, many objects may be prevented from being garbage collected, with potentially large effects on performance.

The fix for this sort of problem is simple: null out references once they become obsolete. In the case of our Stack class, the reference to an item becomes obsolete as soon as it's popped off the stack. The corrected version of the pop method looks like this:

```
public Object pop() {
    if (size == 0)
        throw new EmptyStackException();
    Object result = elements[--size];
    elements[size] = null; // Eliminate obsolete reference
    return result;
}
```

An added benefit of nulling out obsolete references is that, if they are subsequently dereferenced by mistake, the program will immediately fail with a NullPointerException, rather than quietly doing the wrong thing. It is always beneficial to detect programming errors as quickly as possible.

When programmers are first stung by this problem, they may overcompensate by nulling out every object reference as soon as the program is finished using it. This is neither necessary nor desirable, as it clutters up the program unnecessarily. **Nulling out object references should be the exception rather than the norm.** The best way to eliminate an obsolete reference is to let the variable that contained the reference fall out of scope. This occurs naturally if you define each variable in the narrowest possible scope (Item 45).

So when should you null out a reference? What aspect of the Stack class makes it susceptible to memory leaks? Simply put, it *manages its own memory*. The *storage pool* consists of the elements of the elements array (the object reference cells, not the objects themselves). The elements in the active portion of the array (as defined earlier) are *allocated*, and those in the remainder of the array are *free*. The garbage collector has no way of knowing this; to the garbage collector, all of the object references in the elements array are equally valid. Only the programmer knows that the inactive portion of the array is unimportant. The programmer effectively communicates this fact to the garbage collector by manually nulling out array elements as soon as they become part of the inactive portion.

Generally speaking, **whenever a class manages its own memory, the programmer should be alert for memory leaks**. Whenever an element is freed, any object references contained in the element should be nulled out.

Another common source of memory leaks is caches. Once you put an object reference into a cache, it's easy to forget that it's there and leave it in the cache long after it becomes irrelevant. There are several solutions to this problem. If you're lucky enough to implement a cache for which an entry is relevant exactly so long as there are references to its key outside of the cache, represent the cache as a WeakHashMap; entries will be removed automatically after they become obsolete. Remember that WeakHashMap is useful only if the desired lifetime of cache entries is determined by external references to the key, not the value.

More commonly, the useful lifetime of a cache entry is less well defined, with entries becoming less valuable over time. Under these circumstances, the cache should occasionally be cleansed of entries that have fallen into disuse. This can be done by a background thread (perhaps a Timer or ScheduledThreadPoolExecutor) or as a side effect of adding new entries to the cache. The LinkedHashMap class facilitates the latter approach with its removeEldestEntry method. For more sophisticated caches, you may need to use java.lang.ref directly.

A third common source of memory leaks is listeners and other callbacks. If you implement an API where clients register callbacks but don't deregister them explicitly, they will accumulate unless you take some action. The best way to ensure that callbacks are garbage collected promptly is to store only *weak references* to them, for instance, by storing them only as keys in a WeakHashMap.

Because memory leaks typically do not manifest themselves as obvious failures, they may remain present in a system for years. They are typically discovered only as a result of careful code inspection or with the aid of a debugging tool known as a *heap profiler*. Therefore, it is very desirable to learn to anticipate problems like this before they occur and prevent them from happening.

Item 7:   Avoid finalizers

Finalizers are unpredictable, often dangerous, and generally unnecessary.
Their use can cause erratic behavior, poor performance, and portability problems.
Finalizers have a few valid uses, which we'll cover later in this item, but as a rule
of thumb, you should avoid finalizers.

C++ programmers are cautioned not to think of finalizers as Java's analog of
C++ destructors. In C++, destructors are the normal way to reclaim the resources
associated with an object, a necessary counterpart to constructors. In Java, the garbage collector reclaims the storage associated with an object when it becomes
unreachable, requiring no special effort on the part of the programmer. C++
destructors are also used to reclaim other nonmemory resources. In Java, the `try-`
`finally` block is generally used for this purpose.

One shortcoming of finalizers is that there is no guarantee they'll be executed
promptly [JLS, 12.6]. It can take arbitrarily long between the time that an object
becomes unreachable and the time that its finalizer is executed. This means that
you should **never do anything time-critical in a finalizer.** For example, it is a
grave error to depend on a finalizer to close files, because open file descriptors are
a limited resource. If many files are left open because the JVM is tardy in executing finalizers, a program may fail because it can no longer open files.

The promptness with which finalizers are executed is primarily a function of
the garbage collection algorithm, which varies widely from JVM implementation
to JVM implementation. The behavior of a program that depends on the promptness of finalizer execution may likewise vary. It is entirely possible that such a
program will run perfectly on the JVM on which you test it and then fail miserably
on the JVM favored by your most important customer.

Tardy finalization is not just a theoretical problem. Providing a finalizer for a
class can, under rare conditions, arbitrarily delay reclamation of its instances. A
colleague debugged a long-running GUI application that was mysteriously dying
with an `OutOfMemoryError`. Analysis revealed that at the time of its death, the
application had thousands of graphics objects on its finalizer queue just waiting to
be finalized and reclaimed. Unfortunately, the finalizer thread was running at a
lower priority than another application thread, so objects weren't getting finalized
at the rate they became eligible for finalization. The language specification makes
no guarantees as to which thread will execute finalizers, so there is no portable
way to prevent this sort of problem other than to refrain from using finalizers.

Not only does the language specification provide no guarantee that finalizers
will get executed promptly; it provides no guarantee that they'll get executed at

all. It is entirely possible, even likely, that a program terminates without executing finalizers on some objects that are no longer reachable. As a consequence, you should **never depend on a finalizer to update critical persistent state**. For example, depending on a finalizer to release a persistent lock on a shared resource such as a database is a good way to bring your entire distributed system to a grinding halt.

Don't be seduced by the methods `System.gc` and `System.runFinalization`. They may increase the odds of finalizers getting executed, but they don't guarantee it. The only methods that claim to guarantee finalization are `System.runFinalizersOnExit` and its evil twin, `Runtime.runFinalizersOnExit`. These methods are fatally flawed and have been deprecated [ThreadStop].

In case you are not yet convinced that finalizers should be avoided, here's another tidbit worth considering: if an uncaught exception is thrown during finalization, the exception is ignored, and finalization of that object terminates [JLS, 12.6]. Uncaught exceptions can leave objects in a corrupt state. If another thread attempts to use such a corrupted object, arbitrary nondeterministic behavior may result. Normally, an uncaught exception will terminate the thread and print a stack trace, but not if it occurs in a finalizer—it won't even print a warning.

Oh, and one more thing: **there is a *severe* performance penalty for using finalizers.** On my machine, the time to create and destroy a simple object is about 5.6 ns. Adding a finalizer increases the time to 2,400 ns. In other words, it is about 430 times slower to create and destroy objects with finalizers.

So what should you do instead of writing a finalizer for a class whose objects encapsulate resources that require termination, such as files or threads? Just **provide an *explicit termination method***, and require clients of the class to invoke this method on each instance when it is no longer needed. One detail worth mentioning is that the instance must keep track of whether it has been terminated: the explicit termination method must record in a private field that the object is no longer valid, and other methods must check this field and throw an `IllegalStateException` if they are called after the object has been terminated.

Typical examples of explicit termination methods are the `close` methods on `InputStream`, `OutputStream`, and `java.sql.Connection`. Another example is the `cancel` method on `java.util.Timer`, which performs the necessary state change to cause the thread associated with a `Timer` instance to terminate itself gently. Examples from `java.awt` include `Graphics.dispose` and `Window.dispose`. These methods are often overlooked, with predictably dire performance consequences. A related method is `Image.flush`, which deallocates all the resources associated with an `Image` instance but leaves it in a state where it can still be used, reallocating the resources if necessary.

Explicit termination methods are typically used in combination with the `try-finally` construct to ensure termination. Invoking the explicit termination method inside the `finally` clause ensures that it will get executed even if an exception is thrown while the object is being used:

```
// try-finally block guarantees execution of termination method
Foo foo = new Foo(...);
try {
    // Do what must be done with foo
    ...
} finally {
    foo.terminate();  // Explicit termination method
}
```

So what, if anything, are finalizers good for? There are perhaps two legitimate uses. One is to act as a "safety net" in case the owner of an object forgets to call its explicit termination method. While there's no guarantee that the finalizer will be invoked promptly, it may be better to free the resource late than never, in those (hopefully rare) cases when the client fails to call the explicit termination method. But **the finalizer should log a warning if it finds that the resource has not been terminated**, as this indicates a bug in the client code, which should be fixed. If you are considering writing such a safety-net finalizer, think long and hard about whether the extra protection is worth the extra cost.

The four classes cited as examples of the explicit termination method pattern (`FileInputStream`, `FileOutputStream`, `Timer`, and `Connection`) have finalizers that serve as safety nets in case their termination methods aren't called. Unfortunately these finalizers do not log warnings. Such warnings generally can't be added after an API is published, as it would appear to break existing clients.

A second legitimate use of finalizers concerns objects with *native peers*. A native peer is a native object to which a normal object delegates via native methods. Because a native peer is not a normal object, the garbage collector doesn't know about it and can't reclaim it when its Java peer is reclaimed. A finalizer is an appropriate vehicle for performing this task, *assuming the native peer holds no critical resources*. If the native peer holds resources that must be terminated promptly, the class should have an explicit termination method, as described above. The termination method should do whatever is required to free the critical resource. The termination method can be a native method, or it can invoke one.

It is important to note that "finalizer chaining" is not performed automatically. If a class (other than `Object`) has a finalizer and a subclass overrides it, the subclass finalizer must invoke the superclass finalizer manually. You should finalize the subclass in a `try` block and invoke the superclass finalizer in the corresponding `finally` block. This ensures that the superclass finalizer gets executed even if the subclass finalization throws an exception and vice versa. Here's how it looks. Note that this example uses the `Override` annotation (`@Override`), which was added to the platform in release 1.5. You can ignore `Override` annotations for now, or see Item 36 to find out what they mean:

```
// Manual finalizer chaining
@Override protected void finalize() throws Throwable {
    try {
        ... // Finalize subclass state
    } finally {
        super.finalize();
    }
}
```

If a subclass implementor overrides a superclass finalizer but forgets to invoke it, the superclass finalizer will never be invoked. It is possible to defend against such a careless or malicious subclass at the cost of creating an additional object for every object to be finalized. Instead of putting the finalizer on the class requiring finalization, put the finalizer on an anonymous class (Item 22) whose sole purpose is to finalize its enclosing instance. A single instance of the anonymous class, called a *finalizer guardian*, is created for each instance of the enclosing class. The enclosing instance stores the sole reference to its finalizer guardian in a private instance field so the finalizer guardian becomes eligible for finalization at the same time as the enclosing instance. When the guardian is finalized, it performs the finalization activity desired for the enclosing instance, just as if its finalizer were a method on the enclosing class:

```
// Finalizer Guardian idiom
public class Foo {
    // Sole purpose of this object is to finalize outer Foo object
    private final Object finalizerGuardian = new Object() {
        @Override protected void finalize() throws Throwable {
            ... // Finalize outer Foo object
        }
    };
    ... // Remainder omitted
}
```

Note that the public class, `Foo`, has no finalizer (other than the trivial one it inherits from `Object`), so it doesn't matter whether a subclass finalizer calls `super.finalize` or not. This technique should be considered for every nonfinal public class that has a finalizer.

In summary, don't use finalizers except as a safety net or to terminate noncritical native resources. In those rare instances where you do use a finalizer, remember to invoke `super.finalize`. If you use a finalizer as a safety net, remember to log the invalid usage from the finalizer. Lastly, if you need to associate a finalizer with a public, nonfinal class, consider using a finalizer guardian, so finalization can take place even if a subclass finalizer fails to invoke `super.finalize`.

CHAPTER 3

Methods Common to All Objects

ALTHOUGH Object is a concrete class, it is designed primarily for extension. All of its nonfinal methods (equals, hashCode, toString, clone, and finalize) have explicit *general contracts* because they are designed to be overridden. It is the responsibility of any class overriding these methods to obey their general contracts; failure to do so will prevent other classes that depend on the contracts (such as HashMap and HashSet) from functioning properly in conjunction with the class.

This chapter tells you when and how to override the nonfinal Object methods. The finalize method is omitted from this chapter because it was discussed in Item 7. While not an Object method, Comparable.compareTo is discussed in this chapter because it has a similar character.

Item 8: Obey the general contract when overriding equals

Overriding the equals method seems simple, but there are many ways to get it wrong, and consequences can be dire. The easiest way to avoid problems is not to override the equals method, in which case each instance of the class is equal only to itself. This is the right thing to do if any of the following conditions apply:

- **Each instance of the class is inherently unique.** This is true for classes such as Thread that represent active entities rather than values. The equals implementation provided by Object has exactly the right behavior for these classes.

- **You don't care whether the class provides a "logical equality" test.** For example, java.util.Random could have overridden equals to check whether two Random instances would produce the same sequence of random numbers going forward, but the designers didn't think that clients would need or want this functionality. Under these circumstances, the equals implementation inherited from Object is adequate.

- **A superclass has already overridden equals, and the superclass behavior is appropriate for this class.** For example, most Set implementations inherit their equals implementation from AbstractSet, List implementations from AbstractList, and Map implementations from AbstractMap.

- **The class is private or package-private, and you are certain that its equals method will never be invoked.** Arguably, the equals method *should* be overridden under these circumstances, in case it is accidentally invoked:

```
@Override public boolean equals(Object o) {
    throw new AssertionError(); // Method is never called
}
```

So when is it appropriate to override Object.equals? When a class has a notion of *logical equality* that differs from mere object identity, and a superclass has not already overridden equals to implement the desired behavior. This is generally the case for *value classes*. A value class is simply a class that represents a value, such as Integer or Date. A programmer who compares references to value objects using the equals method expects to find out whether they are logically equivalent, not whether they refer to the same object. Not only is overriding the equals method necessary to satisfy programmer expectations; it enables instances to serve as map keys or set elements with predictable, desirable behavior.

One kind of value class that does *not* require the equals method to be overridden is a class that uses instance control (Item 1) to ensure that at most one object exists with each value. Enum types (Item 30) fall into this category. For these classes, logical equality is the same as object identity, so Object's equals method functions as a logical equals method.

When you override the equals method, you must adhere to its general contract. Here is the contract, copied from the specification for Object [JavaSE6]:

The equals method implements an *equivalence relation*. It is:
- *Reflexive*: For any non-null reference value x, x.equals(x) must return true.

- *Symmetric*: For any non-null reference values x and y, x.equals(y) must return true if and only if y.equals(x) returns true.

- *Transitive*: For any non-null reference values x, y, z, if x.equals(y) returns true and y.equals(z) returns true, then x.equals(z) must return true.

- *Consistent*: For any non-null reference values x and y, multiple invocations of x.equals(y) consistently return true or consistently return false, provided no information used in equals comparisons on the objects is modified.

- For any non-null reference value x, x.equals(null) must return false.

Unless you are mathematically inclined, this might look a bit scary, but do not ignore it! If you violate it, you may well find that your program behaves erratically or crashes, and it can be very difficult to pin down the source of the failure. To paraphrase John Donne, no class is an island. Instances of one class are frequently passed to another. Many classes, including all collections classes, depend on the objects passed to them obeying the equals contract.

Now that you are aware of the dangers of violating the equals contract, let's go over the contract in detail. The good news is that, appearances notwithstanding, the contract really isn't very complicated. Once you understand it, it's not hard to adhere to it. Let's examine the five requirements in turn:

Reflexivity—The first requirement says merely that an object must be equal to itself. It is hard to imagine violating this requirement unintentionally. If you were to violate it and then add an instance of your class to a collection, the collection's contains method might well say that the collection didn't contain the instance that you just added.

Symmetry—The second requirement says that any two objects must agree on whether they are equal. Unlike the first requirement, it's not hard to imagine violating this one unintentionally. For example, consider the following class, which implements a case-insensitive string. The case of the string is preserved by toString but ignored in comparisons:

```java
// Broken - violates symmetry!
public final class CaseInsensitiveString {
    private final String s;

    public CaseInsensitiveString(String s) {
        if (s == null)
            throw new NullPointerException();
        this.s = s;
    }

    // Broken - violates symmetry!
    @Override public boolean equals(Object o) {
        if (o instanceof CaseInsensitiveString)
            return s.equalsIgnoreCase(
                ((CaseInsensitiveString) o).s);
        if (o instanceof String)  // One-way interoperability!
            return s.equalsIgnoreCase((String) o);
        return false;
    }
    ...   // Remainder omitted
}
```

The well-intentioned `equals` method in this class naively attempts to interoperate with ordinary strings. Let's suppose that we have one case-insensitive string and one ordinary one:

```
CaseInsensitiveString cis = new CaseInsensitiveString("Polish");
String s = "polish";
```

As expected, `cis.equals(s)` returns `true`. The problem is that while the `equals` method in `CaseInsensitiveString` knows about ordinary strings, the `equals` method in `String` is oblivious to case-insensitive strings. Therefore `s.equals(cis)` returns `false`, a clear violation of symmetry. Suppose you put a case-insensitive string into a collection:

```
List<CaseInsensitiveString> list =
    new ArrayList<CaseInsensitiveString>();
list.add(cis);
```

What does `list.contains(s)` return at this point? Who knows? In Sun's current implementation, it happens to return `false`, but that's just an implementation artifact. In another implementation, it could just as easily return `true` or throw a runtime exception. **Once you've violated the `equals` contract, you simply don't know how other objects will behave when confronted with your object.**

To eliminate the problem, merely remove the ill-conceived attempt to interoperate with `String` from the `equals` method. Once you do this, you can refactor the method to give it a single return:

```
@Override public boolean equals(Object o) {
    return o instanceof CaseInsensitiveString &&
        ((CaseInsensitiveString) o).s.equalsIgnoreCase(s);
}
```

Transitivity—The third requirement of the `equals` contract says that if one object is equal to a second and the second object is equal to a third, then the first object must be equal to the third. Again, it's not hard to imagine violating this requirement unintentionally. Consider the case of a subclass that adds a new *value component* to its superclass. In other words, the subclass adds a piece of information that affects `equals` comparisons. Let's start with a simple immutable two-dimensional integer point class:

```
public class Point {
    private final int x;
    private final int y;
    public Point(int x, int y) {
        this.x = x;
        this.y = y;
    }

    @Override public boolean equals(Object o) {
        if (!(o instanceof Point))
            return false;
        Point p = (Point)o;
        return p.x == x && p.y == y;
    }

    ...  // Remainder omitted
}
```

Suppose you want to extend this class, adding the notion of color to a point:

```
public class ColorPoint extends Point {
    private final Color color;

    public ColorPoint(int x, int y, Color color) {
        super(x, y);
        this.color = color;
    }

    ...  // Remainder omitted
}
```

How should the `equals` method look? If you leave it out entirely, the implementation is inherited from `Point` and color information is ignored in `equals` comparisons. While this does not violate the `equals` contract, it is clearly unacceptable. Suppose you write an `equals` method that returns `true` only if its argument is another color point with the same position and color:

```
// Broken - violates symmetry!
@Override public boolean equals(Object o) {
    if (!(o instanceof ColorPoint))
        return false;
    return super.equals(o) && ((ColorPoint) o).color == color;
}
```

The problem with this method is that you might get different results when comparing a point to a color point and vice versa. The former comparison ignores color, while the latter comparison always returns `false` because the type of the argument is incorrect. To make this concrete, let's create one point and one color point:

```
Point p = new Point(1, 2);
ColorPoint cp = new ColorPoint(1, 2, Color.RED);
```

Then `p.equals(cp)` returns `true`, while `cp.equals(p)` returns `false`. You might try to fix the problem by having `ColorPoint.equals` ignore color when doing "mixed comparisons":

```
// Broken - violates transitivity!
@Override public boolean equals(Object o) {
    if (!(o instanceof Point))
        return false;

    // If o is a normal Point, do a color-blind comparison
    if (!(o instanceof ColorPoint))
        return o.equals(this);

    // o is a ColorPoint; do a full comparison
    return super.equals(o) && ((ColorPoint) o).color == color;
}
```

This approach does provide symmetry, but at the expense of transitivity:

```
ColorPoint p1 = new ColorPoint(1, 2, Color.RED);
Point p2 = new Point(1, 2);
ColorPoint p3 = new ColorPoint(1, 2, Color.BLUE);
```

Now `p1.equals(p2)` and `p2.equals(p3)` return `true`, while `p1.equals(p3)` returns `false`, a clear violation of transitivity. The first two comparisons are "color-blind," while the third takes color into account.

So what's the solution? It turns out that this is a fundamental problem of equivalence relations in object-oriented languages. **There is no way to extend an instantiable class and add a value component while preserving the equals contract**, unless you are willing to forgo the benefits of object-oriented abstraction.

You may hear it said that you can extend an instantiable class and add a value component while preserving the equals contract by using a getClass test in place of the instanceof test in the equals method:

```java
// Broken - violates Liskov substitution principle (page 40)
@Override public boolean equals(Object o) {
    if (o == null || o.getClass() != getClass())
        return false;
    Point p = (Point) o;
    return p.x == x && p.y == y;
}
```

This has the effect of equating objects only if they have the same implementation class. While this may not seem so bad, the consequences are unacceptable.

Let's suppose we want to write a method to tell whether an integer point is on the unit circle. Here is one way we could do it:

```java
// Initialize UnitCircle to contain all Points on the unit circle
private static final Set<Point> unitCircle;
static {
    unitCircle = new HashSet<Point>();
    unitCircle.add(new Point( 1,  0));
    unitCircle.add(new Point( 0,  1));
    unitCircle.add(new Point(-1,  0));
    unitCircle.add(new Point( 0, -1));
}

public static boolean onUnitCircle(Point p) {
    return unitCircle.contains(p);
}
```

While this may not be the fastest way to implement the functionality, it works fine. But suppose you extend Point in some trivial way that doesn't add a value component, say, by having its constructor keep track of how many instances have been created:

```java
public class CounterPoint extends Point {
    private static final AtomicInteger counter =
        new AtomicInteger();

    public CounterPoint(int x, int y) {
        super(x, y);
        counter.incrementAndGet();
    }
    public int numberCreated() { return counter.get(); }
}
```

The *Liskov substitution principle* says that any important property of a type should also hold for its subtypes, so that any method written for the type should work equally well on its subtypes [Liskov87]. But suppose we pass a CounterPoint instance to the onUnitCircle method. If the Point class uses a getClassbased equals method, the onUnitCircle method will return false regardless of the CounterPoint instance's x and y values. This is so because collections, such as the HashSet used by the onUnitCircle method, use the equals method to test for containment, and no CounterPoint instance is equal to any Point. If, however, you use a proper instanceof-based equals method on Point, the same onUnitCircle method will work fine when presented with a CounterPoint.

While there is no satisfactory way to extend an instantiable class and add a value component, there is a fine workaround. Follow the advice of Item 16, "Favor composition over inheritance." Instead of having ColorPoint extend Point, give ColorPoint a private Point field and a public *view* method (Item 5) that returns the point at the same position as this color point:

```java
// Adds a value component without violating the equals contract
public class ColorPoint {
    private final Point point;
    private final Color color;

    public ColorPoint(int x, int y, Color color) {
        if (color == null)
            throw new NullPointerException();
        point = new Point(x, y);
        this.color = color;
    }

    /**
     * Returns the point-view of this color point.
     */
    public Point asPoint() {
        return point;
    }

    @Override public boolean equals(Object o) {
        if (!(o instanceof ColorPoint))
            return false;
        ColorPoint cp = (ColorPoint) o;
        return cp.point.equals(point) && cp.color.equals(color);
    }

    ...   // Remainder omitted
}
```

There are some classes in the Java platform libraries that do extend an instantiable class and add a value component. For example, `java.sql.Timestamp` extends `java.util.Date` and adds a nanoseconds field. The `equals` implementation for `Timestamp` does violate symmetry and can cause erratic behavior if `Timestamp` and `Date` objects are used in the same collection or are otherwise intermixed. The `Timestamp` class has a disclaimer cautioning programmers against mixing dates and timestamps. While you won't get into trouble as long as you keep them separate, there's nothing to prevent you from mixing them, and the resulting errors can be hard to debug. This behavior of the `Timestamp` class was a mistake and should not be emulated.

Note that you *can* add a value component to a subclass of an *abstract* class without violating the `equals` contract. This is important for the sort of class hierarchies that you get by following the advice in Item 20, "Prefer class hierarchies to tagged classes." For example, you could have an abstract class `Shape` with no value components, a subclass `Circle` that adds a `radius` field, and a subclass `Rectangle` that adds `length` and `width` fields. Problems of the sort shown above won't occur so long as it is impossible to create a superclass instance directly.

Consistency—The fourth requirement of the `equals` contract says that if two objects are equal, they must remain equal for all time unless one (or both) of them is modified. In other words, mutable objects can be equal to different objects at different times while immutable objects can't. When you write a class, think hard about whether it should be immutable (Item 15). If you conclude that it should, make sure that your `equals` method enforces the restriction that equal objects remain equal and unequal objects remain unequal for all time.

Whether or not a class is immutable, **do not write an `equals` method that depends on unreliable resources.** It's extremely difficult to satisfy the consistency requirement if you violate this prohibition. For example, `java.net.URL`'s `equals` method relies on comparison of the IP addresses of the hosts associated with the URLs. Translating a host name to an IP address can require network access, and it isn't guaranteed to yield the same results over time. This can cause the URL `equals` method to violate the `equals` contract and has caused problems in practice. (Unfortunately, this behavior cannot be changed due to compatibility requirements.) With very few exceptions, `equals` methods should perform deterministic computations on memory-resident objects.

"Non-nullity"—The final requirement, which in the absence of a name I have taken the liberty of calling "non-nullity," says that all objects must be unequal to `null`. While it is hard to imagine accidentally returning `true` in response to the invocation `o.equals(null)`, it isn't hard to imagine accidentally throwing a

NullPointerException. The general contract does not allow this. Many classes have equals methods that guard against this with an explicit test for null:

```
@Override public boolean equals(Object o) {
    if (o == null)
        return false;
    ...
}
```

This test is unnecessary. To test its argument for equality, the equals method must first cast its argument to an appropriate type so its accessors may be invoked or its fields accessed. Before doing the cast, the method must use the instanceof operator to check that its argument is of the correct type:

```
@Override public boolean equals(Object o) {
    if (!(o instanceof MyType))
        return false;
    MyType mt = (MyType) o;
    ...
}
```

If this type check were missing and the equals method were passed an argument of the wrong type, the equals method would throw a ClassCastException, which violates the equals contract. But the instanceof operator is specified to return false if its first operand is null, regardless of what type appears in the second operand [JLS, 15.20.2]. Therefore the type check will return false if null is passed in, so you don't need a separate null check.

Putting it all together, here's a recipe for a high-quality equals method:

1. **Use the == operator to check if the argument is a reference to this object.** If so, return true. This is just a performance optimization, but one that is worth doing if the comparison is potentially expensive.

2. **Use the instanceof operator to check if the argument has the correct type.** If not, return false. Typically, the correct type is the class in which the method occurs. Occasionally, it is some interface implemented by this class. Use an interface if the class implements an interface that refines the equals contract to permit comparisons across classes that implement the interface. Collection interfaces such as Set, List, Map, and Map.Entry have this property.

3. **Cast the argument to the correct type.** Because this cast was preceded by an instanceof test, it is guaranteed to succeed.

4. **For each "significant" field in the class, check if that field of the argument matches the corresponding field of this object.** If all these tests succeed, return `true`; otherwise, return `false`. If the type in step 2 is an interface, you must access the argument's fields via interface methods; if the type is a class, you may be able to access the fields directly, depending on their accessibility.

For primitive fields whose type is not `float` or `double`, use the `==` operator for comparisons; for object reference fields, invoke the `equals` method recursively; for `float` fields, use the `Float.compare` method; and for `double` fields, use `Double.compare`. The special treatment of `float` and `double` fields is made necessary by the existence of `Float.NaN`, `-0.0f` and the analogous `double` constants; see the `Float.equals` documentation for details. For array fields, apply these guidelines to each element. If every element in an array field is significant, you can use one of the `Arrays.equals` methods added in release 1.5.

Some object reference fields may legitimately contain `null`. To avoid the possibility of a `NullPointerException`, use this idiom to compare such fields:

```
(field == null ? o.field == null : field.equals(o.field))
```

This alternative may be faster if `field` and `o.field` are often identical:

```
(field == o.field || (field != null && field.equals(o.field)))
```

For some classes, such as `CaseInsensitiveString` above, field comparisons are more complex than simple equality tests. If this is the case, you may want to store a *canonical form* of the field, so the `equals` method can do cheap exact comparisons on these canonical forms rather than more costly inexact comparisons. This technique is most appropriate for *immutable* classes (Item 15); if the object can change, you must keep the canonical form up to date.

The performance of the `equals` method may be affected by the order in which fields are compared. For best performance, you should first compare fields that are more likely to differ, less expensive to compare, or, ideally, both. You must not compare fields that are not part of an object's logical state, such as `Lock` fields used to synchronize operations. You need not compare *redundant fields*, which can be calculated from "significant fields," but doing so may improve the performance of the `equals` method. If a redundant field amounts to a summary description of the entire object, comparing this field will save you the expense of comparing the actual data if the comparison fails. For example, suppose you have a `Polygon` class, and you cache the area. If two polygons have unequal areas, you needn't bother comparing their edges and vertices.

5. **When you are finished writing your `equals` method, ask yourself three questions: Is it symmetric? Is it transitive? Is it consistent?** And don't just ask yourself; write unit tests to check that these properties hold! If they don't, figure out why not, and modify the `equals` method accordingly. Of course your `equals` method also has to satisfy the other two properties (reflexivity and "non-nullity"), but these two usually take care of themselves.

For a concrete example of an `equals` method constructed according to the above recipe, see `PhoneNumber.equals` in Item 9. Here are a few final caveats:

- **Always override `hashCode` when you override `equals`** (Item 9).

- **Don't try to be too clever.** If you simply test fields for equality, it's not hard to adhere to the `equals` contract. If you are overly aggressive in searching for equivalence, it's easy to get into trouble. It is generally a bad idea to take any form of aliasing into account. For example, the `File` class shouldn't attempt to equate symbolic links referring to the same file. Thankfully, it doesn't.

- **Don't substitute another type for `Object` in the `equals` declaration.** It is not uncommon for a programmer to write an `equals` method that looks like this, and then spend hours puzzling over why it doesn't work properly:

```
public boolean equals(MyClass o) {
    ...
}
```

The problem is that this method does not *override* `Object.equals`, whose argument is of type `Object`, but *overloads* it instead (Item 41). It is acceptable to provide such a "strongly typed" `equals` method *in addition to* the normal one as long as the two methods return the same result, but there is no compelling reason to do so. It may provide minor performance gains under certain circumstances, but it isn't worth the added complexity (Item 55).

Consistent use of the `@Override` annotation, as illustrated throughout this item, will prevent you from making this mistake (Item 36). This `equals` method won't compile and the error message will tell you exactly what is wrong:

```
@Override public boolean equals(MyClass o) {
    ...
}
```

Item 9:   Always override `hashCode` when you override `equals`

A common source of bugs is the failure to override the `hashCode` method. **You must override `hashCode` in every class that overrides `equals`.** Failure to do so will result in a violation of the general contract for `Object.hashCode`, which will prevent your class from functioning properly in conjunction with all hash-based collections, including `HashMap`, `HashSet`, and `Hashtable`.

Here is the contract, copied from the `Object` specification [JavaSE6]:

- Whenever it is invoked on the same object more than once during an execution of an application, the `hashCode` method must consistently return the same integer, provided no information used in `equals` comparisons on the object is modified. This integer need not remain consistent from one execution of an application to another execution of the same application.

- If two objects are equal according to the `equals(Object)` method, then calling the `hashCode` method on each of the two objects must produce the same integer result.

- It is not required that if two objects are unequal according to the `equals(Object)` method, then calling the `hashCode` method on each of the two objects must produce distinct integer results. However, the programmer should be aware that producing distinct integer results for unequal objects may improve the performance of hash tables.

The key provision that is violated when you fail to override `hashCode` is the second one: equal objects must have equal hash codes. Two distinct instances may be logically equal according to a class's `equals` method, but to `Object`'s `hashCode` method, they're just two objects with nothing much in common. Therefore `Object`'s `hashCode` method returns two seemingly random numbers instead of two equal numbers as required by the contract.

For example, consider the following simplistic `PhoneNumber` class, whose `equals` method is constructed according to the recipe in Item 8:

```
public final class PhoneNumber {
    private final short areaCode;
    private final short prefix;
    private final short lineNumber;

    public PhoneNumber(int areaCode, int prefix,
                       int lineNumber) {
        rangeCheck(areaCode,     999, "area code");
        rangeCheck(prefix,       999, "prefix");
        rangeCheck(lineNumber, 9999, "line number");
```

```
        this.areaCode  = (short) areaCode;
        this.prefix  = (short) prefix;
        this.lineNumber = (short) lineNumber;
    }

    private static void rangeCheck(int arg, int max,
                                    String name) {
        if (arg < 0 || arg > max)
            throw new IllegalArgumentException(name +": " + arg);
    }

    @Override public boolean equals(Object o) {
        if (o == this)
            return true;
        if (!(o instanceof PhoneNumber))
            return false;
        PhoneNumber pn = (PhoneNumber)o;
        return pn.lineNumber == lineNumber
            && pn.prefix  == prefix
            && pn.areaCode  == areaCode;
    }

    // Broken - no hashCode method!

    ... // Remainder omitted
}
```

Suppose you attempt to use this class with a HashMap:

```
Map<PhoneNumber, String> m
    = new HashMap<PhoneNumber, String>();
m.put(new PhoneNumber(707, 867, 5309), "Jenny");
```

At this point, you might expect m.get(new PhoneNumber(707, 867, 5309)) to return "Jenny", but it returns null. Notice that two PhoneNumber instances are involved: one is used for insertion into the HashMap, and a second, equal, instance is used for (attempted) retrieval. The PhoneNumber class's failure to override hashCode causes the two equal instances to have unequal hash codes, in violation of the hashCode contract. Therefore the get method is likely to look for the phone number in a different hash bucket from the one in which it was stored by the put method. Even if the two instances happen to hash to the same bucket, the get method will almost certainly return null, as HashMap has an optimization that caches the hash code associated with each entry and doesn't bother checking for object equality if the hash codes don't match.

Fixing this problem is as simple as providing a proper hashCode method for the PhoneNumber class. So what should a hashCode method look like? It's trivial to write one that is legal but not good. This one, for example, is always legal but should never be used:

```
// The worst possible legal hash function - never use!
@Override public int hashCode() { return 42; }
```

It's legal because it ensures that equal objects have the same hash code. It's atrocious because it ensures that *every* object has the same hash code. Therefore, every object hashes to the same bucket, and hash tables degenerate to linked lists. Programs that should run in linear time instead run in quadratic time. For large hash tables, this is the difference between working and not working.

A good hash function tends to produce unequal hash codes for unequal objects. This is exactly what is meant by the third provision of the hashCode contract. Ideally, a hash function should distribute any reasonable collection of unequal instances uniformly across all possible hash values. Achieving this ideal can be difficult. Luckily it's not too difficult to achieve a fair approximation. Here is a simple recipe:

1. Store some constant nonzero value, say, 17, in an int variable called result.

2. For each significant field f in your object (each field taken into account by the equals method, that is), do the following:

   a. Compute an int hash code c for the field:
       i.   If the field is a boolean, compute (f ? 1 : 0).
       ii. If the field is a byte, char, short, or int, compute (int) f.
       iii. If the field is a long, compute (int) (f ^ (f >>> 32)).
       iv. If the field is a float, compute Float.floatToIntBits(f).
       v.   If the field is a double, compute Double.doubleToLongBits(f), and then hash the resulting long as in step 2.a.iii.
       vi. If the field is an object reference and this class's equals method compares the field by recursively invoking equals, recursively invoke hashCode on the field. If a more complex comparison is required, compute a "canonical representation" for this field and invoke hashCode on the canonical representation. If the value of the field is null, return 0 (or some other constant, but 0 is traditional).

vii. If the field is an array, treat it as if each element were a separate field. That is, compute a hash code for each significant element by applying these rules recursively, and combine these values per step 2.b. If every element in an array field is significant, you can use one of the `Arrays.hashCode` methods added in release 1.5.

b. Combine the hash code c computed in step 2.a into `result` as follows:

```
result = 31 * result + c;
```

3. Return `result`.

4. When you are finished writing the `hashCode` method, ask yourself whether equal instances have equal hash codes. Write unit tests to verify your intuition! If equal instances have unequal hash codes, figure out why and fix the problem.

You may exclude *redundant fields* from the hash code computation. In other words, you may ignore any field whose value can be computed from fields included in the computation. You *must* exclude any fields that are not used in `equals` comparisons, or you risk violating the second provision of the `hashCode` contract.

A nonzero initial value is used in step 1 so the hash value will be affected by initial fields whose hash value, as computed in step 2.a, is zero. If zero were used as the initial value in step 1, the overall hash value would be unaffected by any such initial fields, which could increase collisions. The value 17 is arbitrary.

The multiplication in step 2.b makes the result depend on the order of the fields, yielding a much better hash function if the class has multiple similar fields. For example, if the multiplication were omitted from a `String` hash function, all anagrams would have identical hash codes. The value 31 was chosen because it is an odd prime. If it were even and the multiplication overflowed, information would be lost, as multiplication by 2 is equivalent to shifting. The advantage of using a prime is less clear, but it is traditional. A nice property of 31 is that the multiplication can be replaced by a shift and a subtraction for better performance: $31 * i == (i << 5) - i$. Modern VMs do this sort of optimization automatically.

Let's apply the above recipe to the `PhoneNumber` class. There are three significant fields, all of type `short`:

```
@Override public int hashCode() {
    int result = 17;
    result = 31 * result + areaCode;
    result = 31 * result + prefix;
    result = 31 * result + lineNumber;
    return result;
}
```

Because this method returns the result of a simple deterministic computation whose only inputs are the three significant fields in a PhoneNumber instance, it is clear that equal PhoneNumber instances have equal hash codes. This method is, in fact, a perfectly good hashCode implementation for PhoneNumber, on a par with those in the Java platform libraries. It is simple, reasonably fast, and does a reasonable job of dispersing unequal phone numbers into different hash buckets.

If a class is immutable and the cost of computing the hash code is significant, you might consider caching the hash code in the object rather than recalculating it each time it is requested. If you believe that most objects of this type will be used as hash keys, then you should calculate the hash code when the instance is created. Otherwise, you might choose to *lazily initialize* it the first time hashCode is invoked (Item 71). It is not clear that our PhoneNumber class merits this treatment, but just to show you how it's done:

```
// Lazily initialized, cached hashCode
private volatile int hashCode;   // (See Item 71)

@Override public int hashCode() {
    int result = hashCode;
    if (result == 0) {
        result = 17;
        result = 31 * result + areaCode;
        result = 31 * result + prefix;
        result = 31 * result + lineNumber;
        hashCode = result;
    }
    return result;
}
```

While the recipe in this item yields reasonably good hash functions, it does not yield state-of-the-art hash functions, nor do the Java platform libraries provide such hash functions as of release 1.6. Writing such hash functions is a research topic, best left to mathematicians and theoretical computer scientists. Perhaps a later release of the platform will provide state-of-the-art hash functions for its classes and utility methods to allow average programmers to construct such hash functions. In the meantime, the techniques described in this item should be adequate for most applications.

Do not be tempted to exclude significant parts of an object from the hash code computation to improve performance. While the resulting hash function may run faster, its poor quality may degrade hash tables' performance to the point where they become unusably slow. In particular, the hash function may, in practice, be confronted with a large collection of instances that differ largely in the regions that you've chosen to ignore. If this happens, the hash function will map all the instances to a very few hash codes, and hash-based collections will display quadratic performance. This is not just a theoretical problem. The String hash function implemented in all releases prior to 1.2 examined at most sixteen characters, evenly spaced throughout the string, starting with the first character. For large collections of hierarchical names, such as URLs, this hash function displayed exactly the pathological behavior noted here.

Many classes in the Java platform libraries, such as String, Integer, and Date, include in their specifications the exact value returned by their hashCode method as a function of the instance value. This is generally *not* a good idea, as it severely limits your ability to improve the hash function in future releases. If you leave the details of a hash function unspecified and a flaw is found or a better hash function discovered, you can change the hash function in a subsequent release, confident that no clients depend on the exact values returned by the hash function.

Item 10: Always override `toString`

While `java.lang.Object` provides an implementation of the `toString` method, the string that it returns is generally not what the user of your class wants to see. It consists of the class name followed by an "at" sign (@) and the unsigned hexadecimal representation of the hash code, for example, "PhoneNumber@163b91." The general contract for `toString` says that the returned string should be "a concise but informative representation that is easy for a person to read" [JavaSE6]. While it could be argued that "PhoneNumber@163b91" is concise and easy to read, it isn't very informative when compared to "(707) 867-5309." The `toString` contract goes on to say, "It is recommended that all subclasses override this method." Good advice, indeed!

While it isn't as important as obeying the `equals` and `hashCode` contracts (Item 8, Item 9), **providing a good `toString` implementation makes your class much more pleasant to use**. The `toString` method is automatically invoked when an object is passed to `println`, `printf`, the string concatenation operator, or `assert`, or printed by a debugger. (The `printf` method was added to the platform in release 1.5, as were related methods including `String.format`, which is roughly equivalent to C's `sprintf`.)

If you've provided a good `toString` method for `PhoneNumber`, generating a useful diagnostic message is as easy as this:

```
System.out.println("Failed to connect: " + phoneNumber);
```

Programmers will generate diagnostic messages in this fashion whether or not you override `toString`, but the messages won't be useful unless you do. The benefits of providing a good `toString` method extend beyond instances of the class to objects containing references to these instances, especially collections. Which would you rather see when printing a map, "{Jenny=PhoneNumber@163b91}" or "{Jenny=(707) 867-5309}"?

When practical, the `toString` method should return *all* of the interesting information contained in the object, as in the phone number example just shown. It is impractical if the object is large or if it contains state that is not conducive to string representation. Under these circumstances, `toString` should return a summary such as "Manhattan white pages (1487536 listings)" or "Thread[main,5,main]". Ideally, the string should be self-explanatory. (The Thread example flunks this test.)

One important decision you'll have to make when implementing a toString method is whether to specify the format of the return value in the documentation. It is recommended that you do this for *value classes*, such as phone numbers or matrices. The advantage of specifying the format is that it serves as a standard, unambiguous, human-readable representation of the object. This representation can be used for input and output and in persistent human-readable data objects, such as XML documents. If you specify the format, it's usually a good idea to provide a matching static factory or constructor so programmers can easily translate back and forth between the object and its string representation. This approach is taken by many value classes in the Java platform libraries, including BigInteger, BigDecimal, and most of the boxed primitive classes.

The disadvantage of specifying the format of the toString return value is that once you've specified it, you're stuck with it for life, assuming your class is widely used. Programmers will write code to parse the representation, to generate it, and to embed it into persistent data. If you change the representation in a future release, you'll break their code and data, and they will yowl. By failing to specify a format, you preserve the flexibility to add information or improve the format in a subsequent release.

Whether or not you decide to specify the format, you should clearly document your intentions. If you specify the format, you should do so precisely. For example, here's a toString method to go with the PhoneNumber class in Item 9:

```
/**
 * Returns the string representation of this phone number.
 * The string consists of fourteen characters whose format
 * is "(XXX) YYY-ZZZZ", where XXX is the area code, YYY is
 * the prefix, and ZZZZ is the line number.  (Each of the
 * capital letters represents a single decimal digit.)
 *
 * If any of the three parts of this phone number is too small
 * to fill up its field, the field is padded with leading zeros.
 * For example, if the value of the line number is 123, the last
 * four characters of the string representation will be "0123".
 *
 * Note that there is a single space separating the closing
 * parenthesis after the area code from the first digit of the
 * prefix.
 */
@Override public String toString() {
    return String.format("(%03d) %03d-%04d",
                         areaCode, prefix, lineNumber);
}
```

If you decide not to specify a format, the documentation comment should read something like this:

```
/**
 * Returns a brief description of this potion. The exact details
 * of the representation are unspecified and subject to change,
 * but the following may be regarded as typical:
 *
 * "[Potion #9: type=love, smell=turpentine, look=india ink]"
 */
@Override public String toString() { ... }
```

After reading this comment, programmers who produce code or persistent data that depends on the details of the format will have no one but themselves to blame when the format is changed.

Whether or not you specify the format, **provide programmatic access to all of the information contained in the value returned by toString.** For example, the PhoneNumber class should contain accessors for the area code, prefix, and line number. If you fail to do this, you *force* programmers who need this information to parse the string. Besides reducing performance and making unnecessary work for programmers, this process is error-prone and results in fragile systems that break if you change the format. By failing to provide accessors, you turn the string format into a de facto API, even if you've specified that it's subject to change.

Item 11: Override `clone` judiciously

The `Cloneable` interface was intended as a *mixin interface* (Item 18) for objects to advertise that they permit cloning. Unfortunately, it fails to serve this purpose. Its primary flaw is that it lacks a `clone` method, and `Object`'s `clone` method is protected. You cannot, without resorting to *reflection* (Item 53), invoke the `clone` method on an object merely because it implements `Cloneable`. Even a reflective invocation may fail, as there is no guarantee that the object has an accessible `clone` method. Despite this flaw and others, the facility is in wide use so it pays to understand it. This item tells you how to implement a well-behaved `clone` method, discusses when it is appropriate to do so, and presents alternatives.

So what *does* `Cloneable` do, given that it contains no methods? It determines the behavior of `Object`'s protected `clone` implementation: if a class implements `Cloneable`, `Object`'s `clone` method returns a field-by-field copy of the object; otherwise it throws `CloneNotSupportedException`. This is a highly atypical use of interfaces and not one to be emulated. Normally, implementing an interface says something about what a class can do for its clients. In the case of `Cloneable`, it modifies the behavior of a protected method on a superclass.

If implementing the `Cloneable` interface is to have any effect on a class, the class and all of its superclasses must obey a fairly complex, unenforceable, and thinly documented protocol. The resulting mechanism is *extralinguistic*: it creates an object without calling a constructor.

The general contract for the `clone` method is weak. Here it is, copied from the specification for `java.lang.Object` [JavaSE6]:

> Creates and returns a copy of this object. The precise meaning of "copy" may depend on the class of the object. The general intent is that, for any object x, the expression
>
> ```
> x.clone() != x
> ```
>
> will be `true`, and the expression
>
> ```
> x.clone().getClass() == x.getClass()
> ```
>
> will be `true`, but these are not absolute requirements. While it is typically the case that
>
> ```
> x.clone().equals(x)
> ```
>
> will be `true`, this is not an absolute requirement. Copying an object will typically entail creating a new instance of its class, but it may require copying of internal data structures as well. No constructors are called.

There are a number of problems with this contract. The provision that "no constructors are called" is too strong. A well-behaved clone method can call constructors to create objects internal to the clone under construction. If the class is final, clone can even return an object created by a constructor.

The provision that x.clone().getClass() should generally be identical to x.getClass(), however, is too weak. In practice, programmers assume that if they extend a class and invoke super.clone from the subclass, the returned object will be an instance of the subclass. The *only* way a superclass can provide this functionality is to return an object obtained by calling super.clone. If a clone method returns an object created by a constructor, it will have the wrong class. Therefore, **if you override the clone method in a nonfinal class, you should return an object obtained by invoking super.clone.** If all of a class's superclasses obey this rule, then invoking super.clone will eventually invoke Object's clone method, creating an instance of the right class. This mechanism is vaguely similar to automatic constructor chaining, except that it isn't enforced.

The Cloneable interface does not, as of release 1.6, spell out in detail the responsibilities that a class takes on when it implements this interface. **In practice, a class that implements Cloneable is expected to provide a properly functioning public clone method.** It is not, in general, possible to do so unless all of the class's superclasses provide a well-behaved clone implementation, whether public or protected.

Suppose you want to implement Cloneable in a class whose superclasses provide well-behaved clone methods. The object you get from super.clone() may or may not be close to what you'll eventually return, depending on the nature of the class. This object will be, from the standpoint of each superclass, a fully functional clone of the original object. The fields declared in your class (if any) will have values identical to those of the object being cloned. If every field contains a primitive value or a reference to an immutable object, the returned object may be exactly what you need, in which case no further processing is necessary. This is the case, for example, for the PhoneNumber class in Item 9. In this case, all you need do in addition to declaring that you implement Cloneable is to provide public access to Object's protected clone method:

```
@Override public PhoneNumber clone() {
    try {
        return (PhoneNumber) super.clone();
    } catch(CloneNotSupportedException e) {
        throw new AssertionError();  // Can't happen
    }
}
```

Note that the above clone method returns PhoneNumber, not Object. As of release 1.5, it is legal and desirable to do this, because *covariant return types* were introduced in release 1.5 as part of generics. In other words, it is now legal for an overriding method's return type to be a subclass of the overridden method's return type. This allows the overriding method to provide more information about the returned object and eliminates the need for casting in the client. Because Object.clone returns Object, PhoneNumber.clone must cast the result of super.clone() before returning it, but this is far preferable to requiring every caller of PhoneNumber.clone to cast the result. The general principle at play here is **never make the client do anything the library can do for the client.**

If an object contains fields that refer to mutable objects, using the simple clone implementation shown above can be disastrous. For example, consider the Stack class in Item 6:

```
public class Stack {
    private Object[] elements;
    private int size = 0;
    private static final int DEFAULT_INITIAL_CAPACITY = 16;

    public Stack() {
        this.elements = new Object[DEFAULT_INITIAL_CAPACITY];
    }

    public void push(Object e) {
        ensureCapacity();
        elements[size++] = e;
    }

    public Object pop() {
        if (size == 0)
            throw new EmptyStackException();
        Object result = elements[--size];
        elements[size] = null; // Eliminate obsolete reference
        return result;
    }

    // Ensure space for at least one more element.
    private void ensureCapacity() {
        if (elements.length == size)
            elements = Arrays.copyOf(elements, 2 * size + 1);
    }
}
```

Suppose you want to make this class cloneable. If its clone method merely returns super.clone(), the resulting Stack instance will have the correct value in its `size` field, but its `elements` field will refer to the same array as the original `Stack` instance. Modifying the original will destroy the invariants in the clone and vice versa. You will quickly find that your program produces nonsensical results or throws a `NullPointerException`.

This situation could never occur as a result of calling the sole constructor in the `Stack` class. **In effect, the `clone` method functions as another constructor; you must ensure that it does no harm to the original object and that it properly establishes invariants on the clone**. In order for the `clone` method on `Stack` to work properly, it must copy the internals of the stack. The easiest way to do this is to call `clone` recursively on the `elements` array:

```
@Override public Stack clone() {
    try {
        Stack result = (Stack) super.clone();
        result.elements = elements.clone();
        return result;
    } catch (CloneNotSupportedException e) {
        throw new AssertionError();
    }
}
```

Note that we do not have to cast the result of `elements.clone()` to `Object[]`. As of release 1.5, calling `clone` on an array returns an array whose compile-time type is the same as that of the array being cloned.

Note also that the above solution would not work if the `elements` field were final, because `clone` would be prohibited from assigning a new value to the field. This is a fundamental problem: **the `clone` architecture is incompatible with normal use of final fields referring to mutable objects**, except in cases where the mutable objects may be safely shared between an object and its clone. In order to make a class cloneable, it may be necessary to remove `final` modifiers from some fields.

It is not always sufficient to call `clone` recursively. For example, suppose you are writing a `clone` method for a hash table whose internals consist of an array of buckets, each of which references the first entry in a linked list of key-value pairs or is `null` if the bucket is empty. For performance, the class implements its own lightweight singly linked list instead of using `java.util.LinkedList` internally:

```
public class HashTable implements Cloneable {
    private Entry[] buckets = ...;
```

```
        private static class Entry {
            final Object key;
            Object value;
            Entry  next;

            Entry(Object key, Object value, Entry next) {
                this.key   = key;
                this.value = value;
                this.next  = next;
            }
        }

        ... // Remainder omitted
    }
```

Suppose you merely clone the bucket array recursively, as we did for Stack:

```
// Broken - results in shared internal state!
@Override public HashTable clone() {
    try {
        HashTable result = (HashTable) super.clone();
        result.buckets = buckets.clone();
        return result;
    } catch (CloneNotSupportedException e) {
        throw new AssertionError();
    }
}
```

Though the clone has its own bucket array, this array references the same linked lists as the original, which can easily cause nondeterministic behavior in both the clone and the original. To fix this problem, you'll have to copy the linked list that comprises each bucket individually. Here is one common approach:

```
public class HashTable implements Cloneable {
    private Entry[] buckets = ...;

    private static class Entry {
        final Object key;
        Object value;
        Entry  next;

        Entry(Object key, Object value, Entry next) {
            this.key   = key;
            this.value = value;
            this.next  = next;
        }
```

```
        // Recursively copy the linked list headed by this Entry
        Entry deepCopy() {
            return new Entry(key, value,
                next == null ? null : next.deepCopy());
        }
    }

    @Override public HashTable clone() {
        try {
            HashTable result = (HashTable) super.clone();
            result.buckets = new Entry[buckets.length];
            for (int i = 0; i < buckets.length; i++)
                if (buckets[i] != null)
                    result.buckets[i] = buckets[i].deepCopy();
            return result;
        } catch (CloneNotSupportedException e) {
            throw new AssertionError();
        }
    }
    ... // Remainder omitted
}
```

The private class `HashTable.Entry` has been augmented to support a "deep copy" method. The `clone` method on `HashTable` allocates a new `buckets` array of the proper size and iterates over the original `buckets` array, deep-copying each nonempty bucket. The deep-copy method on `Entry` invokes itself recursively to copy the entire linked list headed by the entry. While this technique is cute and works fine if the buckets aren't too long, it is not a good way to clone a linked list because it consumes one stack frame for each element in the list. If the list is long, this could easily cause a stack overflow. To prevent this from happening, you can replace the recursion in deepCopy with iteration:

```
// Iteratively copy the linked list headed by this Entry
Entry deepCopy() {
    Entry result = new Entry(key, value, next);

    for (Entry p = result; p.next != null; p = p.next)
        p.next = new Entry(p.next.key, p.next.value, p.next.next);

    return result;
}
```

A final approach to cloning complex objects is to call `super.clone`, set all of the fields in the resulting object to their virgin state, and then call higher-level methods to regenerate the state of the object. In the case of our `HashTable` example, the buckets field would be initialized to a new bucket array, and the put(key, value) method (not shown) would be invoked for each key-value mapping in the hash table being cloned. This approach typically yields a simple, reasonably elegant clone method that generally doesn't run quite as fast as one that directly manipulates the innards of the object and its clone.

Like a constructor, a clone method should not invoke any nonfinal methods on the clone under construction (Item 17). If clone invokes an overridden method, this method will execute before the subclass in which it is defined has had a chance to fix its state in the clone, quite possibly leading to corruption in the clone and the original. Therefore the put(key, value) method discussed in the previous paragraph should be either final or private. (If it is private, it is presumably the "helper method" for a nonfinal public method.)

Object's clone method is declared to throw CloneNotSupportedException, but overriding clone methods can omit this declaration. Public clone methods *should* omit it because methods that don't throw checked exceptions are easier to use (Item 59). If a class that is designed for inheritance (Item 17) overrides clone, the overriding method should mimic the behavior of Object.clone: it should be declared protected, it should be declared to throw CloneNotSupportedException, and the class should not implement Cloneable. This gives subclasses the freedom to implement Cloneable or not, just as if they extended Object directly.

One more detail bears noting. If you decide to make a thread-safe class implement Cloneable, remember that its clone method must be properly synchronized just like any other method (Item 66). Object's clone method is not synchronized, so even if it is otherwise satisfactory, you may have to write a synchronized clone method that invokes super.clone().

To recap, all classes that implement Cloneable should override clone with a public method whose return type is the class itself. This method should first call super.clone and then fix any fields that need to be fixed. Typically, this means copying any mutable objects that comprise the internal "deep structure" of the object being cloned, and replacing the clone's references to these objects with references to the copies. While these internal copies can generally be made by calling clone recursively, this is not always the best approach. If the class contains only primitive fields or references to immutable objects, then it is probably the case that no fields need to be fixed. There are exceptions to this rule. For example, a field representing a serial number or other unique ID or a field representing the object's creation time will need to be fixed, even if it is primitive or immutable.

Is all this complexity really necessary? Rarely. If you extend a class that implements Cloneable, you have little choice but to implement a well-behaved clone method. Otherwise, **you are better off providing an alternative means of object copying, or simply not providing the capability**. For example, it doesn't make sense for immutable classes to support object copying, because copies would be virtually indistinguishable from the original.

A fine approach to object copying is to provide a *copy constructor* or *copy factory*. A copy constructor is simply a constructor that takes a single argument whose type is the class containing the constructor, for example,

```
public Yum(Yum yum);
```

A copy factory is the static factory analog of a copy constructor:

```
public static Yum newInstance(Yum yum);
```

The copy constructor approach and its static factory variant have many advantages over Cloneable/clone: they don't rely on a risk-prone extralinguistic object creation mechanism; they don't demand unenforceable adherence to thinly documented conventions; they don't conflict with the proper use of final fields; they don't throw unnecessary checked exceptions; and they don't require casts. While it is impossible to put a copy constructor or factory in an interface, Cloneable fails to function as an interface because it lacks a public clone method. Therefore you aren't giving up interface functionality by using a copy constructor or factory in preference to a clone method.

Furthermore, a copy constructor or factory can take an argument whose type is an interface implemented by the class. For example, by convention all general-purpose collection implementations provide a constructor whose argument is of type Collection or Map. Interface-based copy constructors and factories, more properly known as *conversion constructors* and *conversion factories*, allow the client to choose the implementation type of the copy rather than forcing the client to accept the implementation type of the original. Suppose you have a HashSet s, and you want to copy it as a TreeSet. The clone method can't offer this functionality, but it's easy with a conversion constructor: new TreeSet(s).

Given all of the problems associated with Cloneable, it's safe to say that other interfaces should not extend it, and that classes designed for inheritance (Item 17) should not implement it. Because of its many shortcomings, some expert programmers simply choose never to override the clone method and never to invoke it except, perhaps, to copy arrays. If you design a class for inheritance, be aware that if you choose not to provide a well-behaved protected clone method, it will be impossible for subclasses to implement Cloneable.

Item 12: Consider implementing Comparable

Unlike the other methods discussed in this chapter, the compareTo method is not declared in Object. Rather, it is the sole method in the Comparable interface. It is similar in character to Object's equals method, except that it permits order comparisons in addition to simple equality comparisons, and it is generic. By implementing Comparable, a class indicates that its instances have a *natural ordering.* Sorting an array of objects that implement Comparable is as simple as this:

```
Arrays.sort(a);
```

It is similarly easy to search, compute extreme values, and maintain automatically sorted collections of Comparable objects. For example, the following program, which relies on the fact that String implements Comparable, prints an alphabetized list of its command-line arguments with duplicates eliminated:

```
public class WordList {
    public static void main(String[] args) {
        Set<String> s = new TreeSet<String>();
        Collections.addAll(s, args);
        System.out.println(s);
    }
}
```

By implementing Comparable, you allow your class to interoperate with all of the many generic algorithms and collection implementations that depend on this interface. You gain a tremendous amount of power for a small amount of effort. Virtually all of the value classes in the Java platform libraries implement Comparable. If you are writing a value class with an obvious natural ordering, such as alphabetical order, numerical order, or chronological order, you should strongly consider implementing the interface:

```
public interface Comparable<T> {
    int compareTo(T t);
}
```

The general contract of the compareTo method is similar to that of equals:

Compares this object with the specified object for order. Returns a negative integer, zero, or a positive integer as this object is less than, equal to, or greater than the specified object. Throws ClassCastException if the specified object's type prevents it from being compared to this object.

In the following description, the notation sgn(*expression*) designates the mathematical *signum* function, which is defined to return -1, 0, or 1, according to whether the value of *expression* is negative, zero, or positive.

- The implementor must ensure sgn(x.compareTo(y)) == -sgn(y.compareTo(x)) for all x and y. (This implies that x.compareTo(y) must throw an exception if and only if y.compareTo(x) throws an exception.)

- The implementor must also ensure that the relation is transitive: (x.compareTo(y) > 0 && y.compareTo(z) > 0) implies x.compareTo(z) > 0.

- Finally, the implementor must ensure that x.compareTo(y) == 0 implies that sgn(x.compareTo(z)) == sgn(y.compareTo(z)), for all z.

- It is strongly recommended, but not strictly required, that (x.compareTo(y) == 0) == (x.equals(y)). Generally speaking, any class that implements the Comparable interface and violates this condition should clearly indicate this fact. The recommended language is "Note: This class has a natural ordering that is inconsistent with equals."

Don't be put off by the mathematical nature of this contract. Like the equals contract (Item 8), this contract isn't as complicated as it looks. Within a class, any reasonable ordering will satisfy it. Across classes, compareTo, unlike equals, doesn't have to work: it is permitted to throw ClassCastException if two object references being compared refer to objects of different classes. Usually, that is exactly what compareTo *should* do, and what it *will* do if the class is properly parameterized. While the contract doesn't preclude interclass comparisons, there are, as of release 1.6, no classes in the Java platform libraries that support them.

Just as a class that violates the hashCode contract can break other classes that depend on hashing, a class that violates the compareTo contract can break other classes that depend on comparison. Classes that depend on comparison include the sorted collections TreeSet and TreeMap, and the utility classes Collections and Arrays, which contain searching and sorting algorithms.

Let's go over the provisions of the compareTo contract. The first provision says that if you reverse the direction of a comparison between two object references, the expected thing happens: if the first object is less than the second, then the second must be greater than the first; if the first object is equal to the second, then the second must be equal to the first; and if the first object is greater than the second, then the second must be less than the first. The second provision says that if one object is greater than a second, and the second is greater than a third, then the first must be greater than the third. The final provision says that all objects that compare as equal must yield the same results when compared to any other object.

One consequence of these three provisions is that the equality test imposed by a compareTo method must obey the same restrictions imposed by the equals contract: reflexivity, symmetry, and transitivity. Therefore the same caveat applies: there is no way to extend an instantiable class with a new value component while preserving the compareTo contract, unless you are willing to forgo the benefits of object-oriented abstraction (Item 8). The same workaround applies, too. If you want to add a value component to a class that implements Comparable, don't extend it; write an unrelated class containing an instance of the first class. Then provide a "view" method that returns this instance. This frees you to implement whatever compareTo method you like on the second class, while allowing its client to view an instance of the second class as an instance of the first class when needed.

The final paragraph of the compareTo contract, which is a strong suggestion rather than a true provision, simply states that the equality test imposed by the compareTo method should generally return the same results as the equals method. If this provision is obeyed, the ordering imposed by the compareTo method is said to be *consistent with equals*. If it's violated, the ordering is said to be *inconsistent with equals*. A class whose compareTo method imposes an order that is inconsistent with equals will still work, but sorted collections containing elements of the class may not obey the general contract of the appropriate collection interfaces (Collection, Set, or Map). This is because the general contracts for these interfaces are defined in terms of the equals method, but sorted collections use the equality test imposed by compareTo in place of equals. It is not a catastrophe if this happens, but it's something to be aware of.

For example, consider the BigDecimal class, whose compareTo method is inconsistent with equals. If you create a HashSet instance and add new BigDecimal("1.0") and new BigDecimal("1.00"), the set will contain two elements because the two BigDecimal instances added to the set are unequal when compared using the equals method. If, however, you perform the same procedure using a TreeSet instead of a HashSet, the set will contain only one element because the two BigDecimal instances are equal when compared using the compareTo method. (See the BigDecimal documentation for details.)

Writing a compareTo method is similar to writing an equals method, but there are a few key differences. Because the Comparable interface is parameterized, the compareTo method is statically typed, so you don't need to type check or cast its argument. If the argument is of the wrong type, the invocation won't even compile. If the argument is null, the invocation should throw a NullPointerException, and it will, as soon as the method attempts to access its members.

The field comparisons in a compareTo method are order comparisons rather than equality comparisons. Compare object reference fields by invoking the compareTo method recursively. If a field does not implement Comparable, or you need to use a nonstandard ordering, you can use an explicit Comparator instead. Either write your own, or use a preexisting one as in this compareTo method for the CaseInsensitiveString class in Item 8.

```
public final class CaseInsensitiveString
        implements Comparable<CaseInsensitiveString> {
    public int compareTo(CaseInsensitiveString cis) {
        return String.CASE_INSENSITIVE_ORDER.compare(s, cis.s);
    }
    ... // Remainder omitted
}
```

Note that the CaseInsensitiveString class implements Comparable<CaseInsensitiveString>. This means that a CaseInsensitiveString reference can be compared only to other CaseInsensitiveString references. It is the normal pattern to follow when declaring a class to implement Comparable. Note also that the parameter of the compareTo method is a CaseInsensitiveString, not an Object. This is required by the aforementioned class declaration.

Compare integral primitive fields using the relational operators < and >. For floating-point fields, use Double.compare or Float.compare in place of the relational operators, which do not obey the general contract for compareTo when applied to floating point values. For array fields, apply these guidelines to each element.

If a class has multiple significant fields, the order in which you compare them is critical. You must start with the most significant field and work your way down. If a comparison results in anything other than zero (which represents equality), you're done; just return the result. If the most significant fields are equal, go on to compare the next-most-significant fields, and so on. If all fields are equal, the objects are equal; return zero. The technique is demonstrated by this compareTo method for the PhoneNumber class in Item 9:

```
public int compareTo(PhoneNumber pn) {
    // Compare area codes
    if (areaCode < pn.areaCode)
        return -1;
    if (areaCode > pn.areaCode)
        return  1;
```

```
        // Area codes are equal, compare prefixes
        if (prefix < pn.prefix)
            return -1;
        if (prefix > pn.prefix)
            return  1;

        // Area codes and prefixes are equal, compare line numbers
        if (lineNumber < pn.lineNumber)
            return -1;
        if (lineNumber > pn.lineNumber)
            return  1;

        return 0;  // All fields are equal
    }
```

While this method works, it can be improved. Recall that the contract for com-pareTo does not specify the magnitude of the return value, only the sign. You can take advantage of this to simplify the code and probably make it run a bit faster:

```
public int compareTo(PhoneNumber pn) {
    // Compare area codes
    int areaCodeDiff = areaCode - pn.areaCode;
    if (areaCodeDiff != 0)
        return areaCodeDiff;

    // Area codes are equal, compare prefixes
    int prefixDiff = prefix - pn.prefix;
    if (prefixDiff != 0)
        return prefixDiff;

    // Area codes and prefixes are equal, compare line numbers
    return lineNumber - pn.lineNumber;
}
```

This trick works fine here but should be used with extreme caution. Don't use it unless you're certain the fields in question are non-negative or, more generally, that the difference between the lowest and highest possible field values is less than or equal to Integer.MAX_VALUE (2^{31}-1). The reason this trick doesn't always work is that a signed 32-bit integer isn't big enough to hold the difference between two arbitrary signed 32-bit integers. If i is a large positive int and j is a large negative int, (i - j) will overflow and return a negative value. The resulting compareTo method will return incorrect results for some arguments and violate the first and second provisions of the compareTo contract. This is not a purely theoretical prob-lem: it has caused failures in real systems. These failures can be difficult to debug, as the broken compareTo method works properly for most input values.

CHAPTER 4

Classes and Interfaces

CLASSES and interfaces lie at the heart of the Java programming language. They are its basic units of abstraction. The language provides many powerful elements that you can use to design classes and interfaces. This chapter contains guidelines to help you make the best use of these elements so that your classes and interfaces are usable, robust, and flexible.

Item 13: Minimize the accessibility of classes and members

The single most important factor that distinguishes a well-designed module from a poorly designed one is the degree to which the module hides its internal data and other implementation details from other modules. A well-designed module hides all of its implementation details, cleanly separating its API from its implementation. Modules then communicate only through their APIs and are oblivious to each others' inner workings. This concept, known as *information hiding* or *encapsulation*, is one of the fundamental tenets of software design [Parnas72].

Information hiding is important for many reasons, most of which stem from the fact that it *decouples* the modules that comprise a system, allowing them to be developed, tested, optimized, used, understood, and modified in isolation. This speeds up system development because modules can be developed in parallel. It eases the burden of maintenance because modules can be understood more quickly and debugged with little fear of harming other modules. While information hiding does not, in and of itself, cause good performance, it enables effective performance tuning: once a system is complete and profiling has determined which modules are causing performance problems (Item 55), those modules can be optimized without affecting the correctness of other modules. Information hiding increases software reuse because modules that aren't tightly coupled often prove useful in other contexts besides the ones for which they were developed.

Finally, information hiding decreases the risk in building large systems, because individual modules may prove successful even if the system does not.

Java has many facilities to aid in information hiding. The *access control* mechanism [JLS, 6.6] specifies the *accessibility* of classes, interfaces, and members. The accessibility of an entity is determined by the location of its declaration and by which, if any, of the access modifiers (`private`, `protected`, and `public`) is present on the declaration. Proper use of these modifiers is essential to information hiding.

The rule of thumb is simple: **make each class or member as inaccessible as possible.** In other words, use the lowest possible access level consistent with the proper functioning of the software that you are writing.

For top-level (non-nested) classes and interfaces, there are only two possible access levels: *package-private* and *public*. If you declare a top-level class or interface with the `public` modifier, it will be public; otherwise, it will be package-private. If a top-level class or interface can be made package-private, it should be. By making it package-private, you make it part of the implementation rather than the exported API, and you can modify it, replace it, or eliminate it in a subsequent release without fear of harming existing clients. If you make it public, you are obligated to support it forever to maintain compatibility.

If a package-private top-level class (or interface) is used by only one class, consider making the top-level class a private nested class of the sole class that uses it (Item 22). This reduces its accessibility from all the classes in its package to the one class that uses it. But it is far more important to reduce the accessibility of a gratuitously public class than of a package-private top-level class: the public class is part of the package's API, while the package-private top-level class is already part of its implementation.

For members (fields, methods, nested classes, and nested interfaces), there are four possible access levels, listed here in order of increasing accessibility:

- **private**—The member is accessible only from the top-level class where it is declared.

- **package-private**—The member is accessible from any class in the package where it is declared. Technically known as *default* access, this is the access level you get if no access modifier is specified.

- **protected**—The member is accessible from subclasses of the class where it is declared (subject to a few restrictions [JLS, 6.6.2]) and from any class in the package where it is declared.

- **public**—The member is accessible from anywhere.

After carefully designing your class's public API, your reflex should be to make all other members private. Only if another class in the same package really needs to access a member should you remove the `private` modifier, making the member package-private. If you find yourself doing this often, you should reexamine the design of your system to see if another decomposition might yield classes that are better decoupled from one another. That said, both private and package-private members are part of a class's implementation and do not normally impact its exported API. These fields can, however, "leak" into the exported API if the class implements `Serializable` (Item 74, Item 75).

For members of public classes, a huge increase in accessibility occurs when the access level goes from package-private to protected. A protected member is part of the class's exported API and must be supported forever. Also, a protected member of an exported class represents a public commitment to an implementation detail (Item 17). The need for protected members should be relatively rare.

There is one rule that restricts your ability to reduce the accessibility of methods. If a method overrides a superclass method, it is not permitted to have a lower access level in the subclass than it does in the superclass [JLS, 8.4.8.3]. This is necessary to ensure that an instance of the subclass is usable anywhere that an instance of the superclass is usable. If you violate this rule, the compiler will generate an error message when you try to compile the subclass. A special case of this rule is that if a class implements an interface, all of the class methods that are also present in the interface must be declared public. This is so because all members of an interface are implicitly public [JLS, 9.1.5].

To facilitate testing, you may be tempted to make a class, interface, or member more accessible. This is fine up to a point. It is acceptable to make a private member of a public class package-private in order to test it, but it is not acceptable to raise the accessibility any higher than that. In other words, it is not acceptable to make a class, interface, or member a part of a package's exported API to facilitate testing. Luckily, it isn't necessary either, as tests can be made to run as part of the package being tested, thus gaining access to its package-private elements.

Instance fields should never be public (Item 14). If an instance field is non-final, or is a final reference to a mutable object, then by making the field public, you give up the ability to limit the values that can be stored in the field. This means you also give up the ability to enforce invariants involving the field. Also, you give up the ability to take any action when the field is modified, so **classes with public mutable fields are not thread-safe**. Even if a field is final and refers to an immutable object, by making the field public you give up the flexibility to switch to a new internal data representation in which the field does not exist.

The same advice applies to static fields, with the one exception. You can expose constants via public static final fields, assuming the constants form an integral part of the abstraction provided by the class. By convention, such fields have names consisting of capital letters, with words separated by underscores (Item 56). It is critical that these fields contain either primitive values or references to immutable objects (Item 15). A final field containing a reference to a mutable object has all the disadvantages of a nonfinal field. While the reference cannot be modified, the referenced object can be modified—with disastrous results.

Note that a nonzero-length array is always mutable, so **it is wrong for a class to have a public static final array field, or an accessor that returns such a field**. If a class has such a field or accessor, clients will be able to modify the contents of the array. This is a frequent source of security holes:

```
// Potential security hole!
public static final Thing[] VALUES = { ... };
```

Beware of the fact that many IDEs generate accessors that return references to private array fields, resulting in exactly this problem. There are two ways to fix the problem. You can make the public array private and add a public immutable list:

```
private static final Thing[] PRIVATE_VALUES = { ... };
public static final List<Thing> VALUES =
    Collections.unmodifiableList(Arrays.asList(PRIVATE_VALUES));
```

Alternatively, you can make the array private and add a public method that returns a copy of a private array:

```
private static final Thing[] PRIVATE_VALUES = { ... };
public static final Thing[] values() {
    return PRIVATE_VALUES.clone();
}
```

To choose between these alternatives, think about what the client is likely to do with the result. Which return type will be more convenient? Which will give better performance?

To summarize, you should always reduce accessibility as much as possible. After carefully designing a minimal public API, you should prevent any stray classes, interfaces, or members from becoming a part of the API. With the exception of public static final fields, public classes should have no public fields. Ensure that objects referenced by public static final fields are immutable.

Item 14: In public classes, use accessor methods, not public fields

Occasionally, you may be tempted to write degenerate classes that serve no purpose other than to group instance fields:

```
// Degenerate classes like this should not be public!
class Point {
    public double x;
    public double y;
}
```

Because the data fields of such classes are accessed directly, these classes do not offer the benefits of *encapsulation* (Item 13). You can't change the representation without changing the API, you can't enforce invariants, and you can't take auxiliary action when a field is accessed. Hard-line object-oriented programmers feel that such classes are anathema and should always be replaced by classes with private fields and public *accessor methods* (getters) and, for mutable classes, *mutators* (setters):

```
// Encapsulation of data by accessor methods and mutators
class Point {
    private double x;
    private double y;

    public Point(double x, double y) {
        this.x = x;
        this.y = y;
    }

    public double getX() { return x; }
    public double getY() { return y; }

    public void setX(double x) { this.x = x; }
    public void setY(double y) { this.y = y; }
}
```

Certainly, the hard-liners are correct when it comes to public classes: **if a class is accessible outside its package, provide accessor methods,** to preserve the flexibility to change the class's internal representation. If a public class exposes its data fields, all hope of changing its representation is lost, as client code can be distributed far and wide.

However, **if a class is package-private or is a private nested class, there is nothing inherently wrong with exposing its data fields**—assuming they do an adequate job of describing the abstraction provided by the class. This approach generates less visual clutter than the accessor-method approach, both in the class definition and in the client code that uses it. While the client code is tied to the class's internal representation, this code is confined to the package containing the class. If a change in representation becomes desirable, you can make the change without touching any code outside the package. In the case of a private nested class, the scope of the change is further restricted to the enclosing class.

Several classes in the Java platform libraries violate the advice that public classes should not expose fields directly. Prominent examples include the Point and Dimension classes in the java.awt package. Rather than examples to be emulated, these classes should be regarded as cautionary tales. As described in Item 55, the decision to expose the internals of the Dimension class resulted in a serious performance problem that is still with us today.

While it's never a good idea for a public class to expose fields directly, it is less harmful if the fields are immutable. You can't change the representation of such a class without changing its API, and you can't take auxiliary actions when a field is read, but you can enforce invariants. For example, this class guarantees that each instance represents a valid time:

```
// Public class with exposed immutable fields - questionable
public final class Time {
    private static final int HOURS_PER_DAY    = 24;
    private static final int MINUTES_PER_HOUR = 60;

    public final int hour;
    public final int minute;

    public Time(int hour, int minute) {
        if (hour < 0 || hour >= HOURS_PER_DAY)
            throw new IllegalArgumentException("Hour: " + hour);
        if (minute < 0 || minute >= MINUTES_PER_HOUR)
            throw new IllegalArgumentException("Min: " + minute);
        this.hour = hour;
        this.minute = minute;
    }
    ... // Remainder omitted
}
```

In summary, public classes should never expose mutable fields. It is less harmful, though still questionable, for public classes to expose immutable fields. It is, however, sometimes desirable for package-private or private nested classes to expose fields, whether mutable or immutable.

Item 15: Minimize mutability

An immutable class is simply a class whose instances cannot be modified. All of the information contained in each instance is provided when it is created and is fixed for the lifetime of the object. The Java platform libraries contain many immutable classes, including String, the boxed primitive classes, and BigInteger and BigDecimal. There are many good reasons for this: Immutable classes are easier to design, implement, and use than mutable classes. They are less prone to error and are more secure.

To make a class immutable, follow these five rules:

1. **Don't provide any methods that modify the object's state** (known as *mutators*).

2. **Ensure that the class can't be extended.** This prevents careless or malicious subclasses from compromising the immutable behavior of the class by behaving as if the object's state has changed. Preventing subclassing is generally accomplished by making the class final, but there is an alternative that we'll discuss later.

3. **Make all fields final.** This clearly expresses your intent in a manner that is enforced by the system. Also, it is necessary to ensure correct behavior if a reference to a newly created instance is passed from one thread to another without synchronization, as spelled out in the *memory model* [JLS, 17.5; Goetz06, 16].

4. **Make all fields private.** This prevents clients from obtaining access to mutable objects referred to by fields and modifying these objects directly. While it is technically permissible for immutable classes to have public final fields containing primitive values or references to immutable objects, it is not recommended because it precludes changing the internal representation in a later release (Item 13).

5. **Ensure exclusive access to any mutable components.** If your class has any fields that refer to mutable objects, ensure that clients of the class cannot obtain references to these objects. Never initialize such a field to a client-provided object reference or return the object reference from an accessor. Make *defensive copies* (Item 39) in constructors, accessors, and readObject methods (Item 76).

Many of the example classes in previous items are immutable. One such class is PhoneNumber in Item 9, which has accessors for each attribute but no corresponding mutators. Here is a slightly more complex example:

```java
public final class Complex {
    private final double re;
    private final double im;

    public Complex(double re, double im) {
        this.re = re;
        this.im = im;
    }

    // Accessors with no corresponding mutators
    public double realPart()      { return re; }
    public double imaginaryPart() { return im; }

    public Complex add(Complex c) {
        return new Complex(re + c.re, im + c.im);
    }

    public Complex subtract(Complex c) {
        return new Complex(re - c.re, im - c.im);
    }

    public Complex multiply(Complex c) {
        return new Complex(re * c.re - im * c.im,
                           re * c.im + im * c.re);
    }

    public Complex divide(Complex c) {
        double tmp = c.re * c.re + c.im * c.im;
        return new Complex((re * c.re + im * c.im) / tmp,
                           (im * c.re - re * c.im) / tmp);
    }

    @Override public boolean equals(Object o) {
        if (o == this)
            return true;
        if (!(o instanceof Complex))
            return false;
        Complex c = (Complex) o;

        // See page 43 to find out why we use compare instead of ==
        return Double.compare(re, c.re) == 0 &&
                Double.compare(im, c.im) == 0;
    }
```

```
@Override public int hashCode() {
    int result = 17 + hashDouble(re);
    result = 31 * result + hashDouble(im);
    return result;
}

private static int hashDouble(double val) {
    long longBits = Double.doubleToLongBits(val);
    return (int) (longBits ^ (longBits >>> 32));
}

@Override public String toString() {
    return "(" + re + " + " + im + "i)";
}
}
```

This class represents a *complex number* (a number with both real and imaginary parts). In addition to the standard Object methods, it provides accessors for the real and imaginary parts and provides the four basic arithmetic operations: addition, subtraction, multiplication, and division. Notice how the arithmetic operations create and return a new Complex instance rather than modifying this instance. This pattern is used in most nontrivial immutable classes. It is known as the *functional* approach because methods return the result of applying a function to their operand without modifying it. Contrast this to the more common *procedural* or *imperative* approach in which methods apply a procedure to their operand, causing its state to change.

The functional approach may appear unnatural if you're not familiar with it, but it enables immutability, which has many advantages. **Immutable objects are simple.** An immutable object can be in exactly one state, the state in which it was created. If you make sure that all constructors establish class invariants, then it is guaranteed that these invariants will remain true for all time, with no further effort on your part or on the part of the programmer who uses the class. Mutable objects, on the other hand, can have arbitrarily complex state spaces. If the documentation does not provide a precise description of the state transitions performed by mutator methods, it can be difficult or impossible to use a mutable class reliably.

Immutable objects are inherently thread-safe; they require no synchronization. They cannot be corrupted by multiple threads accessing them concurrently. This is far and away the easiest approach to achieving thread safety. In fact, no thread can ever observe any effect of another thread on an immutable object. Therefore, **immutable objects can be shared freely.** Immutable classes should take advantage of this by encouraging clients to reuse existing instances wherever possible. One easy way to do this is to provide public static final constants for frequently used values. For example, the `Complex` class might provide these constants:

```
public static final Complex ZERO = new Complex(0, 0);
public static final Complex ONE  = new Complex(1, 0);
public static final Complex I    = new Complex(0, 1);
```

This approach can be taken one step further. An immutable class can provide static factories (Item 1) that cache frequently requested instances to avoid creating new instances when existing ones would do. All the boxed primitive classes and `BigInteger` do this. Using such static factories causes clients to share instances instead of creating new ones, reducing memory footprint and garbage collection costs. Opting for static factories in place of public constructors when designing a new class gives you the flexibility to add caching later, without modifying clients.

A consequence of the fact that immutable objects can be shared freely is that you never have to make *defensive copies* (Item 39). In fact, you never have to make any copies at all because the copies would be forever equivalent to the originals. Therefore, you need not and should not provide a `clone` method or *copy constructor* (Item 11) on an immutable class. This was not well understood in the early days of the Java platform, so the `String` class does have a copy constructor, but it should rarely, if ever, be used (Item 5).

Not only can you share immutable objects, but you can share their internals. For example, the `BigInteger` class uses a sign-magnitude representation internally. The sign is represented by an `int`, and the magnitude is represented by an `int` array. The `negate` method produces a new `BigInteger` of like magnitude and opposite sign. It does not need to copy the array; the newly created `BigInteger` points to the same internal array as the original.

Immutable objects make great building blocks for other objects, whether mutable or immutable. It's much easier to maintain the invariants of a complex object if you know that its component objects will not change underneath it. A special case of this principle is that immutable objects make great map keys and set elements: you don't have to worry about their values changing once they're in the map or set, which would destroy the map or set's invariants.

The only real disadvantage of immutable classes is that they require a separate object for each distinct value. Creating these objects can be costly, especially if they are large. For example, suppose that you have a million-bit `BigInteger` and you want to change its low-order bit:

```
BigInteger moby = ...;
moby = moby.flipBit(0);
```

The `flipBit` method creates a new `BigInteger` instance, also a million bits long, that differs from the original in only one bit. The operation requires time and space proportional to the size of the `BigInteger`. Contrast this to `java.util.BitSet`. Like `BigInteger`, `BitSet` represents an arbitrarily long sequence of bits, but unlike `BigInteger`, `BitSet` is mutable. The `BitSet` class provides a method that allows you to change the state of a single bit of a million-bit instance in constant time.

The performance problem is magnified if you perform a multistep operation that generates a new object at every step, eventually discarding all objects except the final result. There are two approaches to coping with this problem. The first is to guess which multistep operations will be commonly required and provide them as primitives. If a multistep operation is provided as a primitive, the immutable class does not have to create a separate object at each step. Internally, the immutable class can be arbitrarily clever. For example, `BigInteger` has a package-private mutable "companion class" that it uses to speed up multistep operations such as modular exponentiation. It is much harder to use the mutable companion class than to use `BigInteger` for all of the reasons outlined earlier, but luckily you don't have to: the implementors of `BigInteger` did the hard work for you.

The package-private mutable companion class approach works fine if you can accurately predict which complex multistage operations clients will want to perform on your immutable class. If not, then your best bet is to provide a *public* mutable companion class. The main example of this approach in the Java platform libraries is the `String` class, whose mutable companion is `StringBuilder` (and the largely obsolete `StringBuffer`). Arguably, `BitSet` plays the role of mutable companion to `BigInteger` under certain circumstances.

Now that you know how to make an immutable class and you understand the pros and cons of immutability, let's discuss a few design alternatives. Recall that to guarantee immutability, a class must not permit itself to be subclassed. Typically this is done by making the class final, but there is another, more flexible way to do it. The alternative to making an immutable class final is to make all of its constructors private or package-private, and to add public *static factories* in place of the public constructors (Item 1).

To make this concrete, here's how `Complex` would look if you took this approach:

```
// Immutable class with static factories instead of constructors
public class Complex {
    private final double re;
    private final double im;

    private Complex(double re, double im) {
        this.re = re;
        this.im = im;
    }

    public static Complex valueOf(double re, double im) {
        return new Complex(re, im);
    }

    ... // Remainder unchanged
}
```

While this approach is not commonly used, it is often the best alternative. It is the most flexible because it allows the use of multiple package-private implementation classes. To its clients that reside outside its package, the immutable class is effectively final because it is impossible to extend a class that comes from another package and that lacks a public or protected constructor. Besides allowing the flexibility of multiple implementation classes, this approach makes it possible to tune the performance of the class in subsequent releases by improving the object-caching capabilities of the static factories.

Static factories have many other advantages over constructors, as discussed in Item 1. For example, suppose that you want to provide a means of creating a complex number based on its polar coordinates. This would be very messy using constructors because the natural constructor would have the same signature that we already used: `Complex(double, double)`. With static factories it's easy. Just add a second static factory with a name that clearly identifies its function:

```
public static Complex valueOfPolar(double r, double theta) {
    return new Complex(r * Math.cos(theta),
                       r * Math.sin(theta));
}
```

It was not widely understood that immutable classes had to be effectively final when `BigInteger` and `BigDecimal` were written, so all of their methods may be overridden. Unfortunately, this could not be corrected after the fact while preserving backward compatibility. If you write a class whose security depends on the immutability of a `BigInteger` or `BigDecimal` argument from an untrusted client, you must check to see that the argument is a "real" `BigInteger` or `BigDecimal`, rather than an instance of an untrusted subclass. If it is the latter, you must defensively copy it under the assumption that it might be mutable (Item 39):

```
public static BigInteger safeInstance(BigInteger val) {
    if (val.getClass() != BigInteger.class)
        return new BigInteger(val.toByteArray());
    return val;
}
```

The list of rules for immutable classes at the beginning of this item says that no methods may modify the object and that all its fields must be final. In fact these rules are a bit stronger than necessary and can be relaxed to improve performance. In truth, no method may produce an *externally visible* change in the object's state. However, some immutable classes have one or more nonfinal fields in which they cache the results of expensive computations the first time they are needed. If the same value is requested again, the cached value is returned, saving the cost of recalculation. This trick works precisely because the object is immutable, which guarantees that the computation would yield the same result if it were repeated.

For example, `PhoneNumber`'s `hashCode` method (Item 9, page 49) computes the hash code the first time it's invoked and caches it in case it's invoked again. This technique, an example of *lazy initialization* (Item 71), is also used by `String`.

One caveat should be added concerning serializability. If you choose to have your immutable class implement `Serializable` and it contains one or more fields that refer to mutable objects, you must provide an explicit `readObject` or `readResolve` method, or use the `ObjectOutputStream.writeUnshared` and `ObjectInputStream.readUnshared` methods, even if the default serialized form is acceptable. Otherwise an attacker could create a mutable instance of your not-quite-immutable class. This topic is covered in detail in Item 76.

To summarize, resist the urge to write a `set` method for every `get` method. **Classes should be immutable unless there's a very good reason to make them mutable.** Immutable classes provide many advantages, and their only disadvantage is the potential for performance problems under certain circumstances. You should always make small value objects, such as `PhoneNumber` and `Complex`, immutable. (There are several classes in the Java platform libraries, such as java.util.Date and java.awt.Point, that should have been immutable but aren't.) You should seriously consider making larger value objects, such as String and BigInteger, immutable as well. You should provide a public mutable companion class for your immutable class *only* once you've confirmed that it's necessary to achieve satisfactory performance (Item 55).

There are some classes for which immutability is impractical. **If a class cannot be made immutable, limit its mutability as much as possible.** Reducing the number of states in which an object can exist makes it easier to reason about the object and reduces the likelihood of errors. Therefore, **make every field final unless there is a compelling reason to make it nonfinal.**

Constructors should create fully initialized objects with all of their invariants established. Don't provide a public initialization method separate from the constructor or static factory unless there is a compelling reason to do so. Similarly, don't provide a "reinitialize" method that enables an object to be reused as if it had been constructed with a different initial state. Such methods generally provide little if any performance benefit at the expense of increased complexity.

The TimerTask class exemplifies these principles. It is mutable, but its state space is kept intentionally small. You create an instance, schedule it for execution, and optionally cancel it. Once a timer task has run to completion or has been canceled, you may not reschedule it.

A final note should be added concerning the Complex class in this item. This example was meant only to illustrate immutability. It is not an industrial-strength complex number implementation. It uses the standard formulas for complex multiplication and division, which are not correctly rounded and provide poor semantics for complex NaNs and infinities [Kahan91, Smith62, Thomas94].

Item 16: Favor composition over inheritance

Inheritance is a powerful way to achieve code reuse, but it is not always the best tool for the job. Used inappropriately, it leads to fragile software. It is safe to use inheritance within a package, where the subclass and the superclass implementations are under the control of the same programmers. It is also safe to use inheritance when extending classes specifically designed and documented for extension (Item 17). Inheriting from ordinary concrete classes across package boundaries, however, is dangerous. As a reminder, this book uses the word "inheritance" to mean *implementation inheritance* (when one class extends another). The problems discussed in this item do not apply to *interface inheritance* (when a class implements an interface or where one interface extends another).

Unlike method invocation, inheritance violates encapsulation [Snyder86]. In other words, a subclass depends on the implementation details of its superclass for its proper function. The superclass's implementation may change from release to release, and if it does, the subclass may break, even though its code has not been touched. As a consequence, a subclass must evolve in tandem with its superclass, unless the superclass's authors have designed and documented it specifically for the purpose of being extended.

To make this concrete, let's suppose we have a program that uses a HashSet. To tune the performance of our program, we need to query the HashSet as to how many elements have been added since it was created (not to be confused with its current size, which goes down when an element is removed). To provide this functionality, we write a HashSet variant that keeps count of the number of attempted element insertions and exports an accessor for this count. The HashSet class contains two methods capable of adding elements, add and addAll, so we override both of these methods:

```
// Broken - Inappropriate use of inheritance!
public class InstrumentedHashSet<E> extends HashSet<E> {
    // The number of attempted element insertions
    private int addCount = 0;

    public InstrumentedHashSet() {
    }

    public InstrumentedHashSet(int initCap, float loadFactor) {
        super(initCap, loadFactor);
    }
```

```
    @Override public boolean add(E e) {
        addCount++;
        return super.add(e);
    }
    @Override public boolean addAll(Collection<? extends E> c) {
        addCount += c.size();
        return super.addAll(c);
    }
    public int getAddCount() {
        return addCount;
    }
}
```

This class looks reasonable, but it doesn't work. Suppose we create an instance and add three elements using the addAll method:

```
InstrumentedHashSet<String> s =
    new InstrumentedHashSet<String>();
s.addAll(Arrays.asList("Snap", "Crackle", "Pop"));
```

We would expect the getAddCount method to return three at this point, but it returns six. What went wrong? Internally, HashSet's addAll method is implemented on top of its add method, although HashSet, quite reasonably, does not document this implementation detail. The addAll method in InstrumentedHash-Set added three to addCount and then invoked HashSet's addAll implementation using super.addAll. This in turn invoked the add method, as overridden in InstrumentedHashSet, once for each element. Each of these three invocations added one more to addCount, for a total increase of six: each element added with the addAll method is double-counted.

We could "fix" the subclass by eliminating its override of the addAll method. While the resulting class would work, it would depend for its proper function on the fact that HashSet's addAll method is implemented on top of its add method. This "self-use" is an implementation detail, not guaranteed to hold in all implementations of the Java platform and subject to change from release to release. Therefore, the resulting InstrumentedHashSet class would be fragile.

It would be slightly better to override the addAll method to iterate over the specified collection, calling the add method once for each element. This would guarantee the correct result whether or not HashSet's addAll method were implemented atop its add method, because HashSet's addAll implementation would no longer be invoked. This technique, however, does not solve all our problems. It amounts to reimplementing superclass methods that may or may not result in self-use, which is difficult, time-consuming, and error-prone. Additionally, it isn't always possible, as some methods cannot be implemented without access to private fields inaccessible to the subclass.

A related cause of fragility in subclasses is that their superclass can acquire new methods in subsequent releases. Suppose a program depends for its security on the fact that all elements inserted into some collection satisfy some predicate. This can be guaranteed by subclassing the collection and overriding each method capable of adding an element to ensure that the predicate is satisfied before adding the element. This works fine until a new method capable of inserting an element is added to the superclass in a subsequent release. Once this happens, it becomes possible to add an "illegal" element merely by invoking the new method, which is not overridden in the subclass. This is not a purely theoretical problem. Several security holes of this nature had to be fixed when Hashtable and Vector were retrofitted to participate in the Collections Framework.

Both of the above problems stem from overriding methods. You might think that it is safe to extend a class if you merely add new methods and refrain from overriding existing methods. While this sort of extension is much safer, it is not without risk. If the superclass acquires a new method in a subsequent release and you have the bad luck to have given the subclass a method with the same signature and a different return type, your subclass will no longer compile [JLS, 8.4.8.3]. If you've given the subclass a method with the same signature and return type as the new superclass method, then you're now overriding it, so you're subject to the two problems described above. Furthermore, it is doubtful that your method will fulfill the contract of the new superclass method, as that contract had not yet been written when you wrote the subclass method.

Luckily, there is a way to avoid all of the problems described earlier. Instead of extending an existing class, give your new class a private field that references an instance of the existing class. This design is called *composition* because the existing class becomes a component of the new one. Each instance method in the new class invokes the corresponding method on the contained instance of the existing class and returns the results. This is known as *forwarding*, and the methods in the new class are known as *forwarding methods*. The resulting class will be rock solid, with no dependencies on the implementation details of the existing class. Even adding new methods to the existing class will have no impact on the new class. To make this concrete, here's a replacement for InstrumentedHashSet that uses the composition-and-forwarding approach. Note that the implementation is broken into two pieces, the class itself and a reusable *forwarding class,* which contains all of the forwarding methods and nothing else:

```java
// Wrapper class - uses composition in place of inheritance
public class InstrumentedSet<E> extends ForwardingSet<E> {
    private int addCount = 0;

    public InstrumentedSet(Set<E> s) {
        super(s);
    }

    @Override public boolean add(E e) {
        addCount++;
        return super.add(e);
    }
    @Override public boolean addAll(Collection<? extends E> c) {
        addCount += c.size();
        return super.addAll(c);
    }
    public int getAddCount() {
        return addCount;
    }
}

// Reusable forwarding class
public class ForwardingSet<E> implements Set<E> {
    private final Set<E> s;
    public ForwardingSet(Set<E> s) { this.s = s; }

    public void clear()               { s.clear();            }
    public boolean contains(Object o) { return s.contains(o); }
    public boolean isEmpty()          { return s.isEmpty();   }
    public int size()                 { return s.size();      }
    public Iterator<E> iterator()     { return s.iterator();  }
    public boolean add(E e)           { return s.add(e);      }
    public boolean remove(Object o)   { return s.remove(o);   }
    public boolean containsAll(Collection<?> c)
                                      { return s.containsAll(c); }
    public boolean addAll(Collection<? extends E> c)
                                      { return s.addAll(c);      }
    public boolean removeAll(Collection<?> c)
                                      { return s.removeAll(c);   }
    public boolean retainAll(Collection<?> c)
                                      { return s.retainAll(c);   }
    public Object[] toArray()         { return s.toArray();   }
    public <T> T[] toArray(T[] a)     { return s.toArray(a);  }
    @Override public boolean equals(Object o)
                                      { return s.equals(o);   }
    @Override public int hashCode()   { return s.hashCode();  }
    @Override public String toString() { return s.toString(); }
}
```

The design of the `InstrumentedSet` class is enabled by the existence of the `Set` interface, which captures the functionality of the `HashSet` class. Besides being robust, this design is extremely flexible. The `InstrumentedSet` class implements the `Set` interface and has a single constructor whose argument is also of type `Set`. In essence, the class transforms one `Set` into another, adding the instrumentation functionality. Unlike the inheritance-based approach, which works only for a single concrete class and requires a separate constructor for each supported constructor in the superclass, the wrapper class can be used to instrument any `Set` implementation and will work in conjunction with any preexisting constructor:

```
Set<Date> s = new InstrumentedSet<Date>(new TreeSet<Date>(cmp));
Set<E> s2 = new InstrumentedSet<E>(new HashSet<E>(capacity));
```

The `InstrumentedSet` class can even be used to temporarily instrument a set instance that has already been used without instrumentation:

```
static void walk(Set<Dog> dogs) {
    InstrumentedSet<Dog> iDogs = new InstrumentedSet<Dog>(dogs);
    ... // Within this method use iDogs instead of dogs
}
```

The `InstrumentedSet` class is known as a *wrapper* class because each `InstrumentedSet` instance contains ("wraps") another `Set` instance. This is also known as the *Decorator* pattern [Gamma95, p. 175], because the `Instrumented-Set` class "decorates" a set by adding instrumentation. Sometimes the combination of composition and forwarding is loosely referred to as *delegation*. Technically it's not delegation unless the wrapper object passes itself to the wrapped object [Lieberman86; Gamma95, p. 20].

The disadvantages of wrapper classes are few. One caveat is that wrapper classes are not suited for use in *callback frameworks*, wherein objects pass self-references to other objects for subsequent invocations ("callbacks"). Because a wrapped object doesn't know of its wrapper, it passes a reference to itself (`this`) and callbacks elude the wrapper. This is known as the *SELF problem* [Lieberman86]. Some people worry about the performance impact of forwarding method invocations or the memory footprint impact of wrapper objects. Neither turn out to have much impact in practice. It's tedious to write forwarding methods, but you have to write the forwarding class for each interface only once, and forwarding classes may be provided for you by the package containing the interface.

Inheritance is appropriate only in circumstances where the subclass really is a *subtype* of the superclass. In other words, a class *B* should extend a class *A* only if an "is-a" relationship exists between the two classes. If you are tempted to have a class B extend a class A, ask yourself the question: Is every B really an A? If you cannot truthfully answer yes to this question, B should not extend A. If the answer is no, it is often the case that B should contain a private instance of A and expose a smaller and simpler API: A is not an essential part of B, merely a detail of its implementation.

There are a number of obvious violations of this principle in the Java platform libraries. For example, a stack is not a vector, so Stack should not extend Vector. Similarly, a property list is not a hash table, so Properties should not extend Hashtable. In both cases, composition would have been preferable.

If you use inheritance where composition is appropriate, you needlessly expose implementation details. The resulting API ties you to the original implementation, forever limiting the performance of your class. More seriously, by exposing the internals you let the client access them directly. At the very least, this can lead to confusing semantics. For example, if p refers to a Properties instance, then p.getProperty(key) may yield different results from p.get(key): the former method takes defaults into account, while the latter method, which is inherited from Hashtable, does not. Most seriously, the client may be able to corrupt invariants of the subclass by modifying the superclass directly. In the case of Properties, the designers intended that only strings be allowed as keys and values, but direct access to the underlying Hashtable allows this invariant to be violated. Once this invariant is violated, it is no longer possible to use other parts of the Properties API (load and store). By the time this problem was discovered, it was too late to correct it because clients depended on the use of nonstring keys and values.

There is one last set of questions you should ask yourself before deciding to use inheritance in place of composition. Does the class that you contemplate extending have any flaws in its API? If so, are you comfortable propagating those flaws into your class's API? Inheritance propagates any flaws in the superclass's API, while composition lets you design a new API that hides these flaws.

To summarize, inheritance is powerful, but it is problematic because it violates encapsulation. It is appropriate only when a genuine subtype relationship exists between the subclass and the superclass. Even then, inheritance may lead to fragility if the subclass is in a different package from the superclass and the superclass is not designed for inheritance. To avoid this fragility, use composition and forwarding instead of inheritance, especially if an appropriate interface to implement a wrapper class exists. Not only are wrapper classes more robust than subclasses, they are also more powerful.

Item 17: Design and document for inheritance or else prohibit it

Item 16 alerted you to the dangers of subclassing a "foreign" class that was not designed and documented for inheritance. So what does it mean for a class to be designed and documented for inheritance?

First, the class must document precisely the effects of overriding any method. In other words, **the class must document its *self-use* of overridable methods.** For each public or protected method or constructor, the documentation must indicate which overridable methods the method or constructor invokes, in what sequence, and how the results of each invocation affect subsequent processing. (By *overridable*, we mean nonfinal and either public or protected.) More generally, a class must document any circumstances under which it might invoke an overridable method. For example, invocations might come from background threads or static initializers.

By convention, a method that invokes overridable methods contains a description of these invocations at the end of its documentation comment. The description begins with the phrase "This implementation." This phrase should not be taken to indicate that the behavior may change from release to release. It connotes that the description concerns the inner workings of the method. Here's an example, copied from the specification for `java.util.AbstractCollection`:

```
public boolean remove(Object o)
```

> Removes a single instance of the specified element from this collection, if it is present (optional operation). More formally, removes an element e such that `(o==null ? e==null : o.equals(e))`, if the collection contains one or more such elements. Returns `true` if the collection contained the specified element (or equivalently, if the collection changed as a result of the call).

> This implementation iterates over the collection looking for the specified element. If it finds the element, it removes the element from the collection using the iterator's `remove` method. Note that this implementation throws an `UnsupportedOperationException` if the iterator returned by this collection's `iterator` method does not implement the `remove` method.

This documentation leaves no doubt that overriding the `iterator` method will affect the behavior of the `remove` method. Furthermore, it describes exactly how the behavior of the `Iterator` returned by the `iterator` method will affect the behavior of the `remove` method. Contrast this to the situation in Item 16, where the programmer subclassing HashSet simply could not say whether overriding the add method would affect the behavior of the addAll method.

But doesn't this violate the dictum that good API documentation should describe *what* a given method does and not *how* it does it? Yes, it does! This is an unfortunate consequence of the fact that inheritance violates encapsulation. To document a class so that it can be safely subclassed, you must describe implementation details that should otherwise be left unspecified.

Design for inheritance involves more than just documenting patterns of self-use. To allow programmers to write efficient subclasses without undue pain, **a class may have to provide hooks into its internal workings in the form of judiciously chosen protected methods** or, in rare instances, protected fields. For example, consider the removeRange method from java.util.AbstractList:

> protected void removeRange(int fromIndex, int toIndex)
>
> Removes from this list all of the elements whose index is between fromIndex, inclusive, and toIndex, exclusive. Shifts any succeeding elements to the left (reduces their index). This call shortens the AbstractList by (toIndex - fromIndex) elements. (If toIndex == fromIndex, this operation has no effect.)
>
> This method is called by the clear operation on this list and its sublists. Overriding this method to take advantage of the internals of the list implementation can substantially improve the performance of the clear operation on this list and its sublists.
>
> This implementation gets a list iterator positioned before fromIndex and repeatedly calls ListIterator.next followed by ListIterator.remove, until the entire range has been removed. Note: If ListIterator.remove requires linear time, this implementation requires quadratic time.
>
> Parameters:w
>
> fromIndex   index of first element to be removed.
>
> toIndex   index after last element to be removed.

This method is of no interest to end users of a List implementation. It is provided solely to make it easy for subclasses to provide a fast clear method on sublists. In the absence of the removeRange method, subclasses would have to make do with quadratic performance when the clear method was invoked on sublists or rewrite the entire subList mechanism from scratch—not an easy task!

So how do you decide what protected members to expose when you design a class for inheritance? Unfortunately, there is no magic bullet. The best you can do is to think hard, take your best guess, and then test it by writing subclasses. You should expose as few protected members as possible, because each one represents a commitment to an implementation detail. On the other hand, you must not expose too few, as a missing protected member can render a class practically unusable for inheritance.

The *only* way to test a class designed for inheritance is to write subclasses. If you omit a crucial protected member, trying to write a subclass will make the omission painfully obvious. Conversely, if several subclasses are written and none uses a protected member, you should probably make it private. Experience shows that three subclasses are usually sufficient to test an extendable class. One or more of these subclasses should be written by someone other than the superclass author.

When you design for inheritance a class that is likely to achieve wide use, realize that you are committing *forever* to the self-use patterns that you document and to the implementation decisions implicit in its protected methods and fields. These commitments can make it difficult or impossible to improve the performance or functionality of the class in a subsequent release. Therefore, **you must test your class by writing subclasses *before* you release it.**

Also, note that the special documentation required for inheritance clutters up normal documentation, which is designed for programmers who create instances of your class and invoke methods on them. As of this writing, there is little in the way of tools or commenting conventions to separate ordinary API documentation from information of interest only to programmers implementing subclasses.

There are a few more restrictions that a class must obey to allow inheritance. **Constructors must not invoke overridable methods**, directly or indirectly. If you violate this rule, program failure will result. The superclass constructor runs before the subclass constructor, so the overriding method in the subclass will get invoked before the subclass constructor has run. If the overriding method depends on any initialization performed by the subclass constructor, the method will not behave as expected. To make this concrete, here's a class that violates this rule:

```
public class Super {
    // Broken - constructor invokes an overridable method
    public Super() {
        overrideMe();
    }
    public void overrideMe() {
    }
}
```

Here's a subclass that overrides the overrideMe, method which is erroneously invoked by Super's sole constructor:

```
public final class Sub extends Super {
    private final Date date; // Blank final, set by constructor

    Sub() {
        date = new Date();
    }

    // Overriding method invoked by superclass constructor
    @Override public void overrideMe() {
        System.out.println(date);
    }

    public static void main(String[] args) {
        Sub sub = new Sub();
        sub.overrideMe();
    }
}
```

You might expect this program to print out the date twice, but it prints out null the first time, because the overrideMe method is invoked by the Super constructor before the Sub constructor has a chance to initialize the date field. Note that this program observes a final field in two different states! Note also that if overrideMe had invoked any method on date, the invocation would have thrown a NullPointerException when the Super constructor invoked overrideMe. The only reason this program doesn't throw a NullPointerException as it stands is that the println method has special provisions for dealing with a null argument.

The Cloneable and Serializable interfaces present special difficulties when designing for inheritance. It is generally not a good idea for a class designed for inheritance to implement either of these interfaces, as they place a substantial burden on programmers who extend the class. There are, however, special actions that you can take to allow subclasses to implement these interfaces without mandating that they do so. These actions are described in Item 11 and Item 74.

If you do decide to implement Cloneable or Serializable in a class designed for inheritance, you should be aware that because the clone and readObject methods behave a lot like constructors, a similar restriction applies: **neither clone nor readObject may invoke an overridable method, directly or indirectly**. In the case of the readObject method, the overriding method will run before the subclass's state has been deserialized. In the case of the clone method, the overriding method will run before the subclass's clone method has a chance to fix the clone's state. In either case, a program failure is likely to follow. In the case of `clone`, the failure can damage the original object as well as the clone. This can happen, for example, if the overriding method assumes it is modifying the clone's copy of the object's deep structure, but the copy hasn't been made yet.

Finally, if you decide to implement `Serializable` in a class designed for inheritance and the class has a `readResolve` or `writeReplace` method, you must make the `readResolve` or `writeReplace` method protected rather than private. If these methods are private, they will be silently ignored by subclasses. This is one more case where an implementation detail becomes part of a class's API to permit inheritance.

By now it should be apparent that **designing a class for inheritance places substantial limitations on the class**. This is not a decision to be undertaken lightly. There are some situations where it is clearly the right thing to do, such as abstract classes, including *skeletal implementations* of interfaces (Item 18). There are other situations where it is clearly the wrong thing to do, such as immutable classes (Item 15).

But what about ordinary concrete classes? Traditionally, they are neither final nor designed and documented for subclassing, but this state of affairs is danger-ous. Each time a change is made in such a class, there is a chance that client classes that extend the class will break. This is not just a theoretical problem. It is not uncommon to receive subclassing-related bug reports after modifying the internals of a nonfinal concrete class that was not designed and documented for inheritance.

The best solution to this problem is to prohibit subclassing in classes that are not designed and documented to be safely subclassed. There are two ways to prohibit subclassing. The easier of the two is to declare the class final. The alternative is to make all the constructors private or package-private and to add public *static* factories in place of the constructors. This alternative, which pro-vides the flexibility to use subclasses internally, is discussed in Item 15. Either approach is acceptable.

This advice may be somewhat controversial, as many programmers have grown accustomed to subclassing ordinary concrete classes to add facilities such as instrumentation, notification, and synchronization or to limit functionality. If a class implements some interface that captures its essence, such as `Set`, `List`, or `Map`, then you should feel no compunction about prohibiting subclassing. The *wrapper class* pattern, described in Item 16, provides a superior alternative to inheritance for augmenting the functionality.

If a concrete class does not implement a standard interface, then you may inconvenience some programmers by prohibiting inheritance. If you feel that you must allow inheritance from such a class, one reasonable approach is to ensure that the class never invokes any of its overridable methods and to document this fact. In other words, eliminate the class's self-use of overridable methods entirely. In doing so, you'll create a class that is reasonably safe to subclass. Overriding a method will never affect the behavior of any other method.

You can eliminate a class's self-use of overridable methods mechanically, without changing its behavior. Move the body of each overridable method to a private "helper method" and have each overridable method invoke its private helper method. Then replace each self-use of an overridable method with a direct invocation of the overridable method's private helper method.

Item 18: Prefer interfaces to abstract classes

The Java programming language provides two mechanisms for defining a type that permits multiple implementations: interfaces and abstract classes. The most obvious difference between the two mechanisms is that abstract classes are permitted to contain implementations for some methods while interfaces are not. A more important difference is that to implement the type defined by an abstract class, a class must be a subclass of the abstract class. Any class that defines all of the required methods and obeys the general contract is permitted to implement an interface, regardless of where the class resides in the class hierarchy. Because Java permits only single inheritance, this restriction on abstract classes severely constrains their use as type definitions.

Existing classes can be easily retrofitted to implement a new interface. All you have to do is add the required methods if they don't yet exist and add an `implements` clause to the class declaration. For example, many existing classes were retrofitted to implement the `Comparable` interface when it was introduced into the platform. Existing classes cannot, in general, be retrofitted to extend a new abstract class. If you want to have two classes extend the same abstract class, you have to place the abstract class high up in the type hierarchy where it subclasses an ancestor of both classes. Unfortunately, this causes great collateral damage to the type hierarchy, forcing all descendants of the common ancestor to extend the new abstract class whether or not it is appropriate for them to do so.

Interfaces are ideal for defining mixins. Loosely speaking, a *mixin* is a type that a class can implement in addition to its "primary type" to declare that it provides some optional behavior. For example, `Comparable` is a mixin interface that allows a class to declare that its instances are ordered with respect to other mutually comparable objects. Such an interface is called a mixin because it allows the optional functionality to be "mixed in" to the type's primary functionality. Abstract classes can't be used to define mixins for the same reason that they can't be retrofitted onto existing classes: a class cannot have more than one parent, and there is no reasonable place in the class hierarchy to insert a mixin.

Interfaces allow the construction of nonhierarchical type frameworks. Type hierarchies are great for organizing some things, but other things don't fall neatly into a rigid hierarchy. For example, suppose we have an interface representing a singer and another representing a songwriter:

```
public interface Singer {
    AudioClip sing(Song s);
}
```

```
public interface Songwriter {
    Song compose(boolean hit);
}
```

In real life, some singers are also songwriters. Because we used interfaces rather than abstract classes to define these types, it is perfectly permissible for a single class to implement both Singer and Songwriter. In fact, we can define a third interface that extends both Singer and Songwriter and adds new methods that are appropriate to the combination:

```
public interface SingerSongwriter extends Singer, Songwriter {
    AudioClip strum();
    void actSensitive();
}
```

You don't always need this level of flexibility, but when you do, interfaces are a lifesaver. The alternative is a bloated class hierarchy containing a separate class for every supported combination of attributes. If there are *n* attributes in the type system, there are 2^n possible combinations that you might have to support. This is what's known as a *combinatorial explosion*. Bloated class hierarchies can lead to bloated classes containing many methods that differ only in the type of their arguments, as there are no types in the class hierarchy to capture common behaviors.

Interfaces enable safe, powerful functionality enhancements via the *wrapper class* idiom, described in Item 16. If you use abstract classes to define types, you leave the programmer who wants to add functionality with no alternative but to use inheritance. The resulting classes are less powerful and more fragile than wrapper classes.

While interfaces are not permitted to contain method implementations, using interfaces to define types does not prevent you from providing implementation assistance to programmers. **You can combine the virtues of interfaces and abstract classes by providing an abstract *skeletal implementation* class to go with each nontrivial interface that you export.** The interface still defines the type, but the skeletal implementation takes all of the work out of implementing it.

By convention, skeletal implementations are called Abstract*Interface*, where *Interface* is the name of the interface they implement. For example, the Collections Framework provides a skeletal implementation to go along with each main collection interface: AbstractCollection, AbstractSet, AbstractList, and AbstractMap. Arguably it would have made sense to call them SkeletalCollection, SkeletalSet, SkeletalList, and SkeletalMap, but the Abstract convention is now firmly established.

When properly designed, skeletal implementations can make it *very* easy for programmers to provide their own implementations of your interfaces. For example, here's a static factory method containing a complete, fully functional List implementation:

```
// Concrete implementation built atop skeletal implementation
static List<Integer> intArrayAsList(final int[] a) {
    if (a == null)
        throw new NullPointerException();

    return new AbstractList<Integer>() {
        public Integer get(int i) {
            return a[i];  // Autoboxing (Item 5)
        }

        @Override public Integer set(int i, Integer val) {
            int oldVal = a[i];
            a[i] = val;      // Auto-unboxing
            return oldVal;  // Autoboxing
        }

        public int size() {
            return a.length;
        }
    };
}
```

When you consider all that a List implementation does for you, this example is an impressive demonstration of the power of skeletal implementations. Incidentally, the example is an *Adapter* [Gamma95, p. 139] that allows an int array to be viewed as a list of Integer instances. Because of all the translation back and forth between int values and Integer instances (boxing and unboxing), its performance is not terribly good. Note that a static factory is provided and that the class is an inaccessible *anonymous class* (Item 22) hidden inside the static factory.

The beauty of skeletal implementations is that they provide the implementation assistance of abstract classes without imposing the severe constraints that abstract classes impose when they serve as type definitions. For most implementors of an interface, extending the skeletal implementation is the obvious choice, but it is strictly optional. If a preexisting class cannot be made to extend the skeletal implementation, the class can always implement the interface manually. Furthermore, the skeletal implementation can still aid the implementor's task. The class implementing the interface can forward invocations of interface methods to a contained instance of a private inner class that extends the skeletal implementation. This technique, known as *simulated multiple inheritance*, is closely related to the wrapper class idiom discussed in Item 16. It provides most of the benefits of multiple inheritance, while avoiding the pitfalls.

Writing a skeletal implementation is a relatively simple, if somewhat tedious, process. First you must study the interface and decide which methods are the primitives in terms of which the others can be implemented. These primitives will be the abstract methods in your skeletal implementation. Then you must provide concrete implementations of all the other methods in the interface. For example, here's a skeletal implementation of the Map.Entry interface:

```
// Skeletal Implementation
public abstract class AbstractMapEntry<K,V>
        implements Map.Entry<K,V> {
    // Primitive operations
    public abstract K getKey();
    public abstract V getValue();

    // Entries in modifiable maps must override this method
    public V setValue(V value) {
        throw new UnsupportedOperationException();
    }

    // Implements the general contract of Map.Entry.equals
    @Override public boolean equals(Object o) {
        if (o == this)
            return true;
        if (!(o instanceof Map.Entry))
            return false;
        Map.Entry<?,?> arg = (Map.Entry) o;
        return equals(getKey(),   arg.getKey()) &&
               equals(getValue(), arg.getValue());
    }
    private static boolean equals(Object o1, Object o2) {
        return o1 == null ? o2 == null : o1.equals(o2);
    }

    // Implements the general contract of Map.Entry.hashCode
    @Override public int hashCode() {
        return hashCode(getKey()) ^ hashCode(getValue());
    }
    private static int hashCode(Object obj) {
        return obj == null ? 0 : obj.hashCode();
    }
}
```

Because skeletal implementations are designed for inheritance, you should follow all of the design and documentation guidelines in Item 17. For brevity's sake, the documentation comments were omitted from the previous example, but good documentation is absolutely essential for skeletal implementations.

A minor variant on the skeletal implementation is the *simple implementation,* exemplified by `AbstractMap.SimpleEntry`. A simple implementation is like a skeletal implementation in that it implements an interface and is designed for inheritance, but it differs in that it isn't abstract: it is the simplest possible working implementation. You can use it as it stands or subclass it as circumstances warrant.

Using abstract classes to define types that permit multiple implementations has one great advantage over using interfaces: **It is far easier to evolve an abstract class than an interface.** If, in a subsequent release, you want to add a new method to an abstract class, you can always add a concrete method containing a reasonable default implementation. All existing implementations of the abstract class will then provide the new method. This does not work for interfaces.

It is, generally speaking, impossible to add a method to a public interface without breaking all existing classes that implement the interface. Classes that previously implemented the interface will be missing the new method and won't compile anymore. You could limit the damage somewhat by adding the new method to the skeletal implementation at the same time as you add it to the interface, but this really wouldn't solve the problem. Any implementation that didn't inherit from the skeletal implementation would still be broken.

Public interfaces, therefore, must be designed carefully. **Once an interface is released and widely implemented, it is almost impossible to change.** You really must get it right the first time. If an interface contains a minor flaw, it will irritate you and its users forever. If an interface is severely deficient, it can doom an API. The best thing to do when releasing a new interface is to have as many programmers as possible implement the interface in as many ways as possible *before* the interface is frozen. This will allow you to discover flaws while you can still correct them.

To summarize, an interface is generally the best way to define a type that permits multiple implementations. An exception to this rule is the case where ease of evolution is deemed more important than flexibility and power. Under these circumstances, you should use an abstract class to define the type, but only if you understand and can accept the limitations. If you export a nontrivial interface, you should strongly consider providing a skeletal implementation to go with it. Finally, you should design all of your public interfaces with the utmost care and test them thoroughly by writing multiple implementations.

Item 19: Use interfaces only to define types

When a class implements an interface, the interface serves as a *type* that can be used to refer to instances of the class. That a class implements an interface should therefore say something about what a client can do with instances of the class. It is inappropriate to define an interface for any other purpose.

One kind of interface that fails this test is the so-called *constant interface*. Such an interface contains no methods; it consists solely of static final fields, each exporting a constant. Classes using these constants implement the interface to avoid the need to qualify constant names with a class name. Here is an example:

```
// Constant interface antipattern - do not use!
public interface PhysicalConstants {
    // Avogadro's number (1/mol)
    static final double AVOGADROS_NUMBER    = 6.02214199e23;

    // Boltzmann constant (J/K)
    static final double BOLTZMANN_CONSTANT = 1.3806503e-23;

    // Mass of the electron (kg)
    static final double ELECTRON_MASS       = 9.10938188e-31;
}
```

The constant interface pattern is a poor use of interfaces. That a class uses some constants internally is an implementation detail. Implementing a constant interface causes this implementation detail to leak into the class's exported API. It is of no consequence to the users of a class that the class implements a constant interface. In fact, it may even confuse them. Worse, it represents a commitment: if in a future release the class is modified so that it no longer needs to use the constants, it still must implement the interface to ensure binary compatibility. If a nonfinal class implements a constant interface, all of its subclasses will have their namespaces polluted by the constants in the interface.

There are several constant interfaces in the Java platform libraries, such as java.io.ObjectStreamConstants. These interfaces should be regarded as anomalies and should not be emulated.

If you want to export constants, there are several reasonable choices. If the constants are strongly tied to an existing class or interface, you should add them to the class or interface. For example, all of the boxed numerical primitive classes, such as Integer and Double, export MIN_VALUE and MAX_VALUE constants. If the constants are best viewed as members of an enumerated type, you should export them with an *enum type* (Item 30). Otherwise, you should export the constants with a noninstantiable *utility class* (Item 4). Here is a utility class version of the PhysicalConstants example above:

```
// Constant utility class
package com.effectivejava.science;

public class PhysicalConstants {
  private PhysicalConstants() { }  // Prevents instantiation

  public static final double AVOGADROS_NUMBER   = 6.02214199e23;
  public static final double BOLTZMANN_CONSTANT = 1.3806503e-23;
  public static final double ELECTRON_MASS      = 9.10938188e-31;
}
```

Normally a utility class requires clients to qualify constant names with a class name, for example, PhysicalConstants.AVOGADROS_NUMBER. If you make heavy use of the constants exported by a utility class, you can avoid the need for qualifying the constants with the class name by making use of the *static import* facility, introduced in release 1.5:

```
// Use of static import to avoid qualifying constants
import static com.effectivejava.science.PhysicalConstants.*;

public class Test {
    double atoms(double mols) {
        return AVOGADROS_NUMBER * mols;
    }
    ...
    // Many more uses of PhysicalConstants justify static import
}
```

In summary, interfaces should be used only to define types. They should not be used to export constants.

Item 20: Prefer class hierarchies to tagged classes

Occasionally you may run across a class whose instances come in two or more flavors and contain a *tag* field indicating the flavor of the instance. For example, consider this class, which is capable of representing a circle or a rectangle:

```java
// Tagged class - vastly inferior to a class hierarchy!
class Figure {
    enum Shape { RECTANGLE, CIRCLE };

    // Tag field - the shape of this figure
    final Shape shape;

    // These fields are used only if shape is RECTANGLE
    double length;
    double width;

    // This field is used only if shape is CIRCLE
    double radius;

    // Constructor for circle
    Figure(double radius) {
        shape = Shape.CIRCLE;
        this.radius = radius;
    }

    // Constructor for rectangle
    Figure(double length, double width) {
        shape = Shape.RECTANGLE;
        this.length = length;
        this.width = width;
    }

    double area() {
        switch(shape) {
          case RECTANGLE:
            return length * width;
          case CIRCLE:
            return Math.PI * (radius * radius);
          default:
            throw new AssertionError();
        }
    }
}
```

Such *tagged classes* have numerous shortcomings. They are cluttered with boilerplate, including enum declarations, tag fields, and switch statements. Readability is further harmed because multiple implementations are jumbled together in a single class. Memory footprint is increased because instances are burdened with irrelevant fields belonging to other flavors. Fields can't be made final unless constructors initialize irrelevant fields, resulting in more boilerplate. Constructors must set the tag field and initialize the right data fields with no help from the compiler: if you initialize the wrong fields, the program will fail at runtime. You can't add a flavor to a tagged class unless you can modify its source file. If you do add a flavor, you must remember to add a case to every switch statement, or the class will fail at runtime. Finally, the data type of an instance gives no clue as to its flavor. In short, **tagged classes are verbose, error-prone, and inefficient.**

Luckily, object-oriented languages such as Java offer a far better alternative for defining a single data type capable of representing objects of multiple flavors: subtyping. **A tagged class is just a pallid imitation of a class hierarchy.**

To transform a tagged class into a class hierarchy, first define an abstract class containing an abstract method for each method in the tagged class whose behavior depends on the tag value. In the Figure class, there is only one such method, which is area. This abstract class is the root of the class hierarchy. If there are any methods whose behavior does not depend on the value of the tag, put them in this class. Similarly, if there are any data fields used by all the flavors, put them in this class. There are no such flavor-independent methods or fields in the Figure class.

Next, define a concrete subclass of the root class for each flavor of the original tagged class. In our example, there are two: circle and rectangle. Include in each subclass the data fields particular to its flavor. In our example, radius is particular to circle, and length and width are particular to rectangle. Also include in each subclass the appropriate implementation of each abstract method in the root class. Here is the class hierarchy corresponding to the original Figure class:

```
// Class hierarchy replacement for a tagged class
abstract class Figure {
    abstract double area();
}

class Circle extends Figure {
    final double radius;

    Circle(double radius) { this.radius = radius; }

    double area() { return Math.PI * (radius * radius); }
}
```

```
class Rectangle extends Figure {
    final double length;
    final double width;

    Rectangle(double length, double width) {
        this.length = length;
        this.width  = width;
    }
    double area() { return length * width; }
}
```

This class hierarchy corrects every shortcoming of tagged classes noted previously. The code is simple and clear, containing none of the boilerplate found in the original. The implementation of each flavor is allotted its own class, and none of these classes are encumbered by irrelevant data fields. All fields are final. The compiler ensures that each class's constructor initializes its data fields, and that each class has an implementation for every abstract method declared in the root class. This eliminates the possibility of a runtime failure due to a missing switch case. Multiple programmers can extend the hierarchy independently and interoperably without access to the source for the root class. There is a separate data type associated with each flavor, allowing programmers to indicate the flavor of a variable and to restrict variables and input parameters to a particular flavor.

Another advantage of class hierarchies is that they can be made to reflect natural hierarchical relationships among types, allowing for increased flexibility and better compile-time type checking. Suppose the tagged class in the original example also allowed for squares. The class hierarchy could be made to reflect the fact that a square is a special kind of rectangle (assuming both are immutable):

```
class Square extends Rectangle {
    Square(double side) {
        super(side, side);
    }
}
```

Note that the fields in the above hierarchy are accessed directly rather than by accessor methods. This was done for brevity and would be unacceptable if the hierarchy were public (Item 14).

In summary, tagged classes are seldom appropriate. If you're tempted to write a class with an explicit tag field, think about whether the tag could be eliminated and the class replaced by a hierarchy. When you encounter an existing class with a tag field, consider refactoring it into a hierarchy.

Item 21: Use function objects to represent strategies

Some languages support *function pointers, delegates, lambda expressions*, or similar facilities that allow programs to store and transmit the ability to invoke a particular function. Such facilities are typically used to allow the caller of a function to specialize its behavior by passing in a second function. For example, the qsort function in C's standard library takes a pointer to a *comparator* function, which qsort uses to compare the elements to be sorted. The comparator function takes two parameters, each of which is a pointer to an element. It returns a negative integer if the element indicated by the first parameter is less than the one indicated by the second, zero if the two elements are equal, and a positive integer if the element indicated by the first parameter is greater than the one indicated by the second. Different sort orders can be obtained by passing in different comparator functions. This is an example of the *Strategy* pattern [Gamma95, p. 315]; the comparator function represents a strategy for sorting elements.

Java does not provide function pointers, but object references can be used to achieve a similar effect. Invoking a method on an object typically performs some operation on *that object*. However, it is possible to define an object whose methods perform operations on *other objects*, passed explicitly to the methods. An instance of a class that exports exactly one such method is effectively a pointer to that method. Such instances are known as *function objects*. For example, consider the following class:

```
class StringLengthComparator {
    public int compare(String s1, String s2) {
        return s1.length() - s2.length();
    }
}
```

This class exports a single method that takes two strings and returns a negative integer if the first string is shorter than the second, zero if the two strings are of equal length, and a positive integer if the first string is longer. This method is a comparator that orders strings based on their length instead of the more typical lexicographic ordering. A reference to a StringLengthComparator object serves as a "function pointer" to this comparator, allowing it to be invoked on arbitrary pairs of strings. In other words, a StringLengthComparator instance is a *concrete strategy* for string comparison.

As is typical for concrete strategy classes, the StringLengthComparator class is *stateless*: it has no fields, hence all instances of the class are functionally equivalent. Thus it should be a singleton to save on unnecessary object creation costs (Item 3, Item 5):

```
class StringLengthComparator {
    private StringLengthComparator() { }
    public static final StringLengthComparator
        INSTANCE = new StringLengthComparator();
    public int compare(String s1, String s2) {
        return s1.length() - s2.length();
    }
}
```

To pass a `StringLengthComparator` instance to a method, we need an appropriate type for the parameter. It would do no good to use `StringLengthComparator` because clients would be unable to pass any other comparison strategy. Instead, we need to define a `Comparator` interface and modify `StringLengthComparator` to implement this interface. In other words, we need to define a *strategy interface* to go with the concrete strategy class. Here it is:

```
// Strategy interface
public interface Comparator<T> {
    public int compare(T t1, T t2);
}
```

This definition of the `Comparator` interface happens to come from the `java.util` package, but there's nothing magic about it: you could just as well have written it yourself. The `Comparator` interface is *generic* (Item 26) so that it is applicable to comparators for objects other than strings. Its `compare` method takes two parameters of type `T` (its *formal type parameter*) rather than `String`. The `StringLengthComparator` class shown above can be made to implement `Comparator<String>` merely by declaring it to do so:

```
class StringLengthComparator implements Comparator<String> {
    ... // class body is identical to the one shown above
}
```

Concrete strategy classes are often declared using anonymous classes (Item 22). The following statement sorts an array of strings according to length:

```
Arrays.sort(stringArray, new Comparator<String>() {
    public int compare(String s1, String s2) {
        return s1.length() - s2.length();
    }
});
```

But note that using an anonymous class in this way will create a new instance each time the call is executed. If it is to be executed repeatedly, consider storing the function object in a private static final field and reusing it. Another advantage of doing this is that you can give the field a descriptive name for the function object.

Because the strategy interface serves as a type for all of its concrete strategy instances, a concrete strategy class needn't be made public to export a concrete strategy. Instead, a "host class" can export a public static field (or static factory method) whose type is the strategy interface, and the concrete strategy class can be a private nested class of the host. In the example that follows, a static member class is used in preference to an anonymous class to allow the concrete strategy class to implement a second interface, `Serializable`:

```
// Exporting a concrete strategy
class Host {
    private static class StrLenCmp
            implements Comparator<String>, Serializable {
        public int compare(String s1, String s2) {
            return s1.length() - s2.length();
        }
    }

    // Returned comparator is serializable
    public static final Comparator<String>
        STRING_LENGTH_COMPARATOR = new StrLenCmp();

    ...  // Bulk of class omitted
}
```

The `String` class uses this pattern to export a case-independent string comparator via its `CASE_INSENSITIVE_ORDER` field.

To summarize, a primary use of function pointers is to implement the Strategy pattern. To implement this pattern in Java, declare an interface to represent the strategy, and a class that implements this interface for each concrete strategy. When a concrete strategy is used only once, it is typically declared and instantiated as an anonymous class. When a concrete strategy is designed for repeated use, it is generally implemented as a private static member class and exported in a public static final field whose type is the strategy interface.

Item 22: Favor static member classes over nonstatic

A *nested class* is a class defined within another class. A nested class should exist only to serve its enclosing class. If a nested class would be useful in some other context, then it should be a top-level class. There are four kinds of nested classes: *static member classes*, *nonstatic member classes*, *anonymous classes*, and *local classes*. All but the first kind are known as *inner classes*. This item tells you when to use which kind of nested class and why.

A static member class is the simplest kind of nested class. It is best thought of as an ordinary class that happens to be declared inside another class and has access to all of the enclosing class's members, even those declared private. A static member class is a static member of its enclosing class and obeys the same accessibility rules as other static members. If it is declared private, it is accessible only within the enclosing class, and so forth.

One common use of a static member class is as a public helper class, useful only in conjunction with its outer class. For example, consider an enum describing the operations supported by a calculator (Item 30). The Operation enum should be a public static member class of the Calculator class. Clients of Calculator could then refer to operations using names like Calculator.Operation.PLUS and Calculator.Operation.MINUS.

Syntactically, the only difference between static and nonstatic member classes is that static member classes have the modifier static in their declarations. Despite the syntactic similarity, these two kinds of nested classes are very different. Each instance of a nonstatic member class is implicitly associated with an *enclosing instance* of its containing class. Within instance methods of a nonstatic member class, you can invoke methods on the enclosing instance or obtain a reference to the enclosing instance using the *qualified this* construct [JLS, 15.8.4]. If an instance of a nested class can exist in isolation from an instance of its enclosing class, then the nested class *must* be a static member class: it is impossible to create an instance of a nonstatic member class without an enclosing instance.

The association between a nonstatic member class instance and its enclosing instance is established when the former is created; it cannot be modified thereafter. Normally, the association is established automatically by invoking a nonstatic member class constructor from within an instance method of the enclosing class. It is possible, although rare, to establish the association manually using the expression enclosingInstance.new MemberClass(args). As you would expect, the association takes up space in the nonstatic member class instance and adds time to its construction.

One common use of a nonstatic member class is to define an *Adapter* [Gamma95, p. 139] that allows an instance of the outer class to be viewed as an instance of some unrelated class. For example, implementations of the Map interface typically use nonstatic member classes to implement their *collection views*, which are returned by Map's keySet, entrySet, and values methods. Similarly, implementations of the collection interfaces, such as Set and List, typically use nonstatic member classes to implement their iterators:

```
// Typical use of a nonstatic member class
public class MySet<E> extends AbstractSet<E> {
    ... // Bulk of the class omitted

    public Iterator<E> iterator() {
        return new MyIterator();
    }

    private class MyIterator implements Iterator<E> {
        ...
    }
}
```

If you declare a member class that does not require access to an enclosing instance, *always* **put the static modifier in its declaration,** making it a static rather than a nonstatic member class. If you omit this modifier, each instance will have an extraneous reference to its enclosing instance. Storing this reference costs time and space, and can result in the enclosing instance being retained when it would otherwise be eligible for garbage collection (Item 6). And should you ever need to allocate an instance without an enclosing instance, you'll be unable to do so, as nonstatic member class instances are required to have an enclosing instance.

A common use of private static member classes is to represent components of the object represented by their enclosing class. For example, consider a Map instance, which associates keys with values. Many Map implementations have an internal Entry object for each key-value pair in the map. While each entry is associated with a map, the methods on an entry (getKey, getValue, and setValue) do not need access to the map. Therefore, it would be wasteful to use a nonstatic member class to represent entries: a private static member class is best. If you accidentally omit the static modifier in the entry declaration, the map will still work, but each entry will contain a superfluous reference to the map, which wastes space and time.

It is doubly important to choose correctly between a static and a nonstatic member class if the class in question is a public or protected member of an exported class. In this case, the member class is an exported API element and cannot be changed from a nonstatic to a static member class in a subsequent release without violating binary compatibility.

Anonymous classes are unlike anything else in the Java programming language. As you would expect, an anonymous class has no name. It is not a member of its enclosing class. Rather than being declared along with other members, it is simultaneously declared and instantiated at the point of use. Anonymous classes are permitted at any point in the code where an expression is legal. Anonymous classes have enclosing instances if and only if they occur in a nonstatic context. But even if they occur in a static context, they cannot have any static members.

There are many limitations on the applicability of anonymous classes. You can't instantiate them except at the point they're declared. You can't perform instanceof tests or do anything else that requires you to name the class. You can't declare an anonymous class to implement multiple interfaces, or to extend a class and implement an interface at the same time. Clients of an anonymous class can't invoke any members except those it inherits from its supertype. Because anonymous classes occur in the midst of expressions, they must be kept short—about ten lines or fewer—or readability will suffer.

One common use of anonymous classes is to create *function objects* (Item 21) on the fly. For example, the sort method invocation on page 104 sorts an array of strings according to their length using an anonymous Comparator instance. Another common use of anonymous classes is to create *process objects*, such as Runnable, Thread, or TimerTask instances. A third common use is within static factory methods (see the intArrayAsList method in Item 18).

Local classes are the least frequently used of the four kinds of nested classes. A local class can be declared anywhere a local variable can be declared and obeys the same scoping rules. Local classes have attributes in common with each of the other kinds of nested classes. Like member classes, they have names and can be used repeatedly. Like anonymous classes, they have enclosing instances only if they are defined in a nonstatic context, and they cannot contain static members. And like anonymous classes, they should be kept short so as not to harm readability.

To recap, there are four different kinds of nested classes, and each has its place. If a nested class needs to be visible outside of a single method or is too long to fit comfortably inside a method, use a member class. If each instance of the member class needs a reference to its enclosing instance, make it nonstatic; otherwise, make it static. Assuming the class belongs inside a method, if you need to create instances from only one location and there is a preexisting type that characterizes the class, make it an anonymous class; otherwise, make it a local class.

CHAPTER 5

Generics

In release 1.5, *generics* were added to Java. Before generics, you had to cast every object you read from a collection. If someone accidentally inserted an object of the wrong type, casts could fail at runtime. With generics, you tell the compiler what types of objects are permitted in each collection. The compiler inserts casts for you automatically and tells you at compile time if you try to insert an object of the wrong type. This results in programs that are both safer and clearer, but these benefits come with complications. This chapter tells you how to maximize the benefits and minimize the complications. For a more detailed treatment of this material, see Langer's tutorial [Langer08] or Naftalin and Wadler's book [Naftalin07].

Item 23: Don't use raw types in new code

First, a few terms. A class or interface whose declaration has one or more *type parameters* is a *generic* class or interface [JLS, 8.1.2, 9.1.2]. For example, as of release 1.5, the List interface has a single type parameter, E, representing the element type of the list. Technically the name of the interface is now List<E> (read "list of E"), but people often call it List for short. Generic classes and interfaces are collectively known as *generic types*.

Each generic type defines a set of *parameterized types*, which consist of the class or interface name followed by an angle-bracketed list of *actual type parameters* corresponding to the generic type's formal type parameters [JLS, 4.4, 4.5]. For example, List<String> (read "list of string") is a parameterized type representing a list whose elements are of type String. (String is the actual type parameter corresponding to the formal type parameter E.)

Finally, each generic type defines a *raw type*, which is the name of the generic type used without any accompanying actual type parameters [JLS, 4.8]. For example, the raw type corresponding to List<E> is List. Raw types behave as if all of the generic type information were erased from the type declaration. For all practical purposes, the raw type List behaves the same way as the interface type List did before generics were added to the platform.

Before release 1.5, this would have been an exemplary collection declaration:

```
// Now a raw collection type - don't do this!

/**
 * My stamp collection. Contains only Stamp instances.
 */
private final Collection stamps = ... ;
```

If you accidentally put a coin into your stamp collection, the erroneous insertion compiles and runs without error:

```
// Erroneous insertion of coin into stamp collection
stamps.add(new Coin( ... ));
```

You don't get an error until you retrieve the coin from the stamp collection:

```
// Now a raw iterator type - don't do this!
for (Iterator i = stamps.iterator(); i.hasNext(); ) {
    Stamp s = (Stamp) i.next(); // Throws ClassCastException
    ... // Do something with the stamp
}
```

As mentioned throughout this book, it pays to discover errors as soon as possible after they are made, ideally at compile time. In this case, you don't discover the error till runtime, long after it has happened, and in code that is far removed from the code containing the error. Once you see the ClassCastException, you have to search through the code base looking for the method invocation that put the coin into the stamp collection. The compiler can't help you, because it can't understand the comment that says, "Contains only Stamp instances."

With generics, you replace the comment with an improved type declaration for the collection that tells the compiler the information that was previously hidden in the comment:

```
// Parameterized collection type - typesafe
private final Collection<Stamp> stamps = ... ;
```

From this declaration the compiler knows that `stamps` should contain only `Stamp` instances and *guarantees* this to be the case, assuming your entire code base is compiled with a compiler from release 1.5 or later and all the code compiles without emitting (or suppressing; see Item 24) any warnings. When `stamps` is declared with a parameterized type, the erroneous insertion generates a compile-time error message that tells you exactly what is wrong:

```
Test.java:9: add(Stamp) in Collection<Stamp> cannot be applied
to (Coin)
    stamps.add(new Coin());
               ^
```

As an added benefit, you no longer have to cast manually when retrieving elements from collections. The compiler inserts invisible casts for you and guarantees that they won't fail (assuming, again, that all of your code was compiled with a generics-aware compiler and did not produce or suppress any warnings). This is true whether you use a for-each loop (Item 46):

```
// for-each loop over a parameterized collection - typesafe
for (Stamp s : stamps) { // No cast
    ... // Do something with the stamp
}
```

or a traditional `for` loop:

```
// for loop with parameterized iterator declaration - typesafe
for (Iterator<Stamp> i = stamps.iterator(); i.hasNext(); ) {
    Stamp s = i.next(); // No cast necessary
    ... // Do something with the stamp
}
```

While the prospect of accidentally inserting a coin into a stamp collection may appear far-fetched, the problem is real. For example, it is easy to imagine someone putting a `java.util.Date` instance into a collection that is supposed to contain only `java.sql.Date` instances.

As noted above, it is still legal to use collection types and other generic types without supplying type parameters, but you should not do it. **If you use raw types, you lose all the safety and expressiveness benefits of generics.** Given that you shouldn't use raw types, why did the language designers allow them? To provide compatibility. The Java platform was about to enter its second decade when generics were introduced, and there was an enormous amount of Java code in existence that did not use generics. It was deemed critical that all of this code remain legal and interoperable with new code that does use generics. It had to be legal to pass instances of parameterized types to methods that were designed for use with ordinary types, and vice versa. This requirement, known as *migration compatibility*, drove the decision to support raw types.

While you shouldn't use raw types such as List in new code, it is fine to use types that are parameterized to allow insertion of arbitrary objects, such as List<Object>. Just what is the difference between the raw type List and the parameterized type List<Object>? Loosely speaking, the former has opted out of generic type checking, while the latter has explicitly told the compiler that it is capable of holding objects of any type. While you can pass a List<String> to a parameter of type List, you can't pass it to a parameter of type List<Object>. There are subtyping rules for generics, and List<String> is a subtype of the raw type List, but not of the parameterized type List<Object> (Item 25). As a consequence, **you lose type safety if you use a raw type like List, but not if you use a parameterized type like List<Object>.**

To make this concrete, consider the following program:

```
// Uses raw type (List) - fails at runtime!
public static void main(String[] args) {
    List<String> strings = new ArrayList<String>();
    unsafeAdd(strings, new Integer(42));
    String s = strings.get(0); // Compiler-generated cast
}

private static void unsafeAdd(List list, Object o) {
    list.add(o);
}
```

This program compiles, but because it uses the raw type List, you get a warning:

```
Test.java:10: warning: unchecked call to add(E) in raw type List
    list.add(o);
        ^
```

And indeed, if you run the program, you get a ClassCastException when the program tries to cast the result of the invocation strings.get(0) to a String. This is a compiler-generated cast, so it's normally guaranteed to succeed, but in this case we ignored a compiler warning and paid the price.

If you replace the raw type List with the parameterized type List<Object> in the unsafeAdd declaration and try to recompile the program, you'll find that it no longer compiles. Here is the error message:

```
Test.java:5: unsafeAdd(List<Object>,Object) cannot be applied
to (List<String>,Integer)
    unsafeAdd(strings, new Integer(42));
    ^
```

You might be tempted to use a raw type for a collection whose element type is unknown and doesn't matter. For example, suppose you want to write a method that takes two sets and returns the number of elements they have in common. Here's how you might write such a method if you were new to generics:

```
// Use of raw type for unknown element type - don't do this!
static int numElementsInCommon(Set s1, Set s2) {
    int result = 0;
    for (Object o1 : s1)
        if (s2.contains(o1))
            result++;
    return result;
}
```

This method works but it uses raw types, which are dangerous. Since release 1.5, Java has provided a safe alternative known as *unbounded wildcard types*. If you want to use a generic type but you don't know or care what the actual type parameter is, you can use a question mark instead. For example, the unbounded wildcard type for the generic type Set<E> is Set<?> (read "set of some type"). It is the most general parameterized Set type, capable of holding *any* set. Here is how the numElementsInCommon method looks with unbounded wildcard types:

```
// Unbounded wildcard type - typesafe and flexible
static int numElementsInCommon(Set<?> s1, Set<?> s2) {
    int result = 0;
    for (Object o1 : s1)
        if (s2.contains(o1))
            result++;
    return result;
}
```

What is the difference between the unbounded wildcard type Set<?> and the raw type Set? Do the question marks really buy you anything? Not to belabor the point, but the wildcard type is safe and the raw type isn't. You can put any element into a collection with a raw type, easily corrupting the collection's type invariant (as demonstrated by the `unsafeAdd` method on page 112); **you can't put any element (other than `null`) into a `Collection<?>`.** Attempting to do so will generate a compile-time error message like this:

```
WildCard.java:13: cannot find symbol
symbol  : method add(String)
location: interface Collection<capture#825 of ?>
          c.add("verboten");
              ^
```

Admittedly this error message leaves something to be desired, but the compiler has done its job, preventing you from corrupting the collection's type invariant. Not only can't you put any element (other than `null`) into a `Collection<?>`, but you can't assume anything about the type of the objects that you get out. If these restrictions are unacceptable, you can use *generic methods* (Item 27) or *bounded wildcard types* (Item 28).

There are two minor exceptions to the rule that you should not use raw types in new code, both of which stem from the fact that generic type information is erased at runtime (Item 25). **You must use raw types in class literals.** The specification does not permit the use of parameterized types (though it does permit array types and primitive types) [JLS, 15.8.2]. In other words, `List.class`, `String[].class`, and `int.class` are all legal, but `List<String>.class` and `List<?>.class` are not.

The second exception to the rule concerns the `instanceof` operator. Because generic type information is erased at runtime, it is illegal to use the `instanceof` operator on parameterized types other than unbounded wildcard types. The use of unbounded wildcard types in place of raw types does not affect the behavior of the `instanceof` operator in any way. In this case, the angle brackets and question marks are just noise. **This is the preferred way to use the `instanceof` operator with generic types:**

```
// Legitimate use of raw type - instanceof operator
if (o instanceof Set) {       // Raw type
    Set<?> m = (Set<?>) o;    // Wildcard type
    ...
}
```

Note that once you've determined that o is a `Set`, you must cast it to the wildcard type `Set<?>`, not the raw type `Set`. This is a checked cast, so it will not cause a compiler warning.

In summary, using raw types can lead to exceptions at runtime, so don't use them in new code. They are provided only for compatibility and interoperability with legacy code that predates the introduction of generics. As a quick review, `Set<Object>` is a parameterized type representing a set that can contain objects of any type, `Set<?>` is a wildcard type representing a set that can contain only objects of some unknown type, and `Set` is a raw type, which opts out of the generic type system. The first two are safe and the last is not.

For quick reference, the terms introduced in this item (and a few introduced elsewhere in this chapter) are summarized in the following table:

Term	**Example**	**Item**
Parameterized type	`List<String>`	Item 23
Actual type parameter	`String`	Item 23
Generic type	`List<E>`	Items 23, 26
Formal type parameter	`E`	Item 23
Unbounded wildcard type	`List<?>`	Item 23
Raw type	`List`	Item 23
Bounded type parameter	`<E extends Number>`	Item 26
Recursive type bound	`<T extends Comparable<T>>`	Item 27
Bounded wildcard type	`List<? extends Number>`	Item 28
Generic method	`static <E> List<E> asList(E[] a)`	Item 27
Type token	`String.class`	Item 29

Item 24: Eliminate unchecked warnings

When you program with generics, you will see many compiler warnings: unchecked cast warnings, unchecked method invocation warnings, unchecked generic array creation warnings, and unchecked conversion warnings. The more experience you acquire with generics, the fewer warnings you'll get, but don't expect newly written code that uses generics to compile cleanly.

Many unchecked warnings are easy to eliminate. For example, suppose you accidentally write this declaration:

```
Set<Lark> exaltation = new HashSet();
```

The compiler will gently remind you what you did wrong:

```
Venery.java:4: warning: [unchecked] unchecked conversion
found   : HashSet, required: Set<Lark>
    Set<Lark> exaltation = new HashSet();
                 ^
```

You can then make the indicated correction, causing the warning to disappear:

```
Set<Lark> exaltation = new HashSet<Lark>();
```

Some warnings will be *much* more difficult to eliminate. This chapter is filled with examples of such warnings. When you get warnings that require some thought, persevere! **Eliminate every unchecked warning that you can.** If you eliminate all warnings, you are assured that your code is typesafe, which is a very good thing. It means that you won't get a ClassCastException at runtime, and it increases your confidence that your program is behaving as you intended.

If you can't eliminate a warning, and you can prove that the code that provoked the warning is typesafe, then (and only then) suppress the warning with an @SuppressWarnings("unchecked") annotation. If you suppress warnings without first proving that the code is typesafe, you are only giving yourself a false sense of security. The code may compile without emitting any warnings, but it can still throw a ClassCastException at runtime. If, however, you ignore unchecked warnings that you know to be safe (instead of suppressing them), you won't notice when a new warning crops up that represents a real problem. The new warning will get lost amidst all the false alarms that you didn't silence.

The SuppressWarnings annotation can be used at any granularity, from an individual local variable declaration to an entire class. **Always use the Suppress-Warnings annotation on the smallest scope possible.** Typically this will be a variable declaration or a very short method or constructor. Never use Suppress-Warnings on an entire class. Doing so could mask critical warnings.

If you find yourself using the SuppressWarnings annotation on a method or constructor that's more than one line long, you may be able to move it onto a local variable declaration. You may have to declare a new local variable, but it's worth it. For example, consider this toArray method, which comes from ArrayList:

```
public <T> T[] toArray(T[] a) {
    if (a.length < size)
        return (T[]) Arrays.copyOf(elements, size, a.getClass());
    System.arraycopy(elements, 0, a, 0, size);
    if (a.length > size)
        a[size] = null;
    return a;
}
```

If you compile ArrayList, the method generates this warning:

```
ArrayList.java:305: warning: [unchecked] unchecked cast
found   : Object[], required: T[]
        return (T[]) Arrays.copyOf(elements, size, a.getClass());
                                   ^
```

It is illegal to put a SuppressWarnings annotation on the return statement, because it isn't a declaration [JLS, 9.7]. You might be tempted to put the annotation on the entire method, but don't. Instead, declare a local variable to hold the return value and annotate its declaration, like so:

```
// Adding local variable to reduce scope of @SuppressWarnings
public <T> T[] toArray(T[] a) {
    if (a.length < size) {
        // This cast is correct because the array we're creating
        // is of the same type as the one passed in, which is T[].
        @SuppressWarnings("unchecked") T[] result =
            (T[]) Arrays.copyOf(elements, size, a.getClass());
        return result;
    }
    System.arraycopy(elements, 0, a, 0, size);
    if (a.length > size)
        a[size] = null;
    return a;
}
```

This method compiles cleanly and minimizes the scope in which unchecked warnings are suppressed.

Every time you use an `@SuppressWarnings("unchecked")` annotation, add a comment saying why it's safe to do so. This will help others understand the code, and more importantly, it will decrease the odds that someone will modify the code so as to make the computation unsafe. If you find it hard to write such a comment, keep thinking. You may end up figuring out that the unchecked operation isn't safe after all.

In summary, unchecked warnings are important. Don't ignore them. Every unchecked warning represents the potential for a `ClassCastException` at runtime. Do your best to eliminate these warnings. If you can't eliminate an unchecked warning and you can prove that the code that provoked it is typesafe, suppress the warning with an `@SuppressWarnings("unchecked")` annotation in the narrowest possible scope. Record the rationale for your decision to suppress the warning in a comment.

Item 25: Prefer lists to arrays

Arrays differ from generic types in two important ways. First, arrays are *covariant*. This scary-sounding word means simply that if Sub is a subtype of Super, then the array type Sub[] is a subtype of Super[]. Generics, by contrast, are *invariant*: for any two distinct types Type1 and Type2, List<Type1> is neither a subtype nor a supertype of List<Type2> [JLS, 4.10; Naftalin07, 2.5]. You might think this means that generics are deficient, but arguably it is arrays that are deficient.

This code fragment is legal:

```
// Fails at runtime!
Object[] objectArray = new Long[1];
objectArray[0] = "I don't fit in"; // Throws ArrayStoreException
```

but this one is not:

```
// Won't compile!
List<Object> ol = new ArrayList<Long>(); // Incompatible types
ol.add("I don't fit in");
```

Either way you can't put a String into a Long container, but with an array you find out that you've made a mistake at runtime; with a list, you find out at compile time. Of course you'd rather find out at compile time.

The second major difference between arrays and generics is that arrays are *reified* [JLS, 4.7]. This means that arrays know and enforce their element types at runtime. As noted above, if you try to store a String into an array of Long, you'll get an ArrayStoreException. Generics, by contrast, are implemented by *erasure* [JLS, 4.6]. This means that they enforce their type constraints only at compile time and discard (or *erase*) their element type information at runtime. Erasure is what allows generic types to interoperate freely with legacy code that does not use generics (Item 23).

Because of these fundamental differences, arrays and generics do not mix well. For example, it is illegal to create an array of a generic type, a parameterized type, or a type parameter. None of these array creation expressions are legal: new List<E>[], new List<String>[], new E[]. All will result in *generic array creation* errors at compile time.

Why is it illegal to create a generic array? Because it isn't typesafe. If it were legal, casts generated by the compiler in an otherwise correct program could fail at runtime with a ClassCastException. This would violate the fundamental guarantee provided by the generic type system.

To make this more concrete, consider the following code fragment:

```
// Why generic array creation is illegal - won't compile!
List<String>[] stringLists = new List<String>[1];  // (1)
List<Integer> intList = Arrays.asList(42);         // (2)
Object[] objects = stringLists;                    // (3)
objects[0] = intList;                              // (4)
String s = stringLists[0].get(0);                  // (5)
```

Let's pretend that line 1, which creates a generic array, is legal. Line 2 creates and initializes a List<Integer> containing a single element. Line 3 stores the List<String> array into an Object array variable, which is legal because arrays are covariant. Line 4 stores the List<Integer> into the sole element of the Object array, which succeeds because generics are implemented by erasure: the runtime type of a List<Integer> instance is simply List, and the runtime type of a List<String>[] instance is List[], so this assignment doesn't generate an ArrayStoreException. Now we're in trouble. We've stored a List<Integer> instance into an array that is declared to hold only List<String> instances. In line 5, we retrieve the sole element from the sole list in this array. The compiler automatically casts the retrieved element to String, but it's an Integer, so we get a ClassCastException at runtime. In order to prevent this from happening, line 1 (which creates a generic array) generates a compile-time error.

Types such as E, List<E>, and List<String> are technically known as *non-reifiable* types [JLS, 4.7]. Intuitively speaking, a non-reifiable type is one whose runtime representation contains less information than its compile-time representation. The only parameterized types that are reifiable are unbounded wildcard types such as List<?> and Map<?,?> (Item 23). It is legal, though infrequently useful, to create arrays of unbounded wildcard types.

The prohibition on generic array creation can be annoying. It means, for example, that it's not generally possible for a generic type to return an array of its element type (but see Item 29 for a partial solution). It also means that you can get confusing warnings when using varargs methods (Item 42) in combination with generic types. This is because every time you invoke a varargs method, an array is created to hold the varargs parameters. If the element type of this array is not reifiable, you get a warning. There is little you can do about these warnings other than to suppress them (Item 24), and to avoid mixing generics and varargs in your APIs.

When you get a generic array creation error, the best solution is often to use the collection type List<E> in preference to the array type E[]. You might sacrifice some performance or conciseness, but in exchange you get better type safety and interoperability.

For example, suppose you have a synchronized list (of the sort returned by Collections.synchronizedList) and a function that takes two values of the type held by the list and returns a third. Now suppose you want to write a method to "reduce" the list by applying the function across it. If the list contains integers and the function adds two integer values, the reduce method returns the sum of all the values in the list. If the function multiplies two integer values, the method returns the product of the values in the list. If the list contains strings and the function concatenates two strings, the method returns a string consisting of all the strings in the list in sequence. In addition to a list and a function, the reduce method takes an initial value for the reduction, which is returned if the list is empty. (The initial value is typically the identity element for the function, which is 0 for addition, 1 for multiplication, and "" for string concatenation.) Here's how the code might have looked without generics:

```
// Reduction without generics, and with concurrency flaw!
static Object reduce(List list, Function f, Object initVal) {
    synchronized(list) {
        Object result = initVal;
        for (Object o : list)
            result = f.apply(result, o);
        return result;
    }
}

interface Function {
    Object apply(Object arg1, Object arg2);
}
```

Now, suppose you've read Item 67, which tells you not to call "alien methods" from a synchronized region. So, you modify the reduce method to copy the contents of the list while holding the lock, which allows you to perform the reduction on the copy. Prior to release 1.5, the natural way to do this would have been using List's toArray method (which locks the list internally):

```
// Reduction without generics or concurrency flaw
static Object reduce(List list, Function f, Object initVal) {
    Object[] snapshot = list.toArray(); // Locks list internally
    Object result = initVal;
    for (Object o : snapshot)
        result = f.apply(result, o);
    return result;
}
```

If you try to do this with generics you'll get into trouble of the sort that we discussed above. Here's a generic version of the Function interface:

```
interface Function<T> {
    T apply(T arg1, T arg2);
}
```

And here's a naive attempt to apply generics to the revised version of the reduce method. This is a *generic method* (Item 27). Don't worry if you don't understand the declaration. For the purposes of this item, you should concentrate on the method body:

```
// Naive generic version of reduction - won't compile!
static <E> E reduce(List<E> list, Function<E> f, E initVal) {
    E[] snapshot = list.toArray();  // Locks list
    E result = initVal;
    for (E e : snapshot)
        result = f.apply(result, e);
    return result;
}
```

If you try to compile this method, you'll get the following error:

```
Reduce.java:12: incompatible types
found    : Object[], required: E[]
         E[] snapshot = list.toArray();  // Locks list
                        ^
```

No big deal, you say, I'll cast the Object array to an E array:

```
E[] snapshot = (E[]) list.toArray();
```

That gets rid of the error, but now you get a warning:

```
Reduce.java:12: warning: [unchecked] unchecked cast
found    : Object[], required: E[]
         E[] snapshot = (E[]) list.toArray();  // Locks list
                        ^
```

The compiler is telling you that it can't check the safety of the cast at runtime because it doesn't know what E is at runtime—remember, element type information is erased from generics at runtime. Will this program work? Yes, it turns out that it will, but it isn't safe. With minor modifications, you could get it to throw a

ClassCastException on a line that doesn't contain an explicit cast. The compile-time type of snapshot is E[] which could be String[], Integer[], or any other kind of array. The runtime type is Object[], and that's dangerous. Casts to arrays of non-reifiable types should be used only under special circumstances (Item 26).

So what should you do? Use a list instead of an array. Here is a version of the reduce method that compiles without error or warning:

```
// List-based generic reduction
static <E> E reduce(List<E> list, Function<E> f, E initVal) {
    List<E> snapshot;
    synchronized(list) {
        snapshot = new ArrayList<E>(list);
    }
    E result = initVal;
    for (E e : snapshot)
        result = f.apply(result, e);
    return result;
}
```

This version is a tad more verbose than the array version, but it's worth it for the peace of mind that comes from knowing you won't get a ClassCastException at runtime.

In summary, arrays and generics have very different type rules. Arrays are covariant and reified; generics are invariant and erased. As a consequence, arrays provide runtime type safety but not compile-time type safety and vice versa for generics. Generally speaking, arrays and generics don't mix well. If you find yourself mixing them and getting compile-time errors or warnings, your first impulse should be to replace the arrays with lists.

Item 26: Favor generic types

It is generally not too difficult to parameterize your collection declarations and make use of the generic types and methods provided by the JDK. Writing your own generic types is a bit more difficult, but it's worth the effort to learn how.

Consider the simple stack implementation from Item 6:

```
// Object-based collection - a prime candidate for generics
public class Stack {
    private Object[] elements;
    private int size = 0;
    private static final int DEFAULT_INITIAL_CAPACITY = 16;

    public Stack() {
        elements = new Object[DEFAULT_INITIAL_CAPACITY];
    }

    public void push(Object e) {
        ensureCapacity();
        elements[size++] = e;
    }

    public Object pop() {
        if (size == 0)
            throw new EmptyStackException();
        Object result = elements[--size];
        elements[size] = null; // Eliminate obsolete reference
        return result;
    }

    public boolean isEmpty() {
        return size == 0;
    }

    private void ensureCapacity() {
        if (elements.length == size)
            elements = Arrays.copyOf(elements, 2 * size + 1);
    }
}
```

This class is a prime candidate for *generification*, in other words, for being compatibly enhanced to take advantage of generic types. As it stands, you have to cast objects that are popped off the stack, and those casts might fail at runtime. The first step in generifying a class is to add one or more type parameters to its declaration. In this case there is one type parameter, representing the element type of the stack, and the conventional name for this parameter is E (Item 56).

The next step is to replace all the uses of the type Object with the appropriate type parameter, and then try to compile the resulting program:

```
// Initial attempt to generify Stack - won't compile!
public class Stack<E> {
    private E[] elements;
    private int size = 0;
    private static final int DEFAULT_INITIAL_CAPACITY = 16;

    public Stack() {
        elements = new E[DEFAULT_INITIAL_CAPACITY];
    }

    public void push(E e) {
        ensureCapacity();
        elements[size++] = e;
    }

    public E pop() {
        if (size==0)
            throw new EmptyStackException();
        E result = elements[--size];
        elements[size] = null; // Eliminate obsolete reference
        return result;
    }
    ... // no changes in isEmpty or ensureCapacity
}
```

You'll generally get at least one error or warning, and this class is no exception. Luckily, this class generates only one error:

```
Stack.java:8: generic array creation
        elements = new E[DEFAULT_INITIAL_CAPACITY];
                   ^
```

As explained in Item 25, you can't create an array of a non-reifiable type, such as E. This problem arises every time you write a generic type that is backed by an array. There are two ways to solve it. The first solution directly circumvents the prohibition on generic array creation: create an array of Object and cast it to the generic array type. Now in place of an error, the compiler will emit a warning. This usage is legal, but it's not (in general) typesafe:

```
Stack.java:8: warning: [unchecked] unchecked cast
found    : Object[], required: E[]
        elements = (E[]) new Object[DEFAULT_INITIAL_CAPACITY];
                   ^
```

The compiler may not be able to prove that your program is typesafe, but you can. You must convince yourself that the unchecked cast will not compromise the type safety of the program. The array in question (elements) is stored in a private field and never returned to the client or passed to any other method. The only elements stored in the array are those passed to the push method, which are of type E, so the unchecked cast can do no harm.

Once you've proved that an unchecked cast is safe, suppress the warning in as narrow a scope as possible (Item 24). In this case, the constructor contains only the unchecked array creation, so it's appropriate to suppress the warning in the entire constructor. With the addition of an annotation to do this, Stack compiles cleanly and you can use it without explicit casts or fear of a ClassCastException:

```
// The elements array will contain only E instances from push(E).
// This is sufficient to ensure type safety, but the runtime
// type of the array won't be E[]; it will always be Object[]!
@SuppressWarnings("unchecked")
public Stack() {
    elements = (E[]) new Object[DEFAULT_INITIAL_CAPACITY];
}
```

The second way to eliminate the generic array creation error in Stack is to change the type of the field elements from E[] to Object[]. If you do this, you'll get a different error:

```
Stack.java:19: incompatible types
found    : Object, required: E
        E result = elements[--size];
                   ^
```

You can change this error into a warning by casting the element retrieved from the array from Object to E:

```
Stack.java:19: warning: [unchecked] unchecked cast
found    : Object, required: E
        E result = (E) elements[--size];
                   ^
```

Because E is a non-reifiable type, there's no way the compiler can check the cast at runtime. Again, you can easily prove to yourself that the unchecked cast is safe, so it's appropriate to suppress the warning. In line with the advice of Item 24, we suppress the warning only on the assignment that contains the unchecked cast, not on the entire pop method:

```
// Appropriate suppression of unchecked warning
public E pop() {
    if (size == 0)
        throw new EmptyStackException();

    // push requires elements to be of type E, so cast is correct
    @SuppressWarnings("unchecked") E result =
        (E) elements[--size];

    elements[size] = null; // Eliminate obsolete reference
    return result;
}
```

Which of the two techniques you choose for dealing with the generic array creation error is largely a matter of taste. All other things being equal, it is riskier to suppress an unchecked cast to an array type than to a scalar type, which would suggest the second solution. But in a more realistic generic class than Stack, you would probably be reading from the array at many points in the code, so choosing the second solution would require many casts to E rather than a single cast to E[], which is why the first solution is used more commonly [Naftalin07, 6.7].

The following program demonstrates the use of our generic Stack class. The program prints its command line arguments in reverse order and converted to uppercase. No explicit cast is necessary to invoke String's toUpperCase method on the elements popped from the stack, and the automatically generated cast is guaranteed to succeed:

```
// Little program to exercise our generic Stack
public static void main(String[] args) {
    Stack<String> stack = new Stack<String>();
    for (String arg : args)
        stack.push(arg);
    while (!stack.isEmpty())
        System.out.println(stack.pop().toUpperCase());
}
```

The foregoing example may appear to contradict Item 25, which encourages the use of lists in preference to arrays. It is not always possible or desirable to use lists inside your generic types. Java doesn't support lists natively, so some generic types, such as `ArrayList`, *must* be implemented atop arrays. Other generic types, such as `HashMap`, are implemented atop arrays for performance.

The great majority of generic types are like our `Stack` example in that their type parameters have no restrictions: you can create a `Stack<Object>`, `Stack<int[]>`, `Stack<List<String>>`, or a `Stack` of any other object reference type. Note that you can't create a `Stack` of a primitive type: trying to create a `Stack<int>` or `Stack<double>` will result in a compile-time error. This is a fundamental limitation of Java's generic type system. You can work around this restriction by using boxed primitive types (Item 49).

There are some generic types that restrict the permissible values of their type parameters. For example, consider `java.util.concurrent.DelayQueue`, whose declaration looks like this:

```
class DelayQueue<E extends Delayed> implements BlockingQueue<E>;
```

The type parameter list (`<E extends Delayed>`) requires that the actual type parameter `E` must be a subtype of `java.util.concurrent.Delayed`. This allows the `DelayQueue` implementation and its clients to take advantage of `Delayed` methods on the elements of a `DelayQueue`, without the need for explicit casting or the risk of a `ClassCastException`. The type parameter `E` is known as a *bounded type parameter*. Note that the subtype relation is defined so that every type is a subtype of itself [JLS, 4.10], so it is legal to create a `DelayQueue<Delayed>`.

In summary, generic types are safer and easier to use than types that require casts in client code. When you design new types, make sure that they can be used without such casts. This will often mean making the types generic. Generify your existing types as time permits. This will make life easier for new users of these types without breaking existing clients (Item 23).

Item 27: Favor generic methods

Just as classes can benefit from generification, so can methods. Static utility methods are particularly good candidates for generification. All of the "algorithm" methods in Collections (such as binarySearch and sort) have been generified.

Writing generic methods is similar to writing generic types. Consider this method, which returns the union of two sets:

```
// Uses raw types - unacceptable! (Item 23)
public static Set union(Set s1, Set s2) {
    Set result = new HashSet(s1);
    result.addAll(s2);
    return result;
}
```

This method compiles, but with two warnings:

```
Union.java:5: warning: [unchecked] unchecked call to
HashSet(Collection<? extends E>) as a member of raw type HashSet
        Set result = new HashSet(s1);
                         ^
Union.java:6: warning: [unchecked] unchecked call to
addAll(Collection<? extends E>) as a member of raw type Set
        result.addAll(s2);
                 ^
```

To fix these warnings and make the method typesafe, modify the method declaration to declare a type parameter representing the element type for the three sets (two arguments and the return value) and use the type parameter in the method. **The type parameter list, which declares the type parameter, goes between the method's modifiers and its return type.** In this example, the type parameter list is <E> and the return type is Set<E>. The naming conventions for type parameters are the same for generic methods as for generic types (Items 26, 56):

```
// Generic method
public static <E> Set<E> union(Set<E> s1, Set<E> s2) {
    Set<E> result = new HashSet<E>(s1);
    result.addAll(s2);
    return result;
}
```

At least for simple generic methods, that's all there is to it. Now the method compiles without generating any warnings and provides type safety as well as ease of use. Here's a simple program to exercise our method. The program contains no casts and compiles without errors or warnings:

```
// Simple program to exercise generic method
public static void main(String[] args) {
    Set<String> guys = new HashSet<String>(
        Arrays.asList("Tom", "Dick", "Harry"));
    Set<String> stooges = new HashSet<String>(
        Arrays.asList("Larry", "Moe", "Curly"));
    Set<String> aflCio = union(guys, stooges);
    System.out.println(aflCio);
}
```

When you run the program, it prints [Moe, Harry, Tom, Curly, Larry, Dick]. The order of the elements is implementation-dependent.

A limitation of the union method is that the types of all three sets (both input parameters and the return value) have to be the same. You can make the method more flexible by using *bounded wildcard types* (Item 28).

One noteworthy feature of generic methods is that you needn't specify the value of the type parameter explicitly as you must when invoking generic constructors. The compiler figures out the value of the type parameters by examining the types of the method arguments. In the case of the program above, the compiler sees that both arguments to union are of type Set<String>, so it knows that the type parameter E must be String. This process is called *type inference*.

As discussed in Item 1, you can exploit the type inference provided by generic method invocation to ease the process of creating parameterized type instances. To refresh your memory, the need to pass the values of type parameters explicitly when invoking generic constructors can be annoying. The type parameters appear redundantly on the left- and right-hand sides of variable declarations:

```
// Parameterized type instance creation with constructor
Map<String, List<String>> anagrams =
    new HashMap<String, List<String>>();
```

To eliminate this redundancy, write a *generic static factory method* corresponding to each constructor that you want to use. For example, here is a generic static factory method corresponding to the parameterless HashMap constructor:

```
// Generic static factory method
public static <K,V> HashMap<K,V> newHashMap() {
    return new HashMap<K,V>();
}
```

With this generic static factory method, you can replace the repetitious declaration above with this concise one:

```
// Parameterized type instance creation with static factory
Map<String, List<String>> anagrams = newHashMap();
```

It would be nice if the language did the same kind of type inference when invoking constructors on generic types as it does when invoking generic methods. Someday it might, but as of release 1.6, it does not.

A related pattern is the *generic singleton factory*. On occasion, you will need to create an object that is immutable but applicable to many different types. Because generics are implemented by erasure (Item 25), you can use a single object for all required type parameterizations, but you need to write a static factory method to repeatedly dole out the object for each requested type parameterization. This pattern is most frequently used for function objects (Item 21) such as `Collections.reverseOrder`, but it is also used for collections such as `Collections.emptySet`.

Suppose you have an interface that describes a function that accepts and returns a value of some type T:

```
public interface UnaryFunction<T> {
    T apply(T arg);
}
```

Now suppose that you want to provide an identity function. It would be wasteful to create a new one each time it's required, as it's stateless. If generics were reified, you would need one identity function per type, but since they're erased you need only a generic singleton. Here's how it looks:

```
// Generic singleton factory pattern
private static UnaryFunction<Object> IDENTITY_FUNCTION =
    new UnaryFunction<Object>() {
        public Object apply(Object arg) { return arg; }
    };

// IDENTITY_FUNCTION is stateless and its type parameter is
// unbounded so it's safe to share one instance across all types.
@SuppressWarnings("unchecked")
public static <T> UnaryFunction<T> identityFunction() {
    return (UnaryFunction<T>) IDENTITY_FUNCTION;
}
```

The cast of IDENTITY_FUNCTION to (UnaryFunction<T>) generates an unchecked cast warning, as UnaryFunction<Object> is not a UnaryFunction<T> for every T. But the identity function is special: it returns its argument unmodified, so we know that it is typesafe to use it as a UnaryFunction<T> whatever the value of T. Therefore, we can confidently suppress the unchecked cast warning that is generated by this cast. Once we've done this, the code compiles without error or warning.

Here is a sample program that uses our generic singleton as a UnaryFunction<String> and a UnaryFunction<Number>. As usual, it contains no casts and compiles without errors or warnings:

```java
// Sample program to exercise generic singleton
public static void main(String[] args) {
    String[] strings = { "jute", "hemp", "nylon" };
    UnaryFunction<String> sameString = identityFunction();
    for (String s : strings)
        System.out.println(sameString.apply(s));

    Number[] numbers = { 1, 2.0, 3L };
    UnaryFunction<Number> sameNumber = identityFunction();
    for (Number n : numbers)
        System.out.println(sameNumber.apply(n));
}
```

It is permissible, though relatively rare, for a type parameter to be bounded by some expression involving that type parameter itself. This is what's known as a *recursive type bound*. The most common use of recursive type bounds is in connection with the Comparable interface, which defines a type's natural ordering:

```java
public interface Comparable<T> {
    int compareTo(T o);
}
```

The type parameter T defines the type to which elements of the type implementing Comparable<T> can be compared. In practice, nearly all types can be compared only to elements of their own type. So, for example, String implements Comparable<String>, Integer implements Comparable<Integer>, and so on.

There are many methods that take a list of elements that implement Comparable, in order to sort the list, search within it, calculate its minimum or maximum, and the like. To do any of these things, it is required that every element in the list be comparable to every other element in the list, in other words, that the elements of the list be *mutually comparable*. Here is how to express that constraint:

```
// Using a recursive type bound to express mutual comparability
public static <T extends Comparable<T>> T max(List<T> list) {...}
```

The type bound `<T extends Comparable<T>>` may be read as "for every type T that can be compared to itself," which corresponds more or less exactly to the notion of mutual comparability.

Here is a method to go with the declaration above. It calculates the maximum value of a list according to its elements' natural order, and it compiles without errors or warnings:

```
// Returns the maximum value in a list - uses recursive type bound
public static <T extends Comparable<T>> T max(List<T> list) {
    Iterator<T> i = list.iterator();
    T result = i.next();
    while (i.hasNext()) {
        T t = i.next();
        if (t.compareTo(result) > 0)
            result = t;
    }
    return result;
}
```

Recursive type bounds can get much more complex than this, but luckily it doesn't happen too often. If you understand this idiom, and its wildcard variant (Item 28), you'll be able to deal with many of the recursive type bounds that you see in practice.

In summary, generic methods, like generic types, are safer and easier to use than methods that require their clients to cast input parameters and return values. Like types, you should make sure that your new methods can be used without casts, which will often mean making them generic. And like types, you should generify your existing methods to make life easier for new users without breaking existing clients (Item 23).

Item 28: Use bounded wildcards to increase API flexibility

As noted in Item 25, parameterized types are *invariant*. In other words, for any two distinct types Type1 and Type2, List<Type1> is neither a subtype nor a supertype of List<Type2>. While it is counterintuitive that List<String> is not a subtype of List<Object>, it really does make sense. You can put any object into a List<Object>, but you can put only strings into a List<String>.

Sometimes you need more flexibility than invariant typing can provide. Consider the stack from Item 26. To refresh your memory, here is its public API:

```
public class Stack<E> {
    public Stack();
    public void push(E e);
    public E pop();
    public boolean isEmpty();
}
```

Suppose we want to add a method that takes a sequence of elements and pushes them all onto the stack. Here's a first attempt:

```
// pushAll method without wildcard type - deficient!
public void pushAll(Iterable<E> src) {
    for (E e : src)
        push(e);
}
```

This method compiles cleanly, but it isn't entirely satisfactory. If the element type of the Iterable src exactly matches that of the stack, it works fine. But suppose you have a Stack<Number> and you invoke push(intVal), where intVal is of type Integer. This works, because Integer is a subtype of Number. So logically, it seems that this should work, too:

```
Stack<Number> numberStack = new Stack<Number>();
Iterable<Integer> integers = ... ;
numberStack.pushAll(integers);
```

If you try it, however, you'll get this error message because, as noted above, parameterized types are invariant:

```
StackTest.java:7: pushAll(Iterable<Number>) in Stack<Number>
cannot be applied to (Iterable<Integer>)
        numberStack.pushAll(integers);
                           ^
```

Luckily, there's a way out. The language provides a special kind of parameterized type call a *bounded wildcard type* to deal with situations like this. The type of the input parameter to pushAll should not be "Iterable of E" but "Iterable of some subtype of E," and there is a wildcard type that means precisely that: Iterable<? extends E>. (The use of the keyword extends is slightly misleading: recall from Item 26 that *subtype* is defined so that every type is a subtype of itself, even though it does not extend itself.) Let's modify pushAll to use this type:

```
// Wildcard type for parameter that serves as an E producer
public void pushAll(Iterable<? extends E> src) {
    for (E e : src)
        push(e);
}
```

With this change, not only does Stack compile cleanly, but so does the client code that wouldn't compile with the original pushAll declaration. Because Stack and its client compile cleanly, you know that everything is typesafe.

Now suppose you want to write a popAll method to go with pushAll. The popAll method pops each element off the stack and adds the elements to the given collection. Here's how a first attempt at writing the popAll method might look:

```
// popAll method without wildcard type - deficient!
public void popAll(Collection<E> dst) {
    while (!isEmpty())
        dst.add(pop());
}
```

Again, this compiles cleanly and works fine if the element type of the destination collection exactly matches that of the stack. But again, it doesn't seem entirely satisfactory. Suppose you have a Stack<Number> and variable of type Object. If you pop an element from the stack and store it in the variable, it compiles and runs without error. So shouldn't you be able to do this, too?

```
Stack<Number> numberStack = new Stack<Number>();
Collection<Object> objects = ... ;
numberStack.popAll(objects);
```

If you try to compile this client code against the version of popAll above, you'll get an error very similar to the one that we got with our first version of pushAll: Collection<Object> is not a subtype of Collection<Number>. Once again, wildcard types provide a way out. The type of the input parameter to popAll should not be "collection of E" but "collection of some supertype of E" (where supertype is defined such that E is a supertype of itself [JLS, 4.10]). Again, there is a wildcard type that means precisely that: Collection<? super E>. Let's modify popAll to use it:

```
// Wildcard type for parameter that serves as an E consumer
public void popAll(Collection<? super E> dst) {
    while (!isEmpty())
        dst.add(pop());
}
```

With this change, both Stack and the client code compile cleanly.

The lesson is clear. **For maximum flexibility, use wildcard types on input parameters that represent producers or consumers.** If an input parameter is both a producer and a consumer, then wildcard types will do you no good: you need an exact type match, which is what you get without any wildcards.

Here is a mnemonic to help you remember which wildcard type to use:

PECS stands for producer-extends, consumer-super.

In other words, if a parameterized type represents a T producer, use <? extends T>; if it represents a T consumer, use <? super T>. In our Stack example, pushAll's src parameter produces E instances for use by the Stack, so the appropriate type for src is Iterable<? extends E>; popAll's dst parameter consumes E instances from the Stack, so the appropriate type for dst is Collection<? super E>. The PECS mnemonic captures the fundamental principle that guides the use of wildcard types. Naftalin and Wadler call it the *Get and Put Principle* [Naftalin07, 2.4].

With this mnemonic in mind, let's take a look at some method declarations from previous items. The reduce method in Item 25 has this declaration:

```
static <E> E reduce(List<E> list, Function<E> f, E initVal)
```

Although lists can both consume and produce values, the reduce method uses its list parameter only as an E **producer**, so its declaration should use a wildcard type that **extends** E. The parameter f represents a function that both consumes and produces E instances, so a wildcard type would be inappropriate for it. Here's the resulting method declaration:

```
// Wildcard type for parameter that serves as an E producer
static <E> E reduce(List<? extends E> list, Function<E> f,
                    E initVal)
```

And would this change make any difference in practice? As it turns out, it would. Suppose you have a List<Integer>, and you want to reduce it with a Function<Number>. This would not compile with the original declaration, but it does once you add the bounded wildcard type.

Now let's look at the union method from Item 27. Here is the declaration:

```
public static <E> Set<E> union(Set<E> s1, Set<E> s2)
```

Both parameters, s1 and s2, are E producers, so the PECS mnemonic tells us that the declaration should be:

```
public static <E> Set<E> union(Set<? extends E> s1,
                               Set<? extends E> s2)
```

Note that the return type is still Set<E>. **Do not use wildcard types as return types.** Rather than providing additional flexibility for your users, it would force them to use wildcard types in client code.

Properly used, wildcard types are nearly invisible to users of a class. They cause methods to accept the parameters they should accept and reject those they should reject. **If the user of a class has to think about wildcard types, there is probably something wrong with the class's API.**

Unfortunately, the type inference rules are quite complex. They take up sixteen pages in the language specification [JLS, 15.12.2.7–8], and they don't always do what you want them to. Looking at the revised declaration for union, you might think that you could do this:

```
Set<Integer> integers = ... ;
Set<Double> doubles = ... ;
Set<Number> numbers = union(integers, doubles);
```

If you try it you'll get this error message:

```
Union.java:14: incompatible types
found : Set<Number & Comparable<? extends Number &
                                      Comparable<?>>>
required: Set<Number>
        Set<Number> numbers = union(integers, doubles);
                                 ^
```

Luckily there is a way to deal with this sort of error. If the compiler doesn't infer the type that you wish it had, you can tell it what type to use with an *explicit type parameter.* This is not something that you have to do very often, which is a good thing, as explicit type parameters aren't very pretty. With the addition of this explicit type parameter, the program compiles cleanly:

```
Set<Number> numbers = Union.<Number>union(integers, doubles);
```

Next let's turn our attention to the max method from Item 27. Here is the original declaration:

```
public static <T extends Comparable<T>> T max(List<T> list)
```

Here is a revised declaration that uses wildcard types:

```
public static <T extends Comparable<? super T>> T max(
        List<? extends T> list)
```

To get the revised declaration from the original one, we apply the PECS transformation twice. The straightforward application is to the parameter list. It produces T instances, so we change the type from List<T> to List<? extends T>. The tricky application is to the type parameter T. This is the first time we've seen a wildcard applied to a type parameter. T was originally specified to extend Comparable<T>, but a comparable of T consumes T instances (and produces integers indicating order relations). Therefore the parameterized type Comparable<T> is replaced by the bounded wildcard type Comparable<? super T>. Comparables are always consumers, so you should **always use Comparable<? super T> in preference to Comparable<T>.** The same is true of comparators, so you should **always use Comparator<? super T> in preference to Comparator<T>.**

The revised max declaration is probably the most complex method declaration in the entire book. Does the added complexity really buy you anything? Yes, it does. Here is a simple example of a list that would be excluded by the original declaration but is permitted by the revised one:

```
List<ScheduledFuture<?>> scheduledFutures = ... ;
```

The reason that you can't apply the original method declaration to this list is that java.util.concurrent.ScheduledFuture does not implement Comparable<ScheduledFuture>. Instead, it is a subinterface of Delayed, which extends Comparable<Delayed>. In other words, a ScheduledFuture instance isn't merely comparable to other ScheduledFuture instances; it's comparable to any Delayed instance, and that's enough to cause the original declaration to reject it.

There is one slight problem with the revised declaration for max: it prevents the method from compiling. Here is the method with the revised declaration:

```
// Won't compile - wildcards can require change in method body!
public static <T extends Comparable<? super T>> T max(
        List<? extends T> list) {
    Iterator<T> i = list.iterator();
    T result = i.next();
    while (i.hasNext()) {
        T t = i.next();
        if (t.compareTo(result) > 0)
            result = t;
    }
    return result;
}
```

Here's what happens when you try to compile it:

```
Max.java:7: incompatible types
found    : Iterator<capture#591 of ? extends T>
required: Iterator<T>
        Iterator<T> i = list.iterator();
                                      ^
```

What does this error message mean, and how do we fix the problem? It means that list is not a List<T>, so its iterator method doesn't return Iterator<T>. It returns an iterator of some subtype of T, so we replace the iterator declaration with this one, which uses a bounded wildcard type:

```
Iterator<? extends T> i = list.iterator();
```

That is the only change that we have to make to the body of the method. The elements returned by the iterator's next method are of some subtype of T, so they can be safely stored in a variable of type T.

There is one more wildcard-related topic that bears discussing. There is a duality between type parameters and wildcards, and many methods can be declared using one or the other. For example, here are two possible declarations for a static method to swap two indexed items in a list. The first uses an unbounded type parameter (Item 27) and the second an unbounded wildcard:

```
// Two possible declarations for the swap method
public static <E> void swap(List<E> list, int i, int j);
public static void swap(List<?> list, int i, int j);
```

Which of these two declarations is preferable, and why? In a public API, the second is better because it's simpler. You pass in a list—any list—and the method swaps the indexed elements. There is no type parameter to worry about. As a rule, **if a type parameter appears only once in a method declaration, replace it with a wildcard.** If it's an unbounded type parameter, replace it with an unbounded wildcard; if it's a bounded type parameter, replace it with a bounded wildcard.

There's one problem with the second declaration for swap, which uses a wildcard in preference to a type parameter: the straightforward implementation won't compile:

```
public static void swap(List<?> list, int i, int j) {
    list.set(i, list.set(j, list.get(i)));
}
```

Trying to compile it produces this less-than-helpful error message:

```
Swap.java:5: set(int,capture#282 of ?) in List<capture#282 of ?>
cannot be applied to (int,Object)
        list.set(i, list.set(j, list.get(i)));
                  ^
```

It doesn't seem right that we can't put an element back into the list that we just took it out of. The problem is that the type of list is List<?>, and you can't put any value except null into a List<?>. Fortunately, there is a way to implement this method without resorting to an unsafe cast or a raw type. The idea is to write a private helper method to *capture* the wildcard type. The helper method must be a generic method in order to capture the type. Here's how it looks:

```
public static void swap(List<?> list, int i, int j) {
    swapHelper(list, i, j);
}

// Private helper method for wildcard capture
private static <E> void swapHelper(List<E> list, int i, int j) {
    list.set(i, list.set(j, list.get(i)));
}
```

The swapHelper method knows that list is a List<E>. Therefore, it knows that any value it gets out of this list is of type E, and that it's safe to put any value of type E into the list. This slightly convoluted implementation of swap compiles cleanly. It allows us to export the nice wildcard-based declaration of swap, while taking advantage of the more complex generic method internally. Clients of the swap method don't have to confront the more complex `swapHelper` declaration, but they do benefit from it

In summary, using wildcard types in your APIs, while tricky, makes the APIs far more flexible. If you write a library that will be widely used, the proper use of wildcard types should be considered mandatory. Remember the basic rule: producer-`extends`, consumer-`super` (PECS). And remember that all comparables and comparators are consumers.

Item 29: Consider typesafe heterogeneous containers

The most common use of generics is for collections, such as Set and Map, and single-element containers, such as ThreadLocal and AtomicReference. In all of these uses, it is the container that is parameterized. This limits you to a fixed number of type parameters per container. Normally that is exactly what you want. A Set has a single type parameter, representing its element type; a Map has two, representing its key and value types; and so forth.

Sometimes, however, you need more flexibility. For example, a database row can have arbitrarily many columns, and it would be nice to be able to access all of them in a typesafe manner. Luckily, there is an easy way to achieve this effect. The idea is to parameterize the *key* instead of the *container*. Then present the parameterized key to the container to insert or retrieve a value. The generic type system is used to guarantee that the type of the value agrees with its key.

As a simple example of this approach, consider a Favorites class that allows its clients to store and retrieve a "favorite" instance of arbitrarily many other classes. The Class object will play the part of the parameterized key. The reason this works is that class Class was generified in release 1.5. The type of a class literal is no longer simply Class, but Class<T>. For example, String.class is of type Class<String>, and Integer.class is of type Class<Integer>. When a class literal is passed among methods to communicate both compile-time and runtime type information, it is called a *type token* [Bracha04].

The API for the Favorites class is simple. It looks just like a simple map, except that the key is parameterized instead of the map. The client presents a Class object when setting and getting favorites. Here is the API:

```
// Typesafe heterogeneous container pattern - API
public class Favorites {
    public <T> void putFavorite(Class<T> type, T instance);
    public <T> T getFavorite(Class<T> type);
}
```

Here is a sample program that exercises the Favorites class, storing, retrieving, and printing a favorite String, Integer, and Class instance:

```
// Typesafe heterogeneous container pattern - client
public static void main(String[] args) {
    Favorites f = new Favorites();
    f.putFavorite(String.class, "Java");
    f.putFavorite(Integer.class, 0xcafebabe);
    f.putFavorite(Class.class, Favorites.class);
```

```
        String favoriteString = f.getFavorite(String.class);
        int favoriteInteger = f.getFavorite(Integer.class);
        Class<?> favoriteClass = f.getFavorite(Class.class);
        System.out.printf("%s %x %s%n", favoriteString,
            favoriteInteger, favoriteClass.getName());
    }
```

As you might expect, this program prints Java cafebabe Favorites.

A Favorites instance is *typesafe*: it will never return an Integer when you ask it for a String. It is also *heterogeneous*: unlike an ordinary map, all the keys are of different types. Therefore, we call Favorites a *typesafe heterogeneous container*.

The implementation of Favorites is surprisingly tiny. Here it is, in its entirety:

```
// Typesafe heterogeneous container pattern - implementation
public class Favorites {
    private Map<Class<?>, Object> favorites =
        new HashMap<Class<?>, Object>();

    public <T> void putFavorite(Class<T> type, T instance) {
        if (type == null)
            throw new NullPointerException("Type is null");
        favorites.put(type, instance);
    }

    public <T> T getFavorite(Class<T> type) {
        return type.cast(favorites.get(type));
    }
}
```

There are a few subtle things going on here. Each Favorites instance is backed by a private Map<Class<?>, Object> called favorites. You might think that you couldn't put anything into this Map because of the unbounded wildcard type, but the truth is quite the opposite. The thing to notice is that the wildcard type is nested: it's not the type of the Map that's a wildcard type but the type of its key. This means that every key can have a *different* parameterized type: one can be Class<String>, the next Class<Integer>, and so on. That's where the heterogeneity comes from.

The next thing to notice is that the value type of the favorites Map is simply Object. In other words, the Map does not guarantee the type relationship between keys and values, which is that every value is of the type represented by its key. In fact, Java's type system is not powerful enough to express this. But we know that it's true, and we take advantage of it when it comes time to retrieve a favorite.

The `putFavorite` implementation is trivial: it simply puts into `favorites` a mapping from the given `Class` object to the given favorite instance. As noted, this discards the "type linkage" between the key and the value; it loses the knowledge that the value is an instance of the key. But that's OK, because the `getFavorites` method can and does reestablish this linkage.

The implementation of the `getFavorite` method is trickier than that of `putFavorite`. First it gets from the `favorites` map the value corresponding to the given `Class` object. This is the correct object reference to return, but it has the wrong compile-time type. Its type is simply `Object` (the value type of the `favorites` map) and we need to return a `T`. So, the `getFavorite` implementation *dynamically casts* the object reference to the type represented by the `Class` object, using `Class`'s cast method.

The `cast` method is the dynamic analog of Java's cast operator. It simply checks that its argument is an instance of the type represented by the `Class` object. If so, it returns the argument; otherwise it throws a `ClassCastException`. We know that the cast invocation in `getFavorite` will never throw `ClassCastException`, assuming the client code compiled cleanly. That is to say, we know that the values in the `favorites` map always match the types of the keys.

So what does the `cast` method do for us, given that it simply returns its argument? The signature of the `cast` method takes full advantage of the fact that class `Class` has been generified. Its return type is the type parameter of the `Class` object:

```
public class Class<T> {
    T cast(Object obj);
}
```

This is precisely what's needed by the `getFavorite` method. It is what allows us to make `Favorites` typesafe without resorting to an unchecked cast to `T`.

There are two limitations to the `Favorites` class that are worth noting. First, a malicious client could easily corrupt the type safety of a `Favorites` instance, simply by using a `Class` object in its raw form. But the resulting client code would generate an unchecked warning when it was compiled. This is no different from the normal collection implementations such as `HashSet` and `HashMap`. You can easily put a `String` into a `HashSet<Integer>` by using the raw type `HashSet` (Item 23). That said, you can have runtime type safety if you're willing to pay for it. The way to ensure that `Favorites` never violates its type invariant is to have the putFavorite method check that instance is indeed an instance of the type represented by type. And we already know how to do this. Just use a dynamic cast:

```
// Achieving runtime type safety with a dynamic cast
public <T> void putFavorite(Class<T> type, T instance) {
    favorites.put(type, type.cast(instance));
}
```

There are collection wrappers in java.util.Collections that play the same trick. They are called checkedSet, checkedList, checkedMap, and so forth. Their static factories take a Class object (or two) in addition to a collection (or map). The static factories are generic methods, ensuring that the compile-time types of the Class object and the collection match. The wrappers add reification to the collections they wrap. For example, the wrapper throws a ClassCastException at runtime if someone tries to put Coin into your Collection<Stamp>. These wrappers are useful for tracking down who adds an incorrectly typed element to a collection in an application that mixes generic and legacy code.

The second limitation of the Favorites class is that it cannot be used on a non-reifiable type (Item 25). In other words, you can store your favorite String or String[], but not your favorite List<String>. If you try to store your favorite List<String>, your program won't compile. The reason is that you can't get a Class object for List<String>: List<String>.class is a syntax error, and it's a good thing, too. List<String> and List<Integer> share a single Class object, which is List.class. It would wreak havoc with the internals of a Favorites object if the "type literals" List<String>.class and List<Integer>.class were legal and returned the same object reference.

There is no entirely satisfactory workaround for the second limitation. There is a technique called *super type tokens* that goes a long way toward addressing the limitation, but this technique has limitations of its own [Gafter07].

The type tokens used by Favorites are unbounded: getFavorite and putFavorite accept any Class object. Sometimes you may need to limit the types that can be passed to a method. This can be achieved with a *bounded type token*, which is simply a type token that places a bound on what type can be represented, using a bounded type parameter (Item 27) or a bounded wildcard (Item 28).

The annotations API (Item 35) makes extensive use of bounded type tokens. For example, here is the method to read an annotation at runtime. This method comes from the AnnotatedElement interface, which is implemented by the reflective types that represent classes, methods, fields, and other program elements:

```
public <T extends Annotation>
    T getAnnotation(Class<T> annotationType);
```

The argument annotationType is a bounded type token representing an annotation type. The method returns the element's annotation of that type, if it has one, or null, if it doesn't. In essence, an annotated element is a typesafe heterogeneous container whose keys are annotation types.

Suppose you have an object of type Class<?> and you want to pass it to a method that requires a bounded type token, such as getAnnotation. You could cast the object to Class<? extends Annotation>, but this cast is unchecked, so it would generate a compile-time warning (Item 24). Luckily, class Class provides an instance method that performs this sort of cast safely (and dynamically). The method is called asSubclass, and it casts the Class object on which it's called to represent a subclass of the class represented by its argument. If the cast succeeds, the method returns its argument; if it fails, it throws a ClassCastException.

Here's how you use the asSubclass method to read an annotation whose type is unknown at compile time. This method compiles without error or warning:

```
// Use of asSubclass to safely cast to a bounded type token
static Annotation getAnnotation(AnnotatedElement element,
                                String annotationTypeName) {
    Class<?> annotationType = null; // Unbounded type token
    try {
        annotationType = Class.forName(annotationTypeName);
    } catch (Exception ex) {
        throw new IllegalArgumentException(ex);
    }
    return element.getAnnotation(
        annotationType.asSubclass(Annotation.class));
}
```

In summary, the normal use of generics, exemplified by the collections APIs, restricts you to a fixed number of type parameters per container. You can get around this restriction by placing the type parameter on the key rather than the container. You can use Class objects as keys for such typesafe heterogeneous containers. A Class object used in this fashion is called a type token. You can also use a custom key type. For example, you could have a DatabaseRow type representing a database row (the container), and a generic type Column<T> as its key.

CHAPTER 6

Enums and Annotations

IN release 1.5, two families of reference types were added to the language: a new kind of class called an *enum type,* and a new kind of interface called an *annotation type.* This chapter discusses best practices for using these new type families.

Item 30: Use enums instead of `int` constants

An *enumerated type* is a type whose legal values consist of a fixed set of constants, such as the seasons of the year, the planets in the solar system, or the suits in a deck of playing cards. Before enum types were added to the language, a common pattern for representing enumerated types was to declare a group of named `int` constants, one for each member of the type:

```
// The int enum pattern - severely deficient!
public static final int APPLE_FUJI         = 0;
public static final int APPLE_PIPPIN       = 1;
public static final int APPLE_GRANNY_SMITH = 2;

public static final int ORANGE_NAVEL  = 0;
public static final int ORANGE_TEMPLE = 1;
public static final int ORANGE_BLOOD  = 2;
```

This technique, known as the *int enum pattern,* has many shortcomings. It provides nothing in the way of type safety and little in the way of convenience. The compiler won't complain if you pass an apple to a method that expects an orange, compare apples to oranges with the == operator, or worse:

```
// Tasty citrus flavored applesauce!
int i = (APPLE_FUJI - ORANGE_TEMPLE) / APPLE_PIPPIN;
```

Note that the name of each apple constant is prefixed with APPLE_ and the name of each orange constant is prefixed with ORANGE_. This is because Java doesn't provide namespaces for int enum groups. Prefixes prevent name clashes when two int enum groups have identically named constants.

Programs that use the int enum pattern are brittle. Because int enums are compile-time constants, they are compiled into the clients that use them. If the int associated with an enum constant is changed, its clients must be recompiled. If they aren't, they will still run, but their behavior will be undefined.

There is no easy way to translate int enum constants into printable strings. If you print such a constant or display it from a debugger, all you see is a number, which isn't very helpful. There is no reliable way to iterate over all the int enum constants in a group, or even to obtain the size of an int enum group.

You may encounter a variant of this pattern in which String constants are used in place of int constants. This variant, known as the *String enum pattern*, is even less desirable. While it does provide printable strings for its constants, it can lead to performance problems because it relies on string comparisons. Worse, it can lead naive users to hard-code string constants into client code instead of using field names. If such a hard-coded string constant contains a typographical error, it will escape detection at compile time and result in bugs at runtime.

Luckily, as of release 1.5, the language provides an alternative that avoids the shortcomings of the int and string enum patterns and provides many added benefits. It is the *enum type* [JLS, 8.9]. Here's how it looks in its simplest form:

```
public enum Apple  { FUJI, PIPPIN, GRANNY_SMITH }
public enum Orange { NAVEL, TEMPLE, BLOOD }
```

On the surface, these enum types may appear similar to those of other languages, such as C, C++, and C#, but appearances are deceiving. Java's enum types are full-fledged classes, far more powerful than their counterparts in these other languages, where enums are essentially int values.

The basic idea behind Java's enum types is simple: they are classes that export one instance for each enumeration constant via a public static final field. Enum types are effectively final, by virtue of having no accessible constructors. Because clients can neither create instances of an enum type nor extend it, there can be no instances but the declared enum constants. In other words, enum types are instance-controlled (page 6). They are a generalization of singletons (Item 3), which are essentially single-element enums. For readers familiar with the first edition of this book, enum types provide linguistic support for the *typesafe enum* pattern [Bloch01, Item 21].

Enums provide compile-time type safety. If you declare a parameter to be of type `Apple`, you are guaranteed that any non-null object reference passed to the parameter is one of the three valid `Apple` values. Attempts to pass values of the wrong type will result in compile-time errors, as will attempts to assign an expression of one enum type to a variable of another, or to use the `==` operator to compare values of different enum types.

Enum types with identically named constants coexist peacefully because each type has its own namespace. You can add or reorder constants in an enum type without recompiling its clients because the fields that export the constants provide a layer of insulation between an enum type and its clients: the constant values are not compiled into the clients as they are in the `int` enum pattern. Finally, you can translate enums into printable strings by calling their `toString` method.

In addition to rectifying the deficiencies of `int` enums, enum types let you add arbitrary methods and fields and implement arbitrary interfaces. They provide high-quality implementations of all the `Object` methods (Chapter 3), they implement `Comparable` (Item 12) and `Serializable` (Chapter 11), and their serialized form is designed to withstand most changes to the enum type.

So why would you want to add methods or fields to an enum type? For starters, you might want to associate data with its constants. Our `Apple` and `Orange` types, for example, might benefit from a method that returns the color of the fruit, or one that returns an image of it. You can augment an enum type with any method that seems appropriate. An enum type can start life as a simple collection of enum constants and evolve over time into a full-featured abstraction.

For a nice example of a rich enum type, consider the eight planets of our solar system. Each planet has a mass and a radius, and from these two attributes you can compute its surface gravity. This in turn lets you compute the weight of an object on the planet's surface, given the mass of the object. Here's how this enum looks. The numbers in parentheses after each enum constant are parameters that are passed to its constructor. In this case, they are the planet's mass and radius:

```java
// Enum type with data and behavior
public enum Planet {
    MERCURY(3.302e+23, 2.439e6),
    VENUS  (4.869e+24, 6.052e6),
    EARTH  (5.975e+24, 6.378e6),
    MARS   (6.419e+23, 3.393e6),
    JUPITER(1.899e+27, 7.149e7),
    SATURN (5.685e+26, 6.027e7),
    URANUS (8.683e+25, 2.556e7),
    NEPTUNE(1.024e+26, 2.477e7);
```

```
    private final double mass;          // In kilograms
    private final double radius;        // In meters
    private final double surfaceGravity; // In m / s^2

    // Universal gravitational constant in m^3 / kg s^2
    private static final double G = 6.67300E-11;

    // Constructor
    Planet(double mass, double radius) {
        this.mass = mass;
        this.radius = radius;
        surfaceGravity = G * mass / (radius * radius);
    }

    public double mass()           { return mass; }
    public double radius()         { return radius; }
    public double surfaceGravity() { return surfaceGravity; }

    public double surfaceWeight(double mass) {
        return mass * surfaceGravity;  // F = ma
    }
}
```

It is easy to write a rich enum type such as Planet. **To associate data with enum constants, declare instance fields and write a constructor that takes the data and stores it in the fields.** Enums are by their nature immutable, so all fields should be final (Item 15). They can be public, but it is better to make them private and provide public accessors (Item 14). In the case of Planet, the constructor also computes and stores the surface gravity, but this is just an optimization. The gravity could be recomputed from the mass and radius each time it was used by the surfaceWeight method, which takes an object's mass and returns its weight on the planet represented by the constant.

While the Planet enum is simple, it is surprisingly powerful. Here is a short program that takes the earth-weight of an object (in any unit) and prints a nice table of the object's weight on all eight planets (in the same unit):

```
public class WeightTable {
    public static void main(String[] args) {
        double earthWeight = Double.parseDouble(args[0]);
        double mass = earthWeight / Planet.EARTH.surfaceGravity();
        for (Planet p : Planet.values())
            System.out.printf("Weight on %s is %f%n",
                              p, p.surfaceWeight(mass));
    }
}
```

Note that `Planet`, like all enums, has a static `values` method that returns an array of its values in the order they were declared. Note also that the `toString` method returns the declared name of each enum value, enabling easy printing by `println` and `printf`. If you're dissatisfied with this string representation, you can change it by overriding the `toString` method. Here is the result of running our little `WeightTable` program with the command line argument 175:

```
Weight on MERCURY is 66.133672
Weight on VENUS is 158.383926
Weight on EARTH is 175.000000
Weight on MARS is 66.430699
Weight on JUPITER is 442.693902
Weight on SATURN is 186.464970
Weight on URANUS is 158.349709
Weight on NEPTUNE is 198.846116
```

If this is the first time you've seen Java's `printf` method in action, note that it differs from C's in that you use %n where you'd use \n in C.

Some behaviors associated with enum constants may need to be used only from within the class or package in which the enum is defined. Such behaviors are best implemented as private or package-private methods. Each constant then carries with it a hidden collection of behaviors that allows the class or package containing the enum to react appropriately when presented with the constant. Just as with other classes, unless you have a compelling reason to expose an enum method to its clients, declare it private or, if need be, package-private (Item 13).

If an enum is generally useful, it should be a top-level class; if its use is tied to a specific top-level class, it should be a member class of that top-level class (Item 22). For example, the `java.math.RoundingMode` enum represents a rounding mode for decimal fractions. These rounding modes are used by the `BigDecimal` class, but they provide a useful abstraction that is not fundamentally tied to `Big-Decimal`. By making `RoundingMode` a top-level enum, the library designers encourage any programmer who needs rounding modes to reuse this enum, leading to increased consistency across APIs.

The techniques demonstrated in the `Planet` example are sufficient for most enum types, but sometimes you need more. There is different data associated with each `Planet` constant, but sometimes you need to associate fundamentally different *behavior* with each constant. For example, suppose you are writing an enum type to represent the operations on a basic four-function calculator, and you want to provide a method to perform the arithmetic operation represented by each constant. One way to achieve this is to switch on the value of the enum:

```
// Enum type that switches on its own value - questionable
public enum Operation {
    PLUS, MINUS, TIMES, DIVIDE;

    // Do the arithmetic op represented by this constant
    double apply(double x, double y) {
        switch(this) {
            case PLUS:   return x + y;
            case MINUS:  return x - y;
            case TIMES:  return x * y;
            case DIVIDE: return x / y;
        }
        throw new AssertionError("Unknown op: " + this);
    }
}
```

This code works, but is isn't very pretty. It won't compile without the throw statement because the end of the method is technically reachable, even though it will never be reached [JLS, 14.21]. Worse, the code is fragile. If you add a new enum constant but forget to add a corresponding case to the switch, the enum will still compile, but it will fail at runtime when you try to apply the new operation.

Luckily, there is a better way to associate a different behavior with each enum constant: declare an abstract apply method in the enum type, and override it with a concrete method for each constant in a *constant-specific class body*. Such methods are knows as *constant-specific method implementations*:

```
// Enum type with constant-specific method implementations
public enum Operation {
    PLUS   { double apply(double x, double y){return x + y;} },
    MINUS  { double apply(double x, double y){return x - y;} },
    TIMES  { double apply(double x, double y){return x * y;} },
    DIVIDE { double apply(double x, double y){return x / y;} };

    abstract double apply(double x, double y);
}
```

If you add a new constant to the second version of Operation, it is unlikely that you'll forget to provide an apply method, as the method immediately follows each constant declaration. In the unlikely event that you do forget, the compiler will remind you, as abstract methods in an enum type must be overridden with concrete methods in all of its constants.

Constant-specific method implementations can be combined with constant-specific data. For example, here is a version of Operation that overrides the toString method to return the symbol commonly associated with the operation:

```
// Enum type with constant-specific class bodies and data
public enum Operation {
    PLUS("+") {
        double apply(double x, double y) { return x + y; }
    },
    MINUS("-") {
        double apply(double x, double y) { return x - y; }
    },
    TIMES("*") {
        double apply(double x, double y) { return x * y; }
    },
    DIVIDE("/") {
        double apply(double x, double y) { return x / y; }
    };
    private final String symbol;
    Operation(String symbol) { this.symbol = symbol; }
    @Override public String toString() { return symbol; }

    abstract double apply(double x, double y);
}
```

In some cases, overriding toString in an enum is very useful. For example, the toString implementation above makes it easy to print arithmetic expressions, as demonstrated by this little program:

```
public static void main(String[] args) {
    double x = Double.parseDouble(args[0]);
    double y = Double.parseDouble(args[1]);
    for (Operation op : Operation.values())
        System.out.printf("%f %s %f = %f%n",
                          x, op, y, op.apply(x, y));
}
```

Running this program with 2 and 4 as command line arguments produces the following output:

```
2.000000 + 4.000000 = 6.000000
2.000000 - 4.000000 = -2.000000
2.000000 * 4.000000 = 8.000000
2.000000 / 4.000000 = 0.500000
```

Enum types have an automatically generated `valueOf(String)` method that translates a constant's name into the constant itself. If you override the `toString` method in an enum type, consider writing a `fromString` method to translate the custom string representation back to the corresponding enum. The following code (with the type name changed appropriately) will do the trick for any enum, so long as each constant has a unique string representation:

```
// Implementing a fromString method on an enum type
private static final Map<String, Operation> stringToEnum
    = new HashMap<String, Operation>();
static { // Initialize map from constant name to enum constant
    for (Operation op : values())
        stringToEnum.put(op.toString(), op);
}
// Returns Operation for string, or null if string is invalid
public static Operation fromString(String symbol) {
    return stringToEnum.get(symbol);
}
```

Note that the `Operation` constants are put into the `stringToEnum` map from a static block that runs after the constants have been created. Trying to make each constant put itself into the map from its own constructor would cause a compilation error. This is a good thing, because it would cause a `NullPointerException` if it were legal. Enum constructors aren't permitted to access the enum's static fields, except for compile-time constant fields. This restriction is necessary because these static fields have not yet been initialized when the constructors run.

A disadvantage of constant-specific method implementations is that they make it harder to share code among enum constants. For example, consider an enum representing the days of the week in a payroll package. This enum has a method that calculates a worker's pay for that day given the worker's base salary (per hour) and the number of hours worked on that day. On the five weekdays, any time worked in excess of a normal shift generates overtime pay; on the two weekend days, all work generates overtime pay. With a `switch` statement, it's easy to do this calculation by applying multiple case labels to each of two code fragments. For brevity's sake, the code in this example uses `double`, but note that `double` is *not* an appropriate data type for a payroll application (Item 48):

```
// Enum that switches on its value to share code - questionable
enum PayrollDay {
    MONDAY, TUESDAY, WEDNESDAY, THURSDAY, FRIDAY,
    SATURDAY, SUNDAY;
    private static final int HOURS_PER_SHIFT = 8;
```

```
double pay(double hoursWorked, double payRate) {
    double basePay = hoursWorked * payRate;

    double overtimePay;       // Calculate overtime pay
    switch(this) {
      case SATURDAY: case SUNDAY:
        overtimePay = hoursWorked * payRate / 2;
        break;
      default: // Weekdays
        overtimePay = hoursWorked <= HOURS_PER_SHIFT ?
          0 : (hoursWorked - HOURS_PER_SHIFT) * payRate / 2;
    }

    return basePay + overtimePay;
  }
}
```

This code is undeniably concise, but it is dangerous from a maintenance perspective. Suppose you add an element to the enum, perhaps a special value to represent a vacation day, but forget to add a corresponding case to the switch statement. The program will still compile, but the pay method will silently pay the worker the same amount for a vacation day as for an ordinary weekday.

To perform the pay calculation safely with constant-specific method implementations, you would have to duplicate the overtime pay computation for each constant, or move the computation into two helper methods (one for weekdays and one for weekend days) and invoke the appropriate helper method from each constant. Either approach would result in a fair amount of boilerplate code, substantially reducing readability and increasing the opportunity for error.

The boilerplate could be reduced by replacing the abstract overtimePay method on PayrollDay with a concrete method that performs the overtime calculation for weekdays. Then only the weekend days would have to override the method. But this would have the same disadvantage as the switch statement: if you added another day without overriding the overtimePay method, you would silently inherit the weekday calculation.

What you really want is to be *forced* to choose an overtime pay strategy each time you add an enum constant. Luckily, there is a nice way to achieve this. The idea is to move the overtime pay computation into a private nested enum, and to pass an instance of this *strategy enum* to the constructor for the PayrollDay enum. The PayrollDay enum then delegates the overtime pay calculation to the strategy enum, eliminating the need for a switch statement or constant-specific method implementation in `PayrollDay`. While this pattern is less concise than the switch statement, it is safer and more flexible:

```java
// The strategy enum pattern
enum PayrollDay {
    MONDAY(PayType.WEEKDAY), TUESDAY(PayType.WEEKDAY),
    WEDNESDAY(PayType.WEEKDAY), THURSDAY(PayType.WEEKDAY),
    FRIDAY(PayType.WEEKDAY),
    SATURDAY(PayType.WEEKEND), SUNDAY(PayType.WEEKEND);

    private final PayType payType;
    PayrollDay(PayType payType) { this.payType = payType; }

    double pay(double hoursWorked, double payRate) {
        return payType.pay(hoursWorked, payRate);
    }
    // The strategy enum type
    private enum PayType {
        WEEKDAY {
            double overtimePay(double hours, double payRate) {
                return hours <= HOURS_PER_SHIFT ? 0 :
                    (hours - HOURS_PER_SHIFT) * payRate / 2;
            }
        },
        WEEKEND {
            double overtimePay(double hours, double payRate) {
                return hours * payRate / 2;
            }
        };
        private static final int HOURS_PER_SHIFT = 8;

        abstract double overtimePay(double hrs, double payRate);

        double pay(double hoursWorked, double payRate) {
            double basePay = hoursWorked * payRate;
            return basePay + overtimePay(hoursWorked, payRate);
        }
    }
}
```

If switch statements on enums are not a good choice for implementing constant-specific behavior on enums, what *are* they good for? **Switches on enums are good for augmenting external enum types with constant-specific behavior.** For example, suppose the Operation enum is not under your control, and you wish it had an instance method to return the inverse of each operation. You can simulate the effect with the following static method:

```
// Switch on an enum to simulate a missing method
public static Operation inverse(Operation op) {
    switch(op) {
        case PLUS:   return Operation.MINUS;
        case MINUS:  return Operation.PLUS;
        case TIMES:  return Operation.DIVIDE;
        case DIVIDE: return Operation.TIMES;
        default:  throw new AssertionError("Unknown op: " + op);
    }
}
```

Enums are, generally speaking, comparable in performance to `int` constants. A minor performance disadvantage of enums over `int` constants is that there is a space and time cost to load and initialize enum types. Except on resource-constrained devices, such as cell phones and toasters, this is unlikely to be noticeable in practice.

So when should you use enums? Anytime you need a fixed set of constants. Of course, this includes "natural enumerated types," such as the planets, the days of the week, and the chess pieces. But it also includes other sets for which you know all the possible values at compile time, such as choices on a menu, operation codes, and command line flags. It is not necessary that the set of constants in an enum type stay fixed for all time. The enum feature was specifically designed to allow for binary compatible evolution of enum types.

In summary, the advantages of enum types over `int` constants are compelling. Enums are far more readable, safer, and more powerful. Many enums require no explicit constructors or members, but many others benefit from associating data with each constant and providing methods whose behavior is affected by this data. Far fewer enums benefit from associating multiple behaviors with a single method. In this relatively rare case, prefer constant-specific methods to enums that switch on their own values. Consider the strategy enum pattern if multiple enum constants share common behaviors.

Item 31: Use instance fields instead of ordinals

Many enums are naturally associated with a single int value. All enums have an ordinal method, which returns the numerical position of each enum constant in its type. You may be tempted to derive an associated int value from the ordinal:

```
// Abuse of ordinal to derive an associated value - DON'T DO THIS
public enum Ensemble {
    SOLO,   DUET,   TRIO, QUARTET, QUINTET,
    SEXTET, SEPTET, OCTET, NONET,  DECTET;

    public int numberOfMusicians() { return ordinal() + 1; }
}
```

While this enum works, it is a maintenance nightmare. If the constants are reordered, the numberOfMusicians method will break. If you want to add a second enum constant associated with an int value that you've already used, you're out of luck. For example, it might be nice to add a constant for *double quartet*, which, like an octet, consists of eight musicians, but there is no way to do it.

Also, you can't add a constant for an int value without adding constants for all intervening int values. For example, suppose you want to add a constant representing a *triple quartet*, which consists of twelve musicians. There is no standard term for an ensemble consisting of eleven musicians, so you are forced to add a dummy constant for the unused int value (11). At best, this is ugly. If many int values are unused, it's impractical.

Luckily, there is a simple solution to these problems. **Never derive a value associated with an enum from its ordinal; store it in an instance field instead:**

```
public enum Ensemble {
    SOLO(1), DUET(2), TRIO(3), QUARTET(4), QUINTET(5),
    SEXTET(6), SEPTET(7), OCTET(8), DOUBLE_QUARTET(8),
    NONET(9), DECTET(10), TRIPLE_QUARTET(12);

    private final int numberOfMusicians;
    Ensemble(int size) { this.numberOfMusicians = size; }
    public int numberOfMusicians() { return numberOfMusicians; }
}
```

The Enum specification has this to say about ordinal: "Most programmers will have no use for this method. It is designed for use by general-purpose enum-based data structures such as EnumSet and EnumMap." Unless you are writing such a data structure, you are best off avoiding the ordinal method entirely.

Item 32: Use `EnumSet` instead of bit fields

If the elements of an enumerated type are used primarily in sets, it is traditional to use the `int` enum pattern (Item 30), assigning a different power of 2 to each constant:

```
// Bit field enumeration constants - OBSOLETE!
public class Text {
    public static final int STYLE_BOLD          = 1 << 0;  // 1
    public static final int STYLE_ITALIC        = 1 << 1;  // 2
    public static final int STYLE_UNDERLINE     = 1 << 2;  // 4
    public static final int STYLE_STRIKETHROUGH = 1 << 3;  // 8

    // Parameter is bitwise OR of zero or more STYLE_ constants
    public void applyStyles(int styles) { ... }
}
```

This representation lets you use the bitwise OR operation to combine several constants into a set, known as a *bit field*:

```
text.applyStyles(STYLE_BOLD | STYLE_ITALIC);
```

The bit field representation also lets you perform set operations such as union and intersection efficiently using bitwise arithmetic. But bit fields have all the disadvantages of `int` enum constants and more. It is even harder to interpret a bit field than a simple `int` enum constant when it is printed as a number. Also, there is no easy way to iterate over all of the elements represented by a bit field.

Some programmers who use enums in preference to `int` constants still cling to the use of bit fields when they need to pass around sets of constants. There is no reason to do this; a better alternative exists. The `java.util` package provides the `EnumSet` class to efficiently represent sets of values drawn from a single enum type. This class implements the `Set` interface, providing all of the richness, type safety, and interoperability you get with any other `Set` implementation. But internally, each `EnumSet` is represented as a bit vector. If the underlying enum type has sixty-four or fewer elements—and most do—the entire `EnumSet` is represented with a single `long` (page 7), so its performance is comparable to that of a bit field. Bulk operations, such as `removeAll` and `retainAll`, are implemented using bitwise arithmetic, just as you'd do manually for bit fields. But you are insulated from the ugliness and error-proneness of manual bit twiddling: the `EnumSet` does the hard work for you.

Here is how the previous example looks when modified to use enums instead of bit fields. It is shorter, clearer, and safer:

```
// EnumSet - a modern replacement for bit fields
public class Text {
    public enum Style { BOLD, ITALIC, UNDERLINE, STRIKETHROUGH }

    // Any Set could be passed in, but EnumSet is clearly best
    public void applyStyles(Set<Style> styles) { ... }
}
```

Here is client code that passes an EnumSet instance to the applyStyles method. EnumSet provides a rich set of static factories for easy set creation, one of which is illustrated in this code:

```
text.applyStyles(EnumSet.of(Style.BOLD, Style.ITALIC));
```

Note that the applyStyles method takes a Set<Style> rather than an Enum-Set<Style>. While it seems likely that all clients would pass an EnumSet to the method, it is good practice to accept the interface type rather than the implementation type. This allows for the possibility of an unusual client to pass in some other Set implementation and has no disadvantages to speak of (page 190).

In summary, **just because an enumerated type will be used in sets, there is no reason to represent it with bit fields**. The EnumSet class combines the conciseness and performance of bit fields with all the many advantages of enum types described in Item 30. The one real disadvantage of EnumSet is that it is not, as of release 1.6, possible to create an immutable EnumSet, but this will likely be remedied in an upcoming release. In the meantime, you can wrap an EnumSet with Collections.unmodifiableSet, but conciseness and performance will suffer.

Item 33: Use EnumMap instead of ordinal indexing

Occasionally you may see code that uses the `ordinal` method (Item 31) to index into an array. For example, consider this simplistic class meant to represent a culinary herb:

```
class Herb {
    enum Type { ANNUAL, PERENNIAL, BIENNIAL }

    final String name;
    final Type type;

    Herb(String name, Type type) {
        this.name = name;
        this.type = type;
    }

    @Override public String toString() {
        return name;
    }
}
```

Now suppose you have an array of herbs representing the plants in a garden, and you want to list these plants organized by type (annual, perennial, or biennial). To do this, you construct three sets, one for each type, and iterate through the garden, placing each herb in the appropriate set. Some programmers would do this by putting the sets into an array indexed by the type's ordinal:

```
// Using ordinal() to index an array - DON'T DO THIS!
Herb[] garden = ... ;

Set<Herb>[] herbsByType =  // Indexed by Herb.Type.ordinal()
    (Set<Herb>[]) new Set[Herb.Type.values().length];
for (int i = 0; i < herbsByType.length; i++)
    herbsByType[i] = new HashSet<Herb>();

for (Herb h : garden)
    herbsByType[h.type.ordinal()].add(h);

// Print the results
for (int i = 0; i < herbsByType.length; i++) {
    System.out.printf("%s: %s%n",
                      Herb.Type.values()[i], herbsByType[i]);
}
```

This technique works, but it is fraught with problems. Because arrays are not compatible with generics (Item 25), the program requires an unchecked cast and will not compile cleanly. Because the array does not know what its index represents, you have to label the output manually. But the most serious problem with this technique is that when you access an array that is indexed by an enum's ordinal, it is your responsibility to use the correct `int` value; `int`s do not provide the type safety of enums. If you use the wrong value, the program will silently do the wrong thing or—if you're lucky—throw an `ArrayIndexOutOfBoundsException`.

Luckily, there is a much better way to achieve the same effect. The array is effectively serving as a map from the enum to a value, so you might as well use a `Map`. More specifically, there is a very fast `Map` implementation designed for use with enum keys, known as `java.util.EnumMap`. Here is how the program looks when it is rewritten to use `EnumMap`:

```
// Using an EnumMap to associate data with an enum
Map<Herb.Type, Set<Herb>> herbsByType =
    new EnumMap<Herb.Type, Set<Herb>>(Herb.Type.class);
for (Herb.Type t : Herb.Type.values())
    herbsByType.put(t, new HashSet<Herb>());
for (Herb h : garden)
    herbsByType.get(h.type).add(h);
System.out.println(herbsByType);
```

This program is shorter, clearer, safer, and comparable in speed to the original version. There is no unsafe cast; no need to label the output manually, as the map keys are enums that know how to translate themselves to printable strings; and no possibility for error in computing array indices. The reason that `EnumMap` is comparable in speed to an ordinal-indexed array is that `EnumMap` uses such an array internally. But it hides this implementation detail from the programmer, combining the richness and type safety of a `Map` with the speed of an array. Note that the `EnumMap` constructor takes the `Class` object of the key type: this is a *bounded type token*, which provides runtime generic type information (Item 29).

You may see an array of arrays indexed (twice!) by ordinals used to represent a mapping from two enum values. For example, this program uses such an array to map two phases to a phase transition (liquid to solid is freezing, liquid to gas is boiling, and so forth):

```
// Using ordinal() to index array of arrays - DON'T DO THIS!
public enum Phase { SOLID, LIQUID, GAS;
    public enum Transition {
        MELT, FREEZE, BOIL, CONDENSE, SUBLIME, DEPOSIT;
```

```
    // Rows indexed by src-ordinal, cols by dst-ordinal
    private static final Transition[][] TRANSITIONS = {
        { null,    MELT,     SUBLIME },
        { FREEZE,  null,     BOIL    },
        { DEPOSIT, CONDENSE, null    }
    };

    // Returns the phase transition from one phase to another
    public static Transition from(Phase src, Phase dst) {
        return TRANSITIONS[src.ordinal()][dst.ordinal()];
    }
  }
}
```

This program works and may even appear elegant, but appearances can be deceiving. Like the simpler herb garden example above, the compiler has no way of knowing the relationship between ordinals and array indices. If you make a mistake in the transition table, or forget to update it when you modify the Phase or Phase.Transition enum type, your program will fail at runtime. The failure may take the form of an ArrayIndexOutOfBoundsException, a NullPointerException, or (worse) silent erroneous behavior. And the size of the table is quadratic in the number of phases, even if the number of non-null entries is smaller.

Again, you can do much better with EnumMap. Because each phase transition is indexed by a *pair* of phase enums, you are best off representing the relationship as a map from one enum (the source phase) to a map from the second enum (the destination phase) to the result (the phase transition). The two phases associated with a phase transition are best captured by associating data with the phase transition enum, which is then used to initialize the nested EnumMap:

```
// Using a nested EnumMap to associate data with enum pairs
public enum Phase {
    SOLID, LIQUID, GAS;

    public enum Transition {
        MELT(SOLID, LIQUID), FREEZE(LIQUID, SOLID),
        BOIL(LIQUID, GAS),   CONDENSE(GAS, LIQUID),
        SUBLIME(SOLID, GAS), DEPOSIT(GAS, SOLID);

        private final Phase src;
        private final Phase dst;

        Transition(Phase src, Phase dst) {
            this.src = src;
            this.dst = dst;
        }
```

```
        // Initialize the phase transition map
        private static final Map<Phase, Map<Phase,Transition>> m =
          new EnumMap<Phase, Map<Phase,Transition>>(Phase.class);
        static {
           for (Phase p : Phase.values())
              m.put(p,new EnumMap<Phase,Transition>(Phase.class));
           for (Transition trans : Transition.values())
              m.get(trans.src).put(trans.dst, trans);
        }

        public static Transition from(Phase src, Phase dst) {
           return m.get(src).get(dst);
        }
      }
    }
```

The code to initialize the phase transition map may look a bit complicated but it isn't too bad. The type of the map is Map<Phase, Map<Phase, Transition>>, which means "map from (source) phase to map from (destination) phase to transition." The first loop in the static initializer block initializes the outer map to contain the three empty inner maps. The second loop in the block initializes the inner maps using the source and destination information provided by each state transition constant.

Now suppose you want to add a new phase to the system: the *plasma*, or ionized gas. There are only two transitions associated with this phase: ionization, which takes a gas to a plasma; and deionization, which takes a plasma to a gas. To update the array-based program, you would have to add one new constant to Phase and two to Phase.Transition, and replace the original nine-element array of arrays with a new sixteen-element version. If you add too many or too few elements to the array, or place an element out of order, you are out of luck: the program will compile, but it will fail at runtime. To update the EnumMap-based version, all you have to do is add PLASMA to the list of phases, and IONIZE(GAS, PLASMA) and DEIONIZE(PLASMA, GAS) to the list of phase transitions. The program takes care of everything else, and you have virtually no opportunity for error. Internally, the map of maps is implemented as an array of arrays, so you pay little in space or time cost for the added clarity, safety, and ease of maintenance.

In summary, **it is rarely appropriate to use ordinals to index arrays: use EnumMap instead.** If the relationship that you are representing is multidimensional, use EnumMap<..., EnumMap<...>>. This is a special case of the general principle that application programmers should rarely, if ever, use Enum.ordinal (Item 31).

Item 34: Emulate extensible enums with interfaces

In almost all respects, enum types are superior to the typesafe enum pattern described in the first edition of this book [Bloch01]. On the face of it, one exception concerns extensibility, which was possible under the original pattern but is not supported by the language construct. In other words, using the pattern, it was possible to have one enumerated type extend another; using the language feature, it is not. This is no accident. For the most part, extensibility of enums turns out to be a bad idea. It is confusing that elements of an extension type are instances of the base type and not vice versa. There is no good way to enumerate over all of the elements of a base type and its extension. Finally, extensibility would complicate many aspects of the design and implementation.

That said, there is at least one compelling use case for extensible enumerated types, which is *operation codes,* also known as *opcodes.* An opcode is an enumerated type whose elements represent operations on some machine, such as the Operation type in Item 30, which represents the functions on a simple calculator. Sometimes it is desirable to let the users of an API provide their own operations, effectively extending the set of operations provided by the API.

Luckily, there is a nice way to achieve this effect using enum types. The basic idea is to take advantage of the fact that enum types can implement arbitrary interfaces by defining an interface for the opcode type and an enum that is the standard implementation of the interface. For example, here is an extensible version of Operation type from Item 30:

```
// Emulated extensible enum using an interface
public interface Operation {
    double apply(double x, double y);
}

public enum BasicOperation  implements Operation {
    PLUS("+") {
        public double apply(double x, double y) { return x + y; }
    },
    MINUS("-") {
        public double apply(double x, double y) { return x - y; }
    },
    TIMES("*") {
        public double apply(double x, double y) { return x * y; }
    },
    DIVIDE("/") {
        public double apply(double x, double y) { return x / y; }
    };
```

```
    private final String symbol;
    BasicOperation(String symbol) {
        this.symbol = symbol;
    }
    @Override public String toString() {
        return symbol;
    }
}
```

While the enum type (BasicOperation) is not extensible, the interface type (Operation) is, and it is the interface type that is used to represent operations in APIs. You can define another enum type that implements this interface and use instances of this new type in place of the base type. For example, suppose you want to define an extension to the operation type above, consisting of the exponentiation and remainder operations. All you have to do is write an enum type that implements the Operation interface:

```
// Emulated extension enum
public enum ExtendedOperation implements Operation {
    EXP("^") {
        public double apply(double x, double y) {
            return Math.pow(x, y);
        }
    },
    REMAINDER("%") {
        public double apply(double x, double y) {
            return x % y;
        }
    };

    private final String symbol;
    ExtendedOperation(String symbol) {
        this.symbol = symbol;
    }
    @Override public String toString() {
        return symbol;
    }
}
```

You can use your new operations anywhere you could use the basic operations, provided that APIs are written to take the interface type (Operation), not the implementation (BasicOperation). Note that you don't have to declare the abstract apply method in the enum as you do in a nonextensible enum with instance-specific method implementations (page 152). This is because the abstract method (apply) is a member of the interface (Operation).

Not only is it possible to pass a single instance of an "extension enum" anywhere a "base enum" is expected; it is possible to pass in an entire extension enum type and use its elements in addition to or instead of those of the base type. For example, here is a version of the test program on page 153 that exercises all of the extended operations defined above:

```
public static void main(String[] args) {
    double x = Double.parseDouble(args[0]);
    double y = Double.parseDouble(args[1]);
    test(ExtendedOperation.class, x, y);
}
private static <T extends Enum<T> & Operation> void test(
        Class<T> opSet, double x, double y) {
    for (Operation op : opSet.getEnumConstants())
        System.out.printf("%f %s %f = %f%n",
                          x, op, y, op.apply(x, y));
}
```

Note that the class literal for the extended operation type (ExtendedOperation.class) is passed from main to test to describe the set of extended operations. The class literal serves as a *bounded type token* (Item 29). The admittedly complex declaration for the opSet parameter (<T extends Enum<T> & Operation> Class<T>) ensures that the Class object represents both an enum and a subtype of Operation, which is exactly what is required to iterate over the elements and perform the operation associated with each one.

A second alternative is to use Collection<? extends Operation>, which is a *bounded wildcard type* (Item 28), as the type for the opSet parameter:

```
public static void main(String[] args) {
    double x = Double.parseDouble(args[0]);
    double y = Double.parseDouble(args[1]);
    test(Arrays.asList(ExtendedOperation.values()), x, y);
}

private static void test(Collection<? extends Operation> opSet,
        double x, double y) {
    for (Operation op : opSet)
        System.out.printf("%f %s %f = %f%n",
                          x, op, y, op.apply(x, y));
}
```

The resulting code is a bit less complex, and the test method is a bit more flexible: it allows the caller to combine operations from multiple implementation types. On the other hand, you forgo the ability to use EnumSet (Item 32) and EnumMap (Item 33) on the specified operations, so you are probably better off with the bounded type token unless you need the flexibility to combine operations of multiple implementation types.

Both programs above will produce this output when run with command line arguments 4 and 2:

```
4.000000 ∧ 2.000000 = 16.000000
4.000000 % 2.000000 = 0.000000
```

A minor disadvantage of the use of interfaces to emulate extensible enums is that implementations cannot be inherited from one enum type to another. In the case of our Operation example, the logic to store and retrieve the symbol associated with an operation is duplicated in BasicOperation and ExtendedOperation. In this case it doesn't matter because very little code is duplicated. If there were a larger amount of shared functionality, you could encapsulate it in a helper class or a static helper method to eliminate the code duplication.

In summary, **while you cannot write an extensible enum type, you can emulate it by writing an interface to go with a basic enum type that implements the interface.** This allows clients to write their own enums that implement the interface. These enums can then be used wherever the basic enum type can be used, assuming APIs are written in terms of the interface.

Item 35: Prefer annotations to naming patterns

Prior to release 1.5, it was common to use *naming patterns* to indicate that some program elements demanded special treatment by a tool or framework. For example, the JUnit testing framework originally required its users to designate test methods by beginning their names with the characters `test` [Beck04]. This technique works, but it has several big disadvantages. First, typographical errors may result in silent failures. For example, suppose you accidentally name a test method `tsetSafetyOverride` instead of `testSafetyOverride`. JUnit will not complain, but it will not execute the test either, leading to a false sense of security.

A second disadvantage of naming patterns is that there is no way to ensure that they are used only on appropriate program elements. For example, suppose you call a class `testSafetyMechanisms` in hopes that JUnit will automatically test all of its methods, regardless of their names. Again, JUnit won't complain, but it won't execute the tests either.

A third disadvantage of naming patterns is that they provide no good way to associate parameter values with program elements. For example, suppose you want to support a category of test that succeeds only if it throws a particular exception. The exception type is essentially a parameter of the test. You could encode the exception type name into the test method name using some elaborate naming pattern, but this would be ugly and fragile (Item 50). The compiler would have no way of knowing to check that the string that was supposed to name an exception actually did. If the named class didn't exist or wasn't an exception, you wouldn't find out until you tried to run the test.

Annotations [JLS, 9.7] solve all of these problems nicely. Suppose you want to define an annotation type to designate simple tests that are run automatically and fail if they throw an exception. Here's how such an annotation type, named `Test`, might look:

```java
// Marker annotation type declaration
import java.lang.annotation.*;

/**
 * Indicates that the annotated method is a test method.
 * Use only on parameterless static methods.
 */
@Retention(RetentionPolicy.RUNTIME)
@Target(ElementType.METHOD)
public @interface Test {
}
```

The declaration for the Test annotation type is itself annotated with Retention and Target annotations. Such annotations on annotation type declarations are known as *meta-annotations*. The @Retention(RetentionPolicy.RUNTIME) meta-annotation indicates that Test annotations should be retained at runtime. Without it, Test annotations would be invisible to the test tool. The @Target(ElementType.METHOD) meta-annotation indicates that the Test annotation is legal only on method declarations: it cannot be applied to class declarations, field declarations, or other program elements.

Note the comment above the Test annotation declaration that says, "Use only on parameterless static methods." It would be nice if the compiler could enforce this restriction, but it can't. There are limits to how much error checking the compiler can do for you even with annotations. If you put a Test annotation on the declaration of an instance method or a method with one or more parameters, the test program will still compile, leaving it to the testing tool to deal with the problem at runtime.

Here is how the Test annotation looks in practice. It is called a *marker annotation*, because it has no parameters but simply "marks" the annotated element. If the programmer were to misspell Test, or to apply the Test annotation to a program element other than a method declaration, the program wouldn't compile:

```
// Program containing marker annotations
public class Sample {
    @Test public static void m1() { }  // Test should pass
    public static void m2() { }
    @Test public static void m3() {     // Test should fail
        throw new RuntimeException("Boom");
    }
    public static void m4() { }
    @Test public void m5() { } // INVALID USE: nonstatic method
    public static void m6() { }
    @Test public static void m7() {     // Test should fail
        throw new RuntimeException("Crash");
    }
    public static void m8() { }
}
```

The Sample class has seven static methods, four of which are annotated as tests. Two of these, m3 and m7, throw exceptions and two, m1 and m5, do not. But one of the annotated methods that does not throw an exception, m5, is an instance method, so it is not a valid use of the annotation. In sum, Sample contains four tests: one will pass, two will fail, and one is invalid. The four methods that are not annotated with the Test annotation will be ignored by the testing tool.

The Test annotations have no direct effect on the semantics of the Sample class. They serve only to provide information for use by interested programs. More generally, annotations never change the semantics of the annotated code, but enable it for special treatment by tools such as this simple test runner:

```
// Program to process marker annotations
import java.lang.reflect.*;

public class RunTests {
    public static void main(String[] args) throws Exception {
        int tests = 0;
        int passed = 0;
        Class testClass = Class.forName(args[0]);
        for (Method m : testClass.getDeclaredMethods()) {
            if (m.isAnnotationPresent(Test.class)) {
                tests++;
                try {
                    m.invoke(null);
                    passed++;
                } catch (InvocationTargetException wrappedExc) {
                    Throwable exc = wrappedExc.getCause();
                    System.out.println(m + " failed: " + exc);
                } catch (Exception exc) {
                    System.out.println("INVALID @Test: " + m);
                }
            }
        }
        System.out.printf("Passed: %d, Failed: %d%n",
                          passed, tests - passed);
    }
}
```

The test runner tool takes a fully qualified class name on the command line and runs all of the class's Test-annotated methods reflectively, by calling Method.invoke. The isAnnotationPresent method tells the tool which methods to run. If a test method throws an exception, the reflection facility wraps it in an InvocationTargetException. The tool catches this exception and prints a failure report containing the original exception thrown by the test method, which is extracted from the InvocationTargetException with the getCause method.

If an attempt to invoke a test method by reflection throws any exception other than InvocationTargetException, it indicates an invalid use of the Test annotation that was not caught at compile time. Such uses include annotation of an instance method, of a method with one or more parameters, or of an inaccessible method. The second catch block in the test runner catches these Test usage errors and prints an appropriate error message. Here is the output that is printed if Run-Tests is run on Sample:

```
public static void Sample.m3() failed: RuntimeException: Boom
INVALID @Test: public void Sample.m5()
public static void Sample.m7() failed: RuntimeException: Crash
Passed: 1, Failed: 3
```

Now let's add support for tests that succeed only if they throw a particular exception. We'll need a new annotation type for this:

```
// Annotation type with a parameter
import java.lang.annotation.*;
/**
 * Indicates that the annotated method is a test method that
 * must throw the designated exception to succeed.
 */
@Retention(RetentionPolicy.RUNTIME)
@Target(ElementType.METHOD)
public @interface ExceptionTest {
    Class<? extends Exception> value();
}
```

The type of the parameter for this annotation is Class<? extends Exception>. This wildcard type is, admittedly, a mouthful. In English, it means "the Class object for some class that extends Exception," and it allows the user of the annotation to specify any exception type. This usage is an example of a *bounded type token* (Item 29). Here's how the annotation looks in practice. Note that class literals are used as the values for the annotation parameter:

```
// Program containing annotations with a parameter
public class Sample2 {
    @ExceptionTest(ArithmeticException.class)
    public static void m1() {  // Test should pass
        int i = 0;
        i = i / i;
    }
    @ExceptionTest(ArithmeticException.class)
    public static void m2() {  // Should fail (wrong exception)
        int[] a = new int[0];
        int i = a[1];
    }
    @ExceptionTest(ArithmeticException.class)
    public static void m3() { }  // Should fail (no exception)
}
```

Now let's modify the test runner tool to process the new annotation. Doing so consists of adding the following code to the `main` method:

```
if (m.isAnnotationPresent(ExceptionTest.class)) {
    tests++;
    try {
        m.invoke(null);
        System.out.printf("Test %s failed: no exception%n", m);
    } catch (InvocationTargetException wrappedEx) {
        Throwable exc = wrappedEx.getCause();
        Class<? extends Exception> excType =
            m.getAnnotation(ExceptionTest.class).value();
        if (excType.isInstance(exc)) {
            passed++;
        } else {
            System.out.printf(
                "Test %s failed: expected %s, got %s%n",
                m, excType.getName(), exc);
        }
    } catch (Exception exc) {
        System.out.println("INVALID @Test: " + m);
    }
}
```

This code is similar to the code we used to process `Test` annotations, with one exception: this code extracts the value of the annotation parameter and uses it to check if the exception thrown by the test is of the right type. There are no explicit casts, hence no danger of a `ClassCastException`. That the test program compiled guarantees that its annotation parameters represent valid exception types, with one caveat: it is possible that the annotation parameters were valid at compile time but a class file representing a specified exception type is no longer present at runtime. In this hopefully rare case, the test runner will throw `TypeNotPresentException`.

Taking our exception testing example one step further, it is possible to envision a test that passes if it throws any one of several specified exceptions. The annotation mechanism has a facility that makes it easy to support this usage. Suppose we change the parameter type of the `ExceptionTest` annotation to be an array of `Class` objects:

```
// Annotation type with an array parameter
@Retention(RetentionPolicy.RUNTIME)
@Target(ElementType.METHOD)
public @interface ExceptionTest {
    Class<? extends Exception>[] value();
}
```

The syntax for array parameters in annotations is flexible. It is optimized for single-element arrays. All of the previous `ExceptionTest` annotations are still valid with the new array-parameter version of `ExceptionTest` and result in single-element arrays. To specify a multiple-element array, surround the elements with curly braces and separate them with commas:

```
// Code containing an annotation with an array parameter
@ExceptionTest({ IndexOutOfBoundsException.class,
                 NullPointerException.class })
public static void doublyBad() {
    List<String> list = new ArrayList<String>();

    // The spec permits this method to throw either
    // IndexOutOfBoundsException or NullPointerException
    list.addAll(5, null);
}
```

It is reasonably straightforward to modify the test runner tool to process the new version of `ExceptionTest`. This code replaces the original version:

```
if (m.isAnnotationPresent(ExceptionTest.class)) {
    tests++;
    try {
        m.invoke(null);
        System.out.printf("Test %s failed: no exception%n", m);
    } catch (Throwable wrappedExc) {
        Throwable exc = wrappedExc.getCause();
        Class<? extends Exception>[] excTypes =
            m.getAnnotation(ExceptionTest.class).value();
        int oldPassed = passed;
        for (Class<? extends Exception> excType : excTypes) {
            if (excType.isInstance(exc)) {
                passed++;
                break;
            }
        }
        if (passed == oldPassed)
            System.out.printf("Test %s failed: %s %n", m, exc);
    }
}
```

The testing framework developed in this item is just a toy, but it clearly demonstrates the superiority of annotations over naming patterns. And it only scratches the surface of what you can do with annotations. If you write a tool that requires programmers to add information to source files, define an appropriate set of annotation types. **There is simply no reason to use naming patterns now that we have annotations.**

That said, with the exception of toolsmiths, most programmers will have no need to define annotation types. **All programmers should, however, *use* the predefined annotation types provided by the Java platform** (Items 36 and 24). Also, consider using any annotations provided by your IDE or static analysis tools. Such annotations can improve the quality of the diagnostic information provided by these tools. Note, however, that these annotations have yet to be standardized, so you will have some work to do if you switch tools, or if a standard emerges.

Item 36: Consistently use the `Override` annotation

When annotations were added to the language in release 1.5, several annotation types were added to the libraries [JLS, 9.6.1]. For the typical programmer, the most important of these is `Override`. This annotation can be used only on method declarations, and it indicates that the annotated method declaration overrides a declaration in a supertype. If you consistently use this annotation, it will protect you from a large class of nefarious bugs. Consider this program, in which the class `Bigram` represents a *bigram*, or ordered pair of letters:

```
// Can you spot the bug?
public class Bigram {
    private final char first;
    private final char second;
    public Bigram(char first, char second) {
        this.first  = first;
        this.second = second;
    }
    public boolean equals(Bigram b) {
        return b.first == first && b.second == second;
    }
    public int hashCode() {
        return 31 * first + second;
    }

    public static void main(String[] args) {
        Set<Bigram> s = new HashSet<Bigram>();
        for (int i = 0; i < 10; i++)
            for (char ch = 'a'; ch <= 'z'; ch++)
                s.add(new Bigram(ch, ch));
        System.out.println(s.size());
    }
}
```

The main program repeatedly adds twenty-six bigrams, each consisting of two identical lowercase letters, to a set. Then it prints the size of the set. You might expect the program to print 26, as sets cannot contain duplicates. If you try running the program, you'll find that it prints not 26 but 260. What is wrong with it?

Clearly, the author of the `Bigram` class intended to override the `equals` method (Item 8) and even remembered to override `hashCode` in tandem (Item 9). Unfortunately, our hapless programmer failed to override `equals`, overloading it instead (Item 41). To override `Object.equals`, you must define an `equals` method whose parameter is of type `Object`, but the parameter of `Bigram`'s `equals` method is not of type `Object`, so `Bigram` inherits the `equals` method from `Object`. This `equals` method tests for object identity, just like the `==` operator. Each of the ten copies of each bigram is distinct from the other nine, so they are deemed unequal by `Object.equals`, which explains why the program prints 260.

Luckily, the compiler can help you find this error, but only if you help the compiler by telling it that you intend to override `Object.equals`. To do this, annotate `Bigram.equals` with `@Override`, as shown below:

```
@Override public boolean equals(Bigram b) {
    return b.first == first && b.second == second;
}
```

If you insert this annotation and try to recompile the program, the compiler will generate an error message like this:

```
Bigram.java:10: method does not override or implement a method
from a supertype
    @Override public boolean equals(Bigram b) {
    ^
```

You will immediately realize what you did wrong, slap yourself on the forehead, and replace the broken `equals` implementation with a correct one (Item 8):

```
@Override public boolean equals(Object o) {
    if (!(o instanceof Bigram))
        return false;
    Bigram b = (Bigram) o;
    return b.first == first && b.second == second;
}
```

Therefore, you should **use the `Override` annotation on every method declaration that you believe to override a superclass declaration**. There is one minor exception to this rule. If you are writing a class that is not labeled abstract, and you believe that it overrides an abstract method, you needn't bother putting the `Override` annotation on that method. In a class that is not declared abstract, the compiler will emit an error message if you fail to override an abstract superclass method. However, you might wish to draw attention to all of the methods in your class that override superclass methods, in which case you should feel free to annotate these methods too.

Modern IDEs provide another reason to use the `Override` annotation consistently. Such IDEs have automated checks known as *code inspections*. If you enable the appropriate code inspection, the IDE will generate a warning if you have a method that doesn't have an Override annotation but does override a superclass method. If you use the Override annotation consistently, these warnings will alert you to unintentional overriding. These warnings complement the compiler's error messages, which alert you to unintentional failure to override. Between the IDE and the compiler, you can be sure that you're overriding methods everywhere you want to override them and nowhere else.

If you are using release 1.6 or a later release, the Override annotation provides even more help in finding bugs. In release 1.6, it became legal to use the Override annotation on method declarations that override declarations from interfaces as well as classes. In a concrete class that is declared to implement an interface, you needn't annotate methods that you believe to override interface methods, because the compiler will emit an error message if your class fails to implement every interface method. Again, you may choose to include these annotations simply to draw attention to interface methods, but it isn't strictly necessary.

In an abstract class or an interface, however, it *is* worth annotating all methods that you believe to override superclass or superinterface methods, whether concrete or abstract. For example, the Set interface adds no new methods to the Collection interface, so it should include Override annotations on all of its method declarations, to ensure that it does not accidentally add any new methods to the Collection interface.

In summary, the compiler can protect you from a great many errors if you use the Override annotation on every method declaration that you believe to override a supertype declaration, with one exception. In concrete classes, you need not annotate methods that you believe to override abstract method declarations (though it is not harmful to do so).

Item 37: Use marker interfaces to define types

A *marker interface* is an interface that contains no method declarations, but merely designates (or "marks") a class that implements the interface as having some property. For example, consider the `Serializable` interface (Chapter 11). By implementing this interface, a class indicates that its instances can be written to an `ObjectOutputStream` (or "serialized").

You may hear it said that marker annotations (Item 35) make marker interfaces obsolete. This assertion is incorrect. Marker interfaces have two advantages over marker annotations. First and foremost, **marker interfaces define a type that is implemented by instances of the marked class; marker annotations do not.** The existence of this type allows you to catch errors at compile time that you couldn't catch until runtime if you used a marker annotation.

In the case of the `Serializable` marker interface, the `ObjectOutput-Stream.write(Object)` method will fail if its argument does not implement the interface. Inexplicably, the authors of the `ObjectOutputStream` API did not take advantage of the `Serializable` interface in declaring the `write` method. The method's argument type should have been `Serializable` rather than `Object`. As it stands, an attempt to call `ObjectOutputStream.write` on an object that doesn't implement `Serializable` will fail only at runtime, but it didn't have to be that way.

Another advantage of marker interfaces over marker annotations is that they can be targeted more precisely. If an annotation type is declared with target `ElementType.TYPE`, it can be applied to *any* class or interface. Suppose you have a marker that is applicable only to implementations of a particular interface. If you define it as a marker interface, you can have it extend the sole interface to which it is applicable, guaranteeing that all marked types are also subtypes of the sole interface to which it is applicable.

Arguably, the `Set` interface is just such a *restricted marker interface*. It is applicable only to `Collection` subtypes, but it adds no methods beyond those defined by `Collection`. It is not generally considered to be a marker interface because it refines the contracts of several `Collection` methods, including `add`, `equals`, and `hashCode`. But it is easy to imagine a marker interface that is applicable only to subtypes of some particular interface and does *not* refine the contracts of any of the interface's methods as such. Such a marker interface might describe some invariant of the entire object or indicate that instances are eligible for processing by a method of some other class (in the way that the `Serializable` interface indicates that instances are eligible for processing by `ObjectOutputStream`).

The chief advantage of marker annotations over marker interfaces is that it is possible to add more information to an annotation type after it is already in use, by adding one or more annotation type elements with defaults [JLS, 9.6]. What starts life as a mere marker annotation type can evolve into a richer annotation type over time. Such evolution is not possible with marker interfaces, as it is not generally possible to add methods to an interface after it has been implemented (Item 18).

Another advantage of marker annotations is that they are part of the larger annotation facility. Therefore, marker annotations allow for consistency in frameworks that permit annotation of a variety of program elements.

So when should you use a marker annotation and when should you use a marker interface? Clearly you must use an annotation if the marker applies to any program element other than a class or interface, as only classes and interfaces can be made to implement or extend an interface. If the marker applies only to classes and interfaces, ask yourself the question, Might I want to write one or more methods that accept only objects that have this marking? If so, you should use a marker interface in preference to an annotation. This will make it possible for you to use the interface as a parameter type for the methods in question, which will result in the very real benefit of compile-time type checking.

If you answered no to the first question, ask yourself one more: Do I want to limit the use of this marker to elements of a particular interface, forever? If so, it makes sense to define the marker as a subinterface of that interface. If you answered no to both questions, you should probably use a marker annotation.

In summary, marker interfaces and marker annotations both have their uses. If you want to define a type that does not have any new methods associated with it, a marker interface is the way to go. If you want to mark program elements other than classes and interfaces, to allow for the possibility of adding more information to the marker in the future, or to fit the marker into a framework that already makes heavy use of annotation types, then a marker annotation is the correct choice. **If you find yourself writing a marker annotation type whose target is `ElementType.TYPE`, take the time to figure out whether it really should be an annotation type, or whether a marker interface would be more appropriate.**

In a sense, this item is the inverse of Item 19, which says, "If you don't want to define a type, don't use an interface." To a first approximation, this item says, "If you do want to define a type, do use an interface."

CHAPTER 7

Methods

THIS chapter discusses several aspects of method design: how to treat parameters and return values, how to design method signatures, and how to document methods. Much of the material in this chapter applies to constructors as well as to methods. Like Chapter 4, this chapter focuses on usability, robustness, and flexibility.

Item 38: Check parameters for validity

Most methods and constructors have some restrictions on what values may be passed into their parameters. For example, it is not uncommon that index values must be non-negative and object references must be non-null. You should clearly document all such restrictions and enforce them with checks at the beginning of the method body. This is a special case of the general principle that you should attempt to detect errors as soon as possible after they occur. Failing to do so makes it less likely that an error will be detected and makes it harder to determine the source of an error once it has been detected.

If an invalid parameter value is passed to a method and the method checks its parameters before execution, it will fail quickly and cleanly with an appropriate exception. If the method fails to check its parameters, several things could happen. The method could fail with a confusing exception in the midst of processing. Worse, the method could return normally but silently compute the wrong result. Worst of all, the method could return normally but leave some object in a compromised state, causing an error at some unrelated point in the code at some undetermined time in the future.

For public methods, use the Javadoc @throws tag to document the exception that will be thrown if a restriction on parameter values is violated (Item 62). Typically the exception will be IllegalArgumentException, IndexOutOfBounds-

Exception, or NullPointerException (Item 60). Once you've documented the restrictions on a method's parameters and you've documented the exceptions that will be thrown if these restrictions are violated, it is a simple matter to enforce the restrictions. Here's a typical example:

```
/**
 * Returns a BigInteger whose value is (this mod m).  This method
 * differs from the remainder method in that it always returns a
 * non-negative BigInteger.
 *
 * @param  m the modulus, which must be positive
 * @return this mod m
 * @throws ArithmeticException if m is less than or equal to 0
 */
public BigInteger mod(BigInteger m) {
    if (m.signum() <= 0)
        throw new ArithmeticException("Modulus <= 0: " + m);
    ... // Do the computation
}
```

For an unexported method, you as the package author control the circumstances under which the method is called, so you can and should ensure that only valid parameter values are ever passed in. Therefore, nonpublic methods should generally check their parameters using *assertions,* as shown below:

```
// Private helper function for a recursive sort
private static void sort(long a[], int offset, int length) {
    assert a != null;
    assert offset >= 0 && offset <= a.length;
    assert length >= 0 && length <= a.length - offset;
    ... // Do the computation
}
```

In essence, these assertions are claims that the asserted condition *will* be true, regardless of how the enclosing package is used by its clients. Unlike normal validity checks, assertions throw AssertionError if they fail. And unlike normal validity checks, they have no effect and essentially no cost unless you enable them, which you do by passing the -ea (or -enableassertions) flag to the java interpreter. For more information on assertions, see Sun's tutorial [Asserts].

It is particularly important to check the validity of parameters that are not used by a method but are stored away for later use. For example, consider the static factory method on page 95, which takes an int array and returns a List view of the array. If a client of this method were to pass in null, the method would throw a `NullPointerException` because the method contains an explicit check. Had the check been omitted, the method would return a reference to a newly created `List` instance that would throw a `NullPointerException` as soon as a client attempted to use it. By that time, the origin of the `List` instance might be difficult to determine, which could greatly complicate the task of debugging.

Constructors represent a special case of the principle that you should check the validity of parameters that are to be stored away for later use. It is critical to check the validity of constructor parameters to prevent the construction of an object that violates its class invariants.

There are exceptions to the rule that you should check a method's parameters before performing its computation. An important exception is the case in which the validity check would be expensive or impractical *and* the validity check is performed implicitly in the process of doing the computation. For example, consider a method that sorts a list of objects, such as `Collections.sort(List)`. All of the objects in the list must be mutually comparable. In the process of sorting the list, every object in the list will be compared to some other object in the list. If the objects aren't mutually comparable, one of these comparisons will throw a `Class-CastException`, which is exactly what the `sort` method should do. Therefore, there would be little point in checking ahead of time that the elements in the list were mutually comparable. Note, however, that indiscriminate reliance on implicit validity checks can result in a loss of failure atomicity (Item 64).

Occasionally, a computation implicitly performs a required validity check but throws the wrong exception if the check fails. In other words, the exception that the computation would naturally throw as the result of an invalid parameter value doesn't match the exception that the method is documented to throw. Under these circumstances, you should use the *exception translation* idiom, described in Item 61, to translate the natural exception into the correct one.

Do not infer from this item that arbitrary restrictions on parameters are a good thing. On the contrary, you should design methods to be as general as it is practical to make them. The fewer restrictions that you place on parameters, the better, assuming the method can do something reasonable with all of the parameter values that it accepts. Often, however, some restrictions are intrinsic to the abstraction being implemented.

To summarize, each time you write a method or constructor, you should think about what restrictions exist on its parameters. You should document these restrictions and enforce them with explicit checks at the beginning of the method body. It is important to get into the habit of doing this. The modest work that it entails will be paid back with interest the first time a validity check fails.

Item 39: Make defensive copies when needed

One thing that makes Java such a pleasure to use is that it is a *safe language*. This means that in the absence of native methods it is immune to buffer overruns, array overruns, wild pointers, and other memory corruption errors that plague unsafe languages such as C and C++. In a safe language, it is possible to write classes and to know with certainty that their invariants will remain true, no matter what happens in any other part of the system. This is not possible in languages that treat all of memory as one giant array.

Even in a safe language, you aren't insulated from other classes without some effort on your part. **You must program defensively, with the assumption that clients of your class will do their best to destroy its invariants.** This may actually be true if someone tries to break the security of your system, but more likely your class will have to cope with unexpected behavior resulting from honest mistakes on the part of programmers using your API. Either way, it is worth taking the time to write classes that are robust in the face of ill-behaved clients.

While it is impossible for another class to modify an object's internal state without some assistance from the object, it is surprisingly easy to provide such assistance without meaning to do so. For example, consider the following class, which purports to represent an immutable time period:

```java
// Broken "immutable" time period class
public final class Period {
    private final Date start;
    private final Date end;

    /**
     * @param  start the beginning of the period
     * @param  end the end of the period; must not precede start
     * @throws IllegalArgumentException if start is after end
     * @throws NullPointerException if start or end is null
     */
    public Period(Date start, Date end) {
        if (start.compareTo(end) > 0)
            throw new IllegalArgumentException(
                start + " after " + end);
        this.start = start;
        this.end   = end;
    }

    public Date start() {
        return start;
    }
```

```
    public Date end() {
        return end;
    }

    ...  // Remainder omitted
}
```

At first glance, this class may appear to be immutable and to enforce the invariant that the start of a period does not follow its end. It is, however, easy to violate this invariant by exploiting the fact that Date is mutable:

```
// Attack the internals of a Period instance
Date start = new Date();
Date end = new Date();
Period p = new Period(start, end);
end.setYear(78);  // Modifies internals of p!
```

To protect the internals of a Period instance from this sort of attack, **it is essential to make a *defensive copy* of each mutable parameter to the constructor** and to use the copies as components of the Period instance in place of the originals:

```
// Repaired constructor - makes defensive copies of parameters
public Period(Date start, Date end) {
    this.start = new Date(start.getTime());
    this.end   = new Date(end.getTime());

    if (this.start.compareTo(this.end) > 0)
      throw new IllegalArgumentException(
          this.start + " after " + this.end);
}
```

With the new constructor in place, the previous attack will have no effect on the Period instance. Note that **defensive copies are made *before* checking the validity of the parameters (Item 38), and the validity check is performed on the copies rather than on the originals.** While this may seem unnatural, it is necessary. It protects the class against changes to the parameters from another thread during the "window of vulnerability" between the time the parameters are checked and the time they are copied. (In the computer security community, this is known as a *time-of-check/time-of-use* or *TOCTOU* attack [Viega01].)

Note also that we did not use Date's clone method to make the defensive copies. Because Date is nonfinal, the clone method is not guaranteed to return an object whose class is java.util.Date: it could return an instance of an untrusted subclass specifically designed for malicious mischief. Such a subclass could, for example, record a reference to each instance in a private static list at the time of its creation and allow the attacker to access this list. This would give the attacker free reign over all instances. To prevent this sort of attack, **do not use the clone method to make a defensive copy of a parameter whose type is subclassable by untrusted parties.**

While the replacement constructor above successfully defends against the previous attack, it is still possible to mutate a Period instance, because its accessors offer access to its mutable internals:

```
// Second attack on the internals of a Period instance
Date start = new Date();
Date end = new Date();
Period p = new Period(start, end);
p.end().setYear(78);   // Modifies internals of p!
```

To defend against the second attack, merely modify the accessors to **return defensive copies of mutable internal fields**:

```
// Repaired accessors - make defensive copies of internal fields
public Date start() {
    return new Date(start.getTime());
}

public Date end() {
    return new Date(end.getTime());
}
```

With the new constructor and the new accessors in place, Period is truly immutable. No matter how malicious or incompetent a programmer, there is simply no way to violate the invariant that the start of a period does not follow its end. This is true because there is no way for any class other than Period itself to gain access to either of the mutable fields in a Period instance. These fields are truly encapsulated within the object.

In the accessors, unlike the constructor, it would be permissible to use the clone method to make the defensive copies. This is so because we know that the class of Period's internal Date objects is java.util.Date, and not some potentially untrusted subclass. That said, you are generally better off using a constructor or static factory, for reasons outlined in Item 11.

Defensive copying of parameters is not just for immutable classes. Anytime you write a method or constructor that enters a client-provided object into an internal data structure, think about whether the client-provided object is potentially mutable. If it is, think about whether your class could tolerate a change in the object after it was entered into the data structure. If the answer is no, you must defensively copy the object and enter the copy into the data structure in place of the original. For example, if you are considering using a client-provided object reference as an element in an internal Set instance or as a key in an internal Map instance, you should be aware that the invariants of the set or map would be destroyed if the object were modified after it is inserted.

The same is true for defensive copying of internal components prior to returning them to clients. Whether or not your class is immutable, you should think twice before returning a reference to an internal component that is mutable. Chances are, you should return a defensive copy. Remember that nonzero-length arrays are always mutable. Therefore, you should always make a defensive copy of an internal array before returning it to a client. Alternatively, you could return an immutable view of the array. Both of these techniques are shown in Item 13.

Arguably, the real lesson in all of this is that you should, where possible, use immutable objects as components of your objects, so that you that don't have to worry about defensive copying (Item 15). In the case of our Period example, it is worth pointing out that experienced programmers often use the primitive long returned by Date.getTime() as an internal time representation instead of using a Date reference. They do this primarily because Date is mutable.

Defensive copying can have a performance penalty associated with it and isn't always justified. If a class trusts its caller not to modify an internal component, perhaps because the class and its client are both part of the same package, then it may be appropriate to dispense with defensive copying. Under these circumstances, the class documentation must make it clear that the caller must not modify the affected parameters or return values.

Even across package boundaries, it is not always appropriate to make a defensive copy of a mutable parameter before integrating it into an object. There are some methods and constructors whose invocation indicates an explicit *handoff* of the object referenced by a parameter. When invoking such a method, the client promises that it will no longer modify the object directly. A method or constructor that expects to take ownership of a client-provided mutable object must make this clear in its documentation.

Classes containing methods or constructors whose invocation indicates a transfer of control cannot defend themselves against malicious clients. Such classes are acceptable only when there is mutual trust between the class and its client or when damage to the class's invariants would harm no one but the client. An example of the latter situation is the wrapper class pattern (Item 16). Depending on the nature of the wrapper class, the client could destroy the class's invariants by directly accessing an object after it has been wrapped, but this typically would harm only the client.

In summary, if a class has mutable components that it gets from or returns to its clients, the class must defensively copy these components. If the cost of the copy would be prohibitive *and* the class trusts its clients not to modify the components inappropriately, then the defensive copy may be replaced by documentation outlining the client's responsibility not to modify the affected components.

Item 40: Design method signatures carefully

This item is a grab bag of API design hints that don't quite deserve items of their own. Taken together, they'll help make your API easier to learn and use and less prone to errors.

Choose method names carefully. Names should always obey the standard naming conventions (Item 56). Your primary goal should be to choose names that are understandable and consistent with other names in the same package. Your secondary goal should be to choose names consistent with the broader consensus, where it exists. When in doubt, look to the Java library APIs for guidance. While there are plenty of inconsistencies—inevitable, given the size and scope of these libraries—there is also a fair amount of consensus.

Don't go overboard in providing convenience methods. Every method should "pull its weight." Too many methods make a class difficult to learn, use, document, test, and maintain. This is doubly true for interfaces, where too many methods complicate life for implementors as well as users. For each action supported by your class or interface, provide a fully functional method. Consider providing a "shorthand" only if it will be used often. **When in doubt, leave it out.**

Avoid long parameter lists. Aim for four parameters or fewer. Most programmers can't remember longer parameter lists. If many of your methods exceed this limit, your API won't be usable without constant reference to its documentation. Modern IDEs help, but you're still much better off with short parameter lists. **Long sequences of identically typed parameters are especially harmful.** Not only won't users be able to remember the order of the parameters, but when they transpose parameters accidentally, their programs will still compile and run. They just won't do what their authors intended.

There are three techniques for shortening overly long parameter lists. One is to break the method up into multiple methods, each of which requires only a subset of the parameters. If done carelessly, this can lead to too many methods, but it can also help *reduce* the method count by increasing orthogonality. For example, consider the `java.util.List` interface. It does not provide methods to find the first or last index of an element in a sublist, both of which would require three parameters. Instead it provides the `subList` method, which takes two parameters and returns a *view* of a sublist. This method can be combined with the `indexOf` or `lastIndexOf` methods, each of which has a single parameter, to yield the desired functionality. Moreover, the `subList` method can be combined with *any* method that operates on a `List` instance to perform arbitrary computations on sublists. The resulting API has a very high power-to-weight ratio.

A second technique for shortening long parameter lists is to create *helper classes* to hold groups of parameters. Typically these helper classes are static member classes (Item 22). This technique is recommended if a frequently occurring sequence of parameters is seen to represent some distinct entity. For example, suppose you are writing a class representing a card game, and you find yourself constantly passing a sequence of two parameters representing a card's rank and its suit. Your API, as well as the internals of your class, would probably benefit if you added a helper class to represent a card and replaced every occurrence of the parameter sequence with a single parameter of the helper class.

A third technique that combines aspects of the first two is to adapt the Builder pattern (Item 2) from object construction to method invocation. If you have a method with many parameters, especially if some of them are optional, it can be beneficial to define an object that represents all of the parameters, and to allow the client to make multiple "setter" calls on this object, each of which sets a single parameter or a small, related group. Once the desired parameters have been set, the client invokes the object's "execute" method, which does any final validity checks on the parameters and performs the actual computation.

For parameter types, favor interfaces over classes (Item 52). If there is an appropriate interface to define a parameter, use it in favor of a class that implements the interface. For example, there is no reason ever to write a method that takes HashMap on input—use Map instead. This lets you pass in a Hashtable, a HashMap, a TreeMap, a submap of a TreeMap, or any Map implementation yet to be written. By using a class instead of an interface, you restrict your client to a particular implementation and force an unnecessary and potentially expensive copy operation if the input data happens to exist in some other form.

Prefer two-element enum types to boolean parameters. It makes your code easier to read and to write, especially if you're using an IDE that supports autocompletion. Also, it makes it easy to add more options later. For example, you might have a Thermometer type with a static factory that takes a value of this enum:

```
public enum TemperatureScale { FAHRENHEIT, CELSIUS }
```

Not only does Thermometer.newInstance(TemperatureScale.CELSIUS) make a lot more sense than Thermometer.newInstance(true), but you can add KELVIN to TemperatureScale in a future release without having to add a new static factory to Thermometer. Also, you can refactor temperature-scale dependencies into methods on the enum constants (Item 30). For example, each scale constant could have a method that took a double value and normalized it to Celsius.

Item 41: Use overloading judiciously

The following program is a well-intentioned attempt to classify collections according to whether they are sets, lists, or some other kind of collection:

```java
// Broken! - What does this program print?
public class CollectionClassifier {
    public static String classify(Set<?> s) {
        return "Set";
    }

    public static String classify(List<?> lst) {
        return "List";
    }

    public static String classify(Collection<?> c) {
        return "Unknown Collection";
    }

    public static void main(String[] args) {
        Collection<?>[] collections = {
            new HashSet<String>(),
            new ArrayList<BigInteger>(),
            new HashMap<String, String>().values()
        };

        for (Collection<?> c : collections)
            System.out.println(classify(c));
    }
}
```

You might expect this program to print Set, followed by List and Unknown Collection, but it doesn't. It prints Unknown Collection three times. Why does this happen? Because the classify method is *overloaded*, and **the choice of which overloading to invoke is made at compile time**. For all three iterations of the loop, the compile-time type of the parameter is the same: Collection<?>. The runtime type is different in each iteration, but this does not affect the choice of overloading. Because the compile-time type of the parameter is Collection<?>, the only applicable overloading is the third one, classify(Collection<?>), and this overloading is invoked in each iteration of the loop.

The behavior of this program is counterintuitive because **selection among overloaded methods is static, while selection among overridden methods is dynamic**. The correct version of an *overridden* method is chosen at runtime, based on the runtime type of the object on which the method is invoked. As a reminder, a method is overridden when a subclass contains a method declaration with the same signature as a method declaration in an ancestor. If an instance method is overridden in a subclass and this method is invoked on an instance of the subclass, the subclass's *overriding method* executes, regardless of the compile-time type of the subclass instance. To make this concrete, consider the following program:

```
class Wine {
    String name() { return "wine"; }
}

class SparklingWine extends Wine {
    @Override String name() { return "sparkling wine"; }
}

class Champagne extends SparklingWine {
    @Override String name() { return "champagne"; }
}

public class Overriding {
    public static void main(String[] args) {
        Wine[] wines = {
            new Wine(), new SparklingWine(), new Champagne()
        };
        for (Wine wine : wines)
            System.out.println(wine.name());
    }
}
```

The name method is declared in class Wine and overridden in classes SparklingWine and Champagne. As you would expect, this program prints out wine, sparkling wine, and champagne, even though the compile-time type of the instance is Wine in each iteration of the loop. The compile-time type of an object has no effect on which method is executed when an overridden method is invoked; the "most specific" overriding method always gets executed. Compare this to overloading, where the runtime type of an object has no effect on which overloading is executed; the selection is made at compile time, based entirely on the compile-time types of the parameters.

In the CollectionClassifier example, the intent of the program was to discern the type of the parameter by dispatching automatically to the appropriate method overloading based on the runtime type of the parameter, just as the name method did in the Wine example. Method overloading simply does not provide this functionality. Assuming a static method is required, the best way to fix the program is to replace all three overloadings of `classify` with a single method that does an explicit `instanceof` test:

```
public static String classify(Collection<?> c) {
    return c instanceof Set  ? "Set" :
            c instanceof List ? "List" : "Unknown Collection";
}
```

Because overriding is the norm and overloading is the exception, overriding sets people's expectations for the behavior of method invocation. As demonstrated by the `CollectionClassifier` example, overloading can easily confound these expectations. It is bad practice to write code whose behavior is likely to confuse programmers. This is especially true for APIs. If the typical user of an API does not know which of several method overloadings will get invoked for a given set of parameters, use of the API is likely to result in errors. These errors will likely manifest themselves as erratic behavior at runtime, and many programmers will be unable to diagnose them. Therefore you should **avoid confusing uses of overloading**.

Exactly what constitutes a confusing use of overloading is open to some debate. **A safe, conservative policy is never to export two overloadings with the same number of parameters.** If a method uses varargs, a conservative policy is not to overload it at all, except as described in Item 42. If you adhere to these restrictions, programmers will never be in doubt as to which overloading applies to any set of actual parameters. The restrictions are not terribly onerous because you can always give methods different names instead of overloading them.

For example, consider the class `ObjectOutputStream`. It has a variant of its `write` method for every primitive type and for several reference types. Rather than overloading the `write` method, these variants have signatures like `writeBoolean(boolean)`, `writeInt(int)`, and `writeLong(long)`. An added benefit of this naming pattern, when compared to overloading, is that it is possible to provide read methods with corresponding names, for example, `readBoolean()`, `readInt()`, and `readLong()`. The `ObjectInputStream` class does, in fact, provide such read methods.

For constructors, you don't have the option of using different names: multiple constructors for a class are *always* overloaded. You do, in many cases, have the option of exporting static factories instead of constructors (Item 1). Also, with constructors you don't have to worry about interactions between overloading and overriding, because constructors can't be overridden. You will probably have occasion to export multiple constructors with the same number of parameters, so it pays to know how to do it safely.

Exporting multiple overloadings with the same number of parameters is unlikely to confuse programmers *if* it is always clear which overloading will apply to any given set of actual parameters. This is the case when at least one corresponding formal parameter in each pair of overloadings has a "radically different" type in the two overloadings. Two types are radically different if it is clearly impossible to cast an instance of either type to the other. Under these circumstances, which overloading applies to a given set of actual parameters is fully determined by the runtime types of the parameters and cannot be affected by their compile-time types, so the major source of confusion goes away. For example, ArrayList has one constructor that takes an int and a second constructor that takes a Collection. It is hard to imagine any confusion over which of these two constructors will be invoked under any circumstances.

Prior to release 1.5, all primitive types were radically different from all reference types, but this is no longer true in the presence of autoboxing, and it has caused real trouble. Consider the following program:

```
public class SetList {
    public static void main(String[] args) {
        Set<Integer> set = new TreeSet<Integer>();
        List<Integer> list = new ArrayList<Integer>();

        for (int i = -3; i < 3; i++) {
            set.add(i);
            list.add(i);
        }
        for (int i = 0; i < 3; i++) {
            set.remove(i);
            list.remove(i);
        }
        System.out.println(set + " " + list);
    }
}
```

The program adds the integers from -3 through 2 to a sorted set and to a list, and then makes three identical calls to remove on both the set and the list. If you're like most people you'd expect the program to remove the non-negative values (0, 1, and 2) from the set and the list, and to print [-3, -2, -1] [-3, -2, -1]. In fact, the program removes the non-negative values from the set and the odd values from the list and prints [-3, -2, -1] [-2, 0, 2]. It is an understatement to call this behavior confusing.

Here's what's happening: The call to set.remove(i) selects the overloading remove(E), where E is the element type of the set (Integer), and autoboxes i from int to Integer. This is the behavior you'd expect, so the program ends up removing the positive values from the set. The call to list.remove(i), on the other hand, selects the overloading remove(int i), which removes the element at the specified *position* from a list. If you start with the list [-3, -2, -1, 0, 1, 2] and remove the zeroth element, then the first, and then the second, you're left with [-2, 0, 2], and the mystery is solved. To fix the problem, cast list.remove's argument to Integer, forcing the correct overloading to be selected. Alternatively, you could invoke Integer.valueOf on i and pass the result to list.remove. Either way, the program prints [-3, -2, -1] [-3, -2, -1], as expected:

```
for (int i = 0; i < 3; i++) {
    set.remove(i);
    list.remove((Integer) i);  // or remove(Integer.valueOf(i))
}
```

The confusing behavior demonstrated by the previous example came about because the List<E> interface has two overloadings of the remove method: remove(E) and remove(int). Prior to release 1.5 when it was "generified," the List interface had a remove(Object) method in place of remove(E), and the corresponding parameter types, Object and int, were radically different. But in the presence of generics and autoboxing, the two parameter types are no longer radically different. In other words, adding generics and autoboxing to the language damaged the List interface. Luckily, few if any other APIs in the Java libraries were similarly damaged, but this tale makes it clear that it is even more important to overload with care now that autoboxing and generics are part of the language.

Array types and classes other than Object are radically different. Also, array types and interfaces other than Serializable and Cloneable are radically different. Two distinct classes are said to be *unrelated* if neither class is a descendant of the other [JLS, 5.5]. For example, String and Throwable are unrelated. It is impossible for any object to be an instance of two unrelated classes, so unrelated classes are radically different.

There are other pairs of types that can't be converted in either direction [JLS, 5.1.12], but once you go beyond the simple cases described above, it becomes very difficult for most programmers to discern which, if any, overloading applies to a set of actual parameters. The rules that determine which overloading is selected are extremely complex. They take up *thirty-three* pages in the language specification [JLS, 15.12.1-3], and few programmers understand all of their subtleties.

There may be times when you feel the need to violate the guidelines in this item, especially when evolving existing classes. For example, the String class has had a contentEquals(StringBuffer) method since release 1.4. In release 1.5, a new interface called CharSequence was added to provide a common interface for StringBuffer, StringBuilder, String, CharBuffer, and other similar types, all of which were retrofitted to implement this interface. At the same time that CharSequence was added to the platform, String was outfitted with an overloading of the contentEquals method that takes a CharSequence.

While the resulting overloading clearly violates the guidelines in this item, it causes no harm as long as both overloaded methods always do exactly the same thing when they are invoked on the same object reference. The programmer may not know which overloading will be invoked, but it is of no consequence so long as they behave identically. The standard way to ensure this behavior is to have the more specific overloading forward to the more general:

```
public boolean contentEquals(StringBuffer sb) {
    return contentEquals((CharSequence) sb);
}
```

While the Java platform libraries largely adhere to the spirit of the advice in this item, there are a number of classes that violate it. For example, the String class exports two overloaded static factory methods, valueOf(char[]) and valueOf(Object), that do completely different things when passed the same object reference. There is no real justification for this, and it should be regarded as an anomaly with the potential for real confusion.

To summarize, just because you can overload methods doesn't mean you should. You should generally refrain from overloading methods with multiple signatures that have the same number of parameters. In some cases, especially where constructors are involved, it may be impossible to follow this advice. In that case, you should at least avoid situations where the same set of parameters can be passed to different overloadings by the addition of casts. If such a situation cannot be avoided, for example, because you are retrofitting an existing class to implement a new interface, you should ensure that all overloadings behave identically when passed the same parameters. If you fail to do this, programmers will be hard pressed to make effective use of the overloaded method or constructor, and they won't understand why it doesn't work.

Item 42: Use varargs judiciously

In release 1.5, varargs methods, formally known as *variable arity methods* [JLS, 8.4.1], were added to the language. Varargs methods accept zero or more arguments of a specified type. The varargs facility works by first creating an array whose size is the number of arguments passed at the call site, then putting the argument values into the array, and finally passing the array to the method.

For example, here is a varargs method that takes a sequence of int arguments and returns their sum. As you would expect, the value of sum(1, 2, 3) is 6, and the value of sum() is 0:

```
// Simple use of varargs
static int sum(int... args) {
    int sum = 0;
    for (int arg : args)
        sum += arg;
    return sum;
}
```

Sometimes it's appropriate to write a method that requires *one* or more arguments of some type, rather than *zero* or more. For example, suppose you want to compute the minimum of a number of int arguments. This function is not well defined if the client passes no arguments. You could check the array length at runtime:

```
// The WRONG way to use varargs to pass one or more arguments!
static int min(int... args) {
    if (args.length == 0)
        throw new IllegalArgumentException("Too few arguments");
    int min = args[0];
    for (int i = 1; i < args.length; i++)
        if (args[i] < min)
            min = args[i];
    return min;
}
```

This solution has several problems. The most serious is that if the client invokes this method with no arguments, it fails at runtime rather than compile time. Another problem is that it is ugly. You have to include an explicit validity check on args, and you can't use a for-each loop unless you initialize min to Integer.MAX_VALUE, which is also ugly.

Luckily there's a much better way to achieve the desired effect. Declare the method to take two parameters, one normal parameter of the specified type and one varargs parameter of this type. This solution corrects all the deficiencies of the previous one:

```
// The right way to use varargs to pass one or more arguments
static int min(int firstArg, int... remainingArgs) {
    int min = firstArg;
    for (int arg : remainingArgs)
        if (arg < min)
            min = arg;
    return min;
}
```

As you can see from this example, varargs are effective in circumstances where you really do want a method with a variable number of arguments. Varargs were designed for `printf`, which was added to the platform in release 1.5, and for the core reflection facility (Item 53), which was retrofitted to take advantage of varargs in that release. Both `printf` and reflection benefit enormously from varargs.

You can retrofit an existing method that takes an array as its final parameter to take a varargs parameter instead with no effect on existing clients. But just because you can doesn't mean that you should! Consider the case of `Arrays.asList`. This method was never designed to gather multiple arguments into a list, but it seemed like a good idea to retrofit it to do so when varargs were added to the platform. As a result, it became possible to do things like this:

```
List<String> homophones = Arrays.asList("to", "too", "two");
```

This usage works, but it was a big mistake to enable it. Prior to release 1.5, this was a common idiom to print the contents of an array:

```
// Obsolete idiom to print an array!
System.out.println(Arrays.asList(myArray));
```

The idiom was necessary because arrays inherit their `toString` implementation from `Object`, so calling `toString` directly on an array produces a useless string such as `[Ljava.lang.Integer;@3e25a5`. The idiom worked only on arrays of object reference types, but if you accidentally tried it on an array of primitives, the program wouldn't compile. For example, this program:

```
public static void main(String[] args) {
    int[] digits = { 3, 1, 4, 1, 5, 9, 2, 6, 5, 4 };
    System.out.println(Arrays.asList(digits));
}
```

would generate this error message in release 1.4:

```
Va.java:6: asList(Object[]) in Arrays can't be applied to (int[])
        System.out.println(Arrays.asList(digits));
                          ^
```

Because of the unfortunate decision to retrofit `Arrays.asList` as a varargs method in release 1.5, this program now compiles without error or warning. Running the program, however, produces output that is both unintended and useless: [[I@3e25a5]. The `Arrays.asList` method, now "enhanced" to use varargs, gathers up the object reference to the `int` array `digits` into a one-element array of arrays and dutifully wraps it into a `List<int[]>` instance. Printing this list causes `toString` to be invoked on the list, which in turn causes `toString` to be invoked on its sole element, the `int` array, with the unfortunate result described above.

On the bright side, the `Arrays.asList` idiom for translating arrays to strings is now obsolete, and the current idiom is far more robust. Also in release 1.5, the `Arrays` class was given a full complement of `Arrays.toString` methods (not varargs methods!) designed specifically to translate arrays of any type into strings. If you use `Arrays.toString` in place of `Arrays.asList`, the program produces the intended result:

```
// The right way to print an array
System.out.println(Arrays.toString(myArray));
```

Instead of retrofitting `Arrays.asList`, it would have been better to add a new method to `Collections` specifically for the purpose of gathering its arguments into a list:

```
public static <T> List<T> gather(T... args) {
    return Arrays.asList(args);
}
```

Such a method would have provided the capability to gather without compromising the type-checking of the existing `Arrays.asList` method.

The lesson is clear. **Don't retrofit every method that has a final array parameter; use varargs *only* when a call really operates on a variable-length sequence of values.**

Two method signatures are particularly suspect:

```
ReturnType1 suspect1(Object... args) { }
<T> ReturnType2 suspect2(T... args) { }
```

Methods with either of these signatures will accept *any* parameter list. Any compile-time type-checking that you had prior to the retrofit will be lost, as demonstrated by what happened to `Arrays.asList`.

Exercise care when using the varargs facility in performance-critical situations. Every invocation of a varargs method causes an array allocation and initialization. If you have determined empirically that you can't afford this cost but you need the flexibility of varargs, there is a pattern that lets you have your cake and eat it too. Suppose you've determined that 95 percent of the calls to a method have three or fewer parameters. Then declare five overloadings of the method, one each with zero through three ordinary parameters, and a single varargs method for use when the number of arguments exceeds three:

```
public void foo() { }
public void foo(int a1) { }
public void foo(int a1, int a2) { }
public void foo(int a1, int a2, int a3) { }
public void foo(int a1, int a2, int a3, int... rest) { }
```

Now you know that you'll pay the cost of the array creation only in the 5 percent of all invocations where the number of parameters exceeds three. Like most performance optimizations, this technique usually isn't appropriate, but when it is, it's a lifesaver.

The `EnumSet` class uses this technique for its static factories to reduce the cost of creating enum sets to a bare minimum. It was appropriate to do this because it was critical that enum sets provide performance-competitive replacements for bit fields (Item 32).

In summary, varargs methods are a convenient way to define methods that require a variable number of arguments, but they should not be overused. They can produce confusing results if used inappropriately.

Item 43: Return empty arrays or collections, not nulls

It is not uncommon to see methods that look something like this:

```
private final List<Cheese> cheesesInStock = ...;

/**
 * @return an array containing all of the cheeses in the shop,
 *     or null if no cheeses are available for purchase.
 */
public Cheese[] getCheeses() {
    if (cheesesInStock.size() == 0)
        return null;
    ...
}
```

There is no reason to make a special case for the situation where no cheeses are available for purchase. Doing so requires extra code in the client to handle the null return value, for example:

```
Cheese[] cheeses = shop.getCheeses();
if (cheeses != null &&
    Arrays.asList(cheeses).contains(Cheese.STILTON))
    System.out.println("Jolly good, just the thing.");
```

instead of:

```
if (Arrays.asList(shop.getCheeses()).contains(Cheese.STILTON))
    System.out.println("Jolly good, just the thing.");
```

This sort of circumlocution is required in nearly every use of a method that returns `null` in place of an empty (zero-length) array or collection. It is error-prone, because the programmer writing the client might forget to write the special-case code to handle a null return. Such an error may go unnoticed for years, as such methods usually return one or more objects. Less significant, but still worthy of note, returning `null` in place of an empty array also complicates the method that returns the array or collection.

It is sometimes argued that a null return value is preferable to an empty array because it avoids the expense of allocating the array. This argument fails on two counts. First, it is inadvisable to worry about performance at this level unless profiling has shown that the method in question is a real contributor to performance problems (Item 55). Second, it is possible to return the same zero-length array from every invocation that returns no items because zero-length arrays are immutable and immutable objects may be shared freely (Item 15). In fact, this is exactly what happens when you use the standard idiom for dumping items from a collection into a typed array:

```
// The right way to return an array from a collection
private final List<Cheese> cheesesInStock = ...;

private static final Cheese[] EMPTY_CHEESE_ARRAY = new Cheese[0];

/**
 * @return an array containing all of the cheeses in the shop.
 */
public Cheese[] getCheeses() {
    return cheesesInStock.toArray(EMPTY_CHEESE_ARRAY);
}
```

In this idiom, an empty-array constant is passed to the toArray method to indicate the desired return type. Normally the toArray method allocates the returned array, but if the collection is empty, it fits in the zero-length input array, and the specification for Collection.toArray(T[]) guarantees that the input array will be returned if it is large enough to hold the collection. Therefore the idiom never allocates an empty array.

In similar fashion, a collection-valued method can be made to return the same immutable empty collection every time it needs to return an empty collection. The Collections.emptySet, emptyList, and emptyMap methods provide exactly what you need, as shown below:

```
// The right way to return a copy of a collection
public List<Cheese> getCheeseList() {
  if (cheesesInStock.isEmpty())
    return Collections.emptyList(); // Always returns same list
  else
    return new ArrayList<Cheese>(cheesesInStock);
}
```

In summary, **there is no reason ever to return null from an array- or collection-valued method instead of returning an empty array or collection.** The null-return idiom is likely a holdover from the C programming language, in which array lengths are returned separately from actual arrays. In C, there is no advantage to allocating an array if zero is returned as the length.

Item 44: Write doc comments for all exposed API elements

If an API is to be usable, it must be documented. Traditionally API documentation was generated manually, and keeping it in sync with code was a chore. The Java programming environment eases this task with the *Javadoc* utility. Javadoc generates API documentation automatically from source code with specially formatted *documentation comments*, more commonly known as *doc comments*.

If you are not familiar with the doc comment conventions, you should learn them. While these conventions are not officially part of the language, they constitute a de facto API that every programmer should know. These conventions are described on Sun's *How to Write Doc Comments* Web page [Javadoc-guide]. While this page has not been updated since release 1.4, it is still an invaluable resource. Two important Javadoc tags were added to Javadoc in release 1.5, {@literal} and {@code} [Javadoc-5.0]. These tags are discussed in this item.

To document your API properly, you must precede *every* exported class, interface, constructor, method, and field declaration with a doc comment. If a class is serializable, you should also document its serialized form (Item 75). In the absence of a doc comment, the best that Javadoc can do is to reproduce the declaration as the sole documentation for the affected API element. It is frustrating and error-prone to use an API with missing documentation comments. To write maintainable code, you should also write doc comments for most unexported classes, interfaces, constructors, methods, and fields.

The doc comment for a method should describe succinctly the contract between the method and its client. With the exception of methods in classes designed for inheritance (Item 17), the contract should say *what* the method does rather than *how* it does its job. The doc comment should enumerate all of the method's *preconditions*, which are the things that have to be true in order for a client to invoke it, and its *postconditions*, which are the things that will be true after the invocation has completed successfully. Typically, preconditions are described implicitly by the @throws tags for unchecked exceptions; each unchecked exception corresponds to a precondition violation. Also, preconditions can be specified along with the affected parameters in their @param tags.

In addition to preconditions and postconditions, methods should document any *side effects*. A side effect is an observable change in the state of the system that is not obviously required in order to achieve the postcondition. For example, if a method starts a background thread, the documentation should make note of it. Finally, documentation comments should describe the *thread safety* of a class or method, as discussed in Item 70.

To describe a method's contract fully, the doc comment should have an @param tag for every parameter, an @return tag unless the method has a void return type, and an @throws tag for every exception thrown by the method, whether checked or unchecked (Item 62). By convention, the text following an @param tag or @return tag should be a noun phrase describing the value represented by the parameter or return value. The text following an @throws tag should consist of the word "if," followed by a clause describing the conditions under which the exception is thrown. Occasionally, arithmetic expressions are used in place of noun phrases. By convention, the phrase or clause following an @param, @return, or @throws tag is not terminated by a period. All of these conventions are illustrated by the following short doc comment:

```
/**
 * Returns the element at the specified position in this list.
 *
 * <p>This method is <i>not</i> guaranteed to run in constant
 * time. In some implementations it may run in time proportional
 * to the element position.
 *
 * @param  index index of element to return; must be
 *         non-negative and less than the size of this list
 * @return the element at the specified position in this list
 * @throws IndexOutOfBoundsException if the index is out of range
 *         ({@code index < 0 || index >= this.size()})
 */
E get(int index);
```

Notice the use of HTML tags in this doc comment (<p> and <i>). The Javadoc utility translates doc comments into HTML, and arbitrary HTML elements in doc comments end up in the resulting HTML document. Occasionally, programmers go so far as to embed HTML tables in their doc comments, although this is rare.

Also notice the use of the Javadoc {@code} tag around the code fragment in the @throws clause. This serves two purposes: it causes the code fragment to be rendered in code font, and it suppresses processing of HTML markup and nested Javadoc tags in the code fragment. The latter property is what allows us to use the less-than sign (<) in the code fragment even though it's an HTML metacharacter. Prior to release 1.5, code fragments were included in doc comments by using HTML tags and HTML escapes. **It is no longer necessary to use the HTML <code> or <tt> tags in doc comments: the Javadoc {@code} tag is preferable because it eliminates the need to escape HTML metacharacters.** To include a multiline code example in a doc comment, use a Javadoc {@code} tag wrapped inside an HTML `<pre>` tag. In other words, precede the multiline code example with the characters `<pre>{@code` and follow it with the characters `}</pre>`.

Finally, notice the use of the word "this" in the doc comment. By convention, the word "this" always refers to the object on which the method is invoked when it is used in the doc comment for an instance method.

Don't forget that you must take special action to generate documentation containing HTML metacharacters, such as the less-than sign (<), the greater-than sign (>), and the ampersand (&). The best way to get these characters into documentation is to surround them with the `{@literal}` tag, which suppress processing of HTML markup and nested Javadoc tags. It is like the `{@code}` tag, except that it doesn't render the text in code font. For example, this Javadoc fragment:

```
* The triangle inequality is {@literal |x + y| < |x| + |y|}.
```

produces the documentation: "The triangle inequality is $|x + y| < |x| + |y|$." The `{@literal}` tag could have been placed around just the less-than sign rather than the entire inequality with the same resulting documentation, but the doc comment would have been less readable in the source code. This illustrates the general principle that doc comments should be readable in both the source code and in the generated documentation. If you can't achieve both, generated documentation readability trumps source code readability.

The first "sentence" of each doc comment (as defined below) becomes the *summary description* of the element to which the comment pertains. For example, the summary description in the doc comment on page 204 is "Returns the element at the specified position in this list." The summary description must stand on its own to describe the functionality of the element it summarizes. To avoid confusion, **no two members or constructors in a class or interface should have the same summary description.** Pay particular attention to overloadings, for which it is often natural to use the same first sentence in a prose description (but unacceptable in doc comments).

Be careful if the intended summary description contains a period, because the period can prematurely terminate the description. For example, a doc comment that begins with the phrase "A college degree, such as B.S., M.S. or Ph.D." will result in the summary description "A college degree, such as B.S., M.S." The problem is that the summary description ends at the first period that is followed by a space, tab, or line terminator (or at the first block tag) [Javadoc-ref]. In this case, the second period in the abbreviation "M.S." is followed by a space. The best solution is to surround the offending period and any associated text with a `{@literal}` tag, so the period is no longer followed by a space in the source code:

```
/**
 * A college degree, such as B.S., {@literal M.S.} or Ph.D.
 * College is a fountain of knowledge where many go to drink.
 */
public class Degree { ... }
```

It is somewhat misleading to say that the summary description is the first *sentence* in a doc comment. Convention dictates that it should seldom be a complete sentence. For methods and constructors, the summary description should be a full verb phrase (including any object) describing the action performed by the method. For example,

- `ArrayList(int initialCapacity)`—Constructs an empty list with the specified initial capacity.

- `Collection.size()`—Returns the number of elements in this collection.

For classes, interfaces, and fields, the summary description should be a noun phrase describing the thing represented by an instance of the class or interface or by the field itself. For example,

- `TimerTask`—A task that can be scheduled for one-time or repeated execution by a `Timer`.

- `Math.PI`—The `double` value that is closer than any other to pi, the ratio of the circumference of a circle to its diameter.

Three features added to the language in release 1.5 require special care in doc comments: generics, enums, and annotations. **When documenting a generic type or method, be sure to document all type parameters:**

```
/**
 * An object that maps keys to values.  A map cannot contain
 * duplicate keys; each key can map to at most one value.
 *
 * (Remainder omitted)
 *
 * @param <K> the type of keys maintained by this map
 * @param <V> the type of mapped values
 */
public interface Map<K, V> {
    ... // Remainder omitted
}
```

When documenting an enum type, be sure to document the constants as well as the type and any public methods. Note that you can put an entire doc comment on one line if it's short:

```
/**
 * An instrument section of a symphony orchestra.
 */
public enum OrchestraSection {
    /** Woodwinds, such as flute, clarinet, and oboe. */
    WOODWIND,

    /** Brass instruments, such as french horn and trumpet. */
    BRASS,

    /** Percussion instruments, such as timpani and cymbals */
    PERCUSSION,

    /** Stringed instruments, such as violin and cello. */
    STRING;
}
```

When documenting an annotation type, be sure to document any members as well as the type itself. Document members with noun phrases, as if they were fields. For the summary description of the type, use a verb phrase that says what it means when a program element has an annotation of this type:

```
/**
 * Indicates that the annotated method is a test method that
 * must throw the designated exception to succeed.
 */
@Retention(RetentionPolicy.RUNTIME)
@Target(ElementType.METHOD)
public @interface ExceptionTest {
    /**
     * The exception that the annotated test method must throw
     * in order to pass. (The test is permitted to throw any
     * subtype of the type described by this class object.)
     */
    Class<? extends Throwable> value();
}
```

As of release 1.5, package-level doc comments should be placed in a file called `package-info.java` instead of `package.html`. In addition to package-level doc comments, `package-info.java` must contain a package declaration and may contain package annotations on this declaration.

Two aspects of a class's exported API that are often neglected are thread-safety and serializability. Whether or not a class is thread-safe, you should document its thread-safety level, as described in Item 70. If a class is serializable, you should document its serialized form, as described in Item 75.

Javadoc has the ability to "inherit" method comments. If an API element does not have a doc comment, Javadoc searches for the most specific applicable doc comment, giving preference to interfaces over superclasses. The details of the search algorithm can be found in *The Javadoc Reference Guide* [Javadoc-ref]. You can also inherit *parts* of doc comments from supertypes using the {@inheritDoc} tag. This means, among other things, that classes can reuse doc comments from interfaces they implement, rather than copying these comments. This facility has the potential to reduce the burden of maintaining multiple sets of nearly identical doc comments, but it is tricky to use and has some limitations. The details are beyond the scope of this book.

A simple way to reduce the likelihood of errors in documentation comments is to run the HTML files generated by Javadoc through an *HTML validity checker*. This will detect many incorrect uses of HTML tags, as well as HTML metacharacters that should have been escaped. Several HTML validity checkers are available for download and you can validate HTML online [W3C-validator].

One caveat should be added concerning documentation comments. While it is necessary to provide documentation comments for all exported API elements, it is not always sufficient. For complex APIs consisting of multiple interrelated classes, it is often necessary to supplement the documentation comments with an external document describing the overall architecture of the API. If such a document exists, the relevant class or package documentation comments should include a link to it.

The conventions described in this item cover the basics. The definitive guide to writing doc comments is Sun's *How to Write Doc Comments* [Javadoc-guide]. There are IDE plug-ins that check for adherence to many of these rules [Burn01].

To summarize, documentation comments are the best, most effective way to document your API. Their use should be considered mandatory for all exported API elements. Adopt a consistent style that adheres to standard conventions. Remember that arbitrary HTML is permissible within documentation comments and that HTML metacharacters must be escaped.

CHAPTER 8

General Programming

THIS chapter is largely devoted to the nuts and bolts of the language. It discusses the treatment of local variables, control structures, the use of libraries, the use of various data types, and the use of two extralinguistic facilities: *reflection* and *native methods*. Finally, it discusses optimization and naming conventions.

Item 45: Minimize the scope of local variables

This item is similar in nature to Item 13, "Minimize the accessibility of classes and members." By minimizing the scope of local variables, you increase the readability and maintainability of your code and reduce the likelihood of error.

Older programming languages, such as C, mandated that local variables must be declared at the head of a block, and some programmers continue to do this out of habit. It's a habit worth breaking. As a gentle reminder, Java lets you declare variables anywhere a statement is legal.

The most powerful technique for minimizing the scope of a local variable is to declare it where it is first used. If a variable is declared before it is used, it's just clutter—one more thing to distract the reader who is trying to figure out what the program does. By the time the variable is used, the reader might not remember the variable's type or initial value.

Declaring a local variable prematurely can cause its scope not only to extend too early, but also to end too late. The scope of a local variable extends from the point where it is declared to the end of the enclosing block. If a variable is declared outside of the block in which it is used, it remains visible after the program exits that block. If a variable is used accidentally before or after its region of intended use, the consequences can be disastrous.

Nearly every local variable declaration should contain an initializer. If you don't yet have enough information to initialize a variable sensibly, you should postpone the declaration until you do. One exception to this rule concerns try-catch statements. If a variable is initialized by a method that throws a checked exception, it must be initialized inside a try block. If the value must be used outside of the try block, then it must be declared before the try block, where it cannot yet be "sensibly initialized." For example, see page 231.

Loops present a special opportunity to minimize the scope of variables. The for loop, in both its traditional and for-each forms, allows you to declare *loop variables*, limiting their scope to the exact region where they're needed. (This region consists of the body of the loop and the code in parentheses between the for keyword and the body.) Therefore, **prefer for loops to while loops**, assuming the contents of the loop variable aren't needed after the loop terminates.

For example, here is the preferred idiom for iterating over a collection (Item 46):

```
// Preferred idiom for iterating over a collection
for (Element e : c) {
    doSomething(e);
}
```

Before release 1.5, this was the preferred idiom (and it still has valid uses):

```
// No for-each loop or generics before release 1.5
for (Iterator i = c.iterator(); i.hasNext(); ) {
    doSomething((Element) i.next());
}
```

To see why these for loops are preferable to a while loop, consider the following code fragment, which contains two while loops and one bug:

```
Iterator<Element> i = c.iterator();
while (i.hasNext()) {
    doSomething(i.next());
}
...

Iterator<Element> i2 = c2.iterator();
while (i.hasNext()) {                    // BUG!
    doSomethingElse(i2.next());
}
```

The second loop contains a copy-and-paste error: it initializes a new loop variable, i2, but uses the old one, i, which is, unfortunately, still in scope. The resulting code compiles without error and runs without throwing an exception, but it does the wrong thing. Instead of iterating over c2, the second loop terminates immediately, giving the false impression that c2 is empty. Because the program errs silently, the error can remain undetected for a long time.

If a similar copy-and-paste error were made in conjunction with either of the for loops (for-each or traditional), the resulting code wouldn't even compile. The element (or iterator) variable from the first loop would not be in scope at the point where the second loop occurred. Here's how it looks for the traditional for loop:

```
for (Iterator<Element> i = c.iterator(); i.hasNext(); ) {
    doSomething(i.next());
}
    ...

// Compile-time error - cannot find symbol i
for (Iterator<Element> i2 = c2.iterator(); i.hasNext(); ) {
    doSomething(i2.next());
}
```

Moreover, if you use a for loop, it's much less likely that you'll make the copy-and-paste error, as there's no incentive to use different variable names in the two loops. The loops are completely independent, so there's no harm in reusing the element (or iterator) variable name. In fact, it's often stylish to do so.

The for loop has one more advantage over the while loop: it is shorter, which enhances readability.

Here is another loop idiom that minimizes the scope of local variables:

```
for (int i = 0, n = expensiveComputation(); i < n; i++) {
    doSomething(i);
}
```

The important thing to notice about this idiom is that it has *two* loop variables, i and n, both of which have exactly the right scope. The second variable, n, is used to store the limit of the first, thus avoiding the cost of a redundant computation on every iteration. As a rule, you should use this idiom if the loop test involves a method invocation that is guaranteed to return the same result on each iteration.

A final technique to minimize the scope of local variables is to **keep methods small and focused**. If you combine two activities in the same method, local variables relevant to one activity may be in the scope of the code performing the other activity. To prevent this from happening, simply separate the method into two: one for each activity.

Item 46: Prefer for-each loops to traditional for loops

Prior to release 1.5, this was the preferred idiom for iterating over a collection:

```
// No longer the preferred idiom to iterate over a collection!
for (Iterator i = c.iterator(); i.hasNext(); ) {
    doSomething((Element) i.next()); // (No generics before 1.5)
}
```

This was the preferred idiom for iterating over an array:

```
// No longer the preferred idiom to iterate over an array!
for (int i = 0; i < a.length; i++) {
    doSomething(a[i]);
}
```

These idioms are better than while loops (Item 45), but they aren't perfect. The iterator and the index variables are both just clutter. Furthermore, they represent opportunities for error. The iterator occurs three times in each loop and the index variable four, which gives you many chances to use the wrong variable. If you do, there is no guarantee that the compiler will catch the problem.

The for-each loop, introduced in release 1.5, gets rid of the clutter and the opportunity for error by hiding the iterator or index variable completely. The resulting idiom applies equally to collections and arrays:

```
// The preferred idiom for iterating over collections and arrays
for (Element e : elements) {
    doSomething(e);
}
```

When you see the colon (:), read it as "in." Thus, the loop above reads as "for each element *e* in *elements*." Note that there is no performance penalty for using the for-each loop, even for arrays. In fact, it may offer a slight performance advantage over an ordinary for loop in some circumstances, as it computes the limit of the array index only once. While you *can* do this by hand (Item 45), programmers don't always do so.

The advantages of the for-each loop over the traditional for loop are even greater when it comes to nested iteration over multiple collections. Here is a common mistake that people make when they try to do nested iteration over two collections:

```
// Can you spot the bug?
enum Suit { CLUB, DIAMOND, HEART, SPADE }
enum Rank { ACE, DEUCE, THREE, FOUR, FIVE, SIX, SEVEN, EIGHT,
            NINE, TEN, JACK, QUEEN, KING }
...
Collection<Suit> suits = Arrays.asList(Suit.values());
Collection<Rank> ranks = Arrays.asList(Rank.values());

List<Card> deck = new ArrayList<Card>();
for (Iterator<Suit> i = suits.iterator(); i.hasNext(); )
    for (Iterator<Rank> j = ranks.iterator(); j.hasNext(); )
        deck.add(new Card(i.next(), j.next()));
```

Don't feel bad if you didn't spot the bug. Many expert programmers have made this mistake at one time or another. The problem is that the next method is called too many times on the iterator for the outer collection (suits). It should be called from the outer loop, so that it is called once per suit, but instead it is called from the inner loop, so it is called once per card. After you run out of suits, the loop throws a NoSuchElementException.

If you're really unlucky and the size of the outer collection is a multiple of the size of the inner collection—perhaps because they're the same collection—the loop will terminate normally, but it won't do what you want. For example, consider this ill-conceived attempt to print all of the possible rolls of a pair of dice:

```
// Same bug, different symptom!
enum Face { ONE, TWO, THREE, FOUR, FIVE, SIX }
...
Collection<Face> faces = Arrays.asList(Face.values());

for (Iterator<Face> i = faces.iterator(); i.hasNext(); )
    for (Iterator<Face> j = faces.iterator(); j.hasNext(); )
        System.out.println(i.next() + " " + j.next());
```

This program doesn't throw an exception but it prints only the six "doubles" (from "ONE ONE" to "SIX SIX"), instead of the expected thirty-six combinations.

To fix the bugs in these examples, you must add a variable in the scope of the outer loop to hold the outer element:

```
// Fixed, but ugly - you can do better!
for (Iterator<Suit> i = suits.iterator(); i.hasNext(); ) {
    Suit suit = i.next();
    for (Iterator<Rank> j = ranks.iterator(); j.hasNext(); )
        deck.add(new Card(suit, j.next()));
}
```

If instead you use a nested for-each loop, the problem simply disappears. The resulting code is as succinct as you could wish for:

```
// Preferred idiom for nested iteration on collections and arrays
for (Suit suit : suits)
    for (Rank rank : ranks)
        deck.add(new Card(suit, rank));
```

Not only does the for-each loop let you iterate over collections and arrays, it lets you iterate over any object that implements the Iterable interface. This simple interface, which consists of a single method, was added to the platform at the same time as the for-each loop. Here is how it looks:

```
public interface Iterable<E> {
    // Returns an iterator over the elements in this iterable
    Iterator<E> iterator();
}
```

It is not hard to implement the Iterable interface. If you are writing a type that represents a group of elements, have it implement Iterable even if you choose not to have it implement Collection. This will allow your users to iterate over your type using the for-each loop, and they will be forever grateful.

In summary, the for-each loop provides compelling advantages over the traditional for loop in clarity and bug prevention, with no performance penalty. You should use it wherever you can. Unfortunately, there are three common situations where you *can't* use a for-each loop:

1. **Filtering**—If you need to traverse a collection and remove selected elements, then you need to use an explicit iterator so that you can call its remove method.

2. **Transforming**—If you need to traverse a list or array and replace some or all of the values of its elements, then you need the list iterator or array index in order to set the value of an element.

3. **Parallel iteration**—If you need to traverse multiple collections in parallel, then you need explicit control over the iterator or index variable, so that all iterators or index variables can be advanced in lockstep (as demonstrated unintentionally in the buggy card and dice examples above).

If you find yourself in any of these situations, use an ordinary for loop, be wary of the traps mentioned in this item, and know that you're doing the best you can.

Item 47: Know and use the libraries

Suppose you want to generate random integers between zero and some upper bound. Faced with this common task, many programmers would write a little method that looks something like this:

```
private static final Random rnd = new Random();

// Common but deeply flawed!
static int random(int n) {
    return Math.abs(rnd.nextInt()) % n;
}
```

This method may look good, but it has three flaws. The first is that if n is a small power of two, the sequence of random numbers it generates will repeat itself after a fairly short period. The second flaw is that if n is not a power of two, some numbers will, on average, be returned more frequently than others. If n is large, this effect can be quite pronounced. This is graphically demonstrated by the following program, which generates a million random numbers in a carefully chosen range and then prints out how many of the numbers fell in the lower half of the range:

```
public static void main(String[] args) {
    int n = 2 * (Integer.MAX_VALUE / 3);
    int low = 0;
    for (int i = 0; i < 1000000; i++)
        if (random(n) < n/2)
            low++;

    System.out.println(low);
}
```

If the random method worked properly, the program would print a number close to half a million, but if you run it, you'll find that it prints a number close to 666,666. Two-thirds of the numbers generated by the random method fall in the lower half of its range!

The third flaw in the random method is that it can, on rare occasions, fail catastrophically, returning a number outside the specified range. This is so because the method attempts to map the value returned by rnd.nextInt() to a non-negative int by calling Math.abs. If nextInt() returns Integer.MIN_VALUE, Math.abs will also return Integer.MIN_VALUE, and the remainder operator (%) will return a negative number, assuming n is not a power of two. This will almost certainly cause your program to fail, and the failure may be difficult to reproduce.

To write a version of the random method that corrects these three flaws, you'd have to know a fair amount about pseudorandom number generators, number theory, and two's complement arithmetic. Luckily, you don't have to do this—it's been done for you. It's called Random.nextInt(int), and it has been a part of the Java platform since release 1.2.

You don't have to concern yourself with the details of how nextInt(int) does its job (although you can study the documentation or the source code if you're curious). A senior engineer with a background in algorithms spent a good deal of time designing, implementing, and testing this method and then showed it to several experts in the field to make sure it was right. Then the library was beta tested, released, and used extensively by millions of programmers for the better part of a decade. No flaws have yet been found in the method, but if a flaw were to be discovered, it would be fixed in the next release. **By using a standard library, you take advantage of the knowledge of the experts who wrote it and the experience of those who used it before you.**

A second advantage of using the libraries is that you don't have to waste your time writing ad hoc solutions to problems that are only marginally related to your work. If you are like most programmers, you'd rather spend your time working on your application than on the underlying plumbing.

A third advantage of using standard libraries is that their performance tends to improve over time, with no effort on your part. Because many people use them and because they're used in industry-standard benchmarks, the organizations that supply these libraries have a strong incentive to make them run faster. Many of the Java platform libraries have been rewritten over the years, sometimes repeatedly, resulting in dramatic performance improvements.

Libraries also tend to gain new functionality over time. If a library is missing something, the developer community will make it known, and the missing functionality may get added to a subsequent release. The Java platform has always been developed with substantial input from the community.

A final advantage of using the standard libraries is that you place your code in the mainstream. Such code is more easily readable, maintainable, and reusable by the multitude of developers.

Given all these advantages, it seems only logical to use library facilities in preference to ad hoc implementations, yet a significant fraction of programmers don't. Why? Perhaps they don't know the library facilities exist. **Numerous features are added to the libraries in every major release, and it pays to keep**

abreast of these additions. Each time there is a major release of the Java platform, Sun publishes a Web page describing its new features. These pages are well worth reading [Java5-feat, Java6-feat]. The libraries are too big to study all the documentation [JavaSE6], but **every programmer should be familiar with the contents of `java.lang`, `java.util`, and, to a lesser extent, `java.io`.** Knowledge of other libraries can be acquired on an as-needed basis.

It is beyond the scope of this item to summarize the facilities in the libraries, but two bear special mention. In release 1.2, a *Collections Framework* was added to the `java.util` package. It should be part of every programmer's basic toolkit. The Collections Framework is a unified architecture for representing and manipulating collections, allowing them to be manipulated independently of the details of their representation. It reduces programming effort while increasing performance. It allows for interoperability among unrelated APIs, reduces effort in designing and learning new APIs, and fosters software reuse. If you want to know more, see the documentation on Sun's Web site [Collections], or read the tutorial [Bloch06].

In release 1.5, a set of concurrency utilities was added, in the package `java.util.concurrent`. This package contains both high-level concurrency utilities to simplify the task of multithreaded programming and low-level concurrency primitives to allow experts to write their own higher-level concurrent abstractions. The high-level parts of `java.util.concurrent` should also be part of every programmer's basic toolkit (Item 68, Item 69).

Occasionally, a library facility can fail to meet your needs. The more specialized your needs, the more likely this is to happen. While your first impulse should be to use the libraries, if you've looked at what they have to offer in some area and it doesn't meet your needs, then use an alternate implementation. There will always be holes in the functionality provided by any finite set of libraries. If the functionality that you need is missing, you may have no choice but to implement it yourself.

To summarize, don't reinvent the wheel. If you need to do something that seems like it should be reasonably common, there may already be a class in the libraries that does what you want. If there is, use it; if you don't know, check. Generally speaking, library code is likely to be better than code that you'd write yourself and is likely to improve over time. This is no reflection on your abilities as a programmer. Economies of scale dictate that library code receives far more attention than most developers could afford to devote to the same functionality.

Item 48: Avoid `float` and `double` if exact answers are required

The `float` and `double` types are designed primarily for scientific and engineering calculations. They perform *binary floating-point arithmetic*, which was carefully designed to furnish accurate approximations quickly over a broad range of magnitudes. They do not, however, provide exact results and should not be used where exact results are required. **The `float` and `double` types are particularly ill-suited for monetary calculations** because it is impossible to represent 0.1 (or any other negative power of ten) as a `float` or `double` exactly.

For example, suppose you have $1.03 in your pocket, and you spend 42¢. How much money do you have left? Here's a naive program fragment that attempts to answer this question:

```
System.out.println(1.03 - .42);
```

Unfortunately, it prints out `0.6100000000000001`. This is not an isolated case. Suppose you have a dollar in your pocket, and you buy nine washers priced at ten cents each. How much change do you get?

```
System.out.println(1.00 - 9 * .10);
```

According to this program fragment, you get $`0.09999999999999998`.

You might think that the problem could be solved merely by rounding results prior to printing, but unfortunately this does not always work. For example, suppose you have a dollar in your pocket, and you see a shelf with a row of delicious candies priced at 10¢, 20¢, 30¢, and so forth, up to a dollar. You buy one of each candy, starting with the one that costs 10¢, until you can't afford to buy the next candy on the shelf. How many candies do you buy, and how much change do you get? Here's a naive program designed to solve this problem:

```
// Broken - uses floating point for monetary calculation!
public static void main(String[] args) {
    double funds = 1.00;
    int itemsBought = 0;
    for (double price = .10; funds >= price; price += .10) {
        funds -= price;
        itemsBought++;
    }
    System.out.println(itemsBought + " items bought.");
    System.out.println("Change: $" + funds);
}
```

If you run the program, you'll find that you can afford three pieces of candy, and you have $0.399999999999999 left. This is the wrong answer! The right way to solve this problem is to **use BigDecimal, int, or long for monetary calculations**.

Here's a straightforward transformation of the previous program to use the BigDecimal type in place of double:

```
public static void main(String[] args) {
    final BigDecimal TEN_CENTS = new BigDecimal(".10");

    int itemsBought = 0;
    BigDecimal funds = new BigDecimal("1.00");
    for (BigDecimal price = TEN_CENTS;
            funds.compareTo(price) >= 0;
            price = price.add(TEN_CENTS)) {
        funds = funds.subtract(price);
        itemsBought++;
    }
    System.out.println(itemsBought + " items bought.");
    System.out.println("Money left over: $" + funds);
}
```

If you run the revised program, you'll find that you can afford four pieces of candy, with $0.00 left over. This is the correct answer.

There are, however, two disadvantages to using BigDecimal: it's less convenient than using a primitive arithmetic type, and it's slower. The latter disadvantage is irrelevant if you're solving a single short problem, but the former may annoy you.

An alternative to using BigDecimal is to use int or long, depending on the amounts involved, and to keep track of the decimal point yourself. In this example, the obvious approach is to do all computation in cents instead of dollars. Here's a straightforward transformation of the program just shown that takes this approach:

```
public static void main(String[] args) {
    int itemsBought = 0;
    int funds = 100;
    for (int price = 10; funds >= price; price += 10) {
        funds -= price;
        itemsBought++;
    }
    System.out.println(itemsBought + " items bought.");
    System.out.println("Money left over: "+ funds + " cents");
}
```

In summary, don't use float or double for any calculations that require an exact answer. Use BigDecimal if you want the system to keep track of the decimal point and you don't mind the inconvenience and cost of not using a primitive type. Using BigDecimal has the added advantage that it gives you full control over rounding, letting you select from eight rounding modes whenever an operation that entails rounding is performed. This comes in handy if you're performing business calculations with legally mandated rounding behavior. If performance is of the essence, you don't mind keeping track of the decimal point yourself, and the quantities aren't too big, use int or long. If the quantities don't exceed nine decimal digits, you can use int; if they don't exceed eighteen digits, you can use long. If the quantities might exceed eighteen digits, you must use BigDecimal.

Item 49:   Prefer primitive types to boxed primitives

Java has a two-part type system, consisting of *primitives*, such as int, double, and boolean, and *reference types*, such as String and List. Every primitive type has a corresponding reference type, called a *boxed primitive*. The boxed primitives corresponding to int, double, and boolean are Integer, Double, and Boolean.

In release 1.5, *autoboxing* and *auto-unboxing* were added to the language. As mentioned in Item 5, these features blur but do not erase the distinction between the primitive and boxed primitive types. There are real differences between the two, and it's important that you remain aware of which you are using, and that you choose carefully between them.

There are three major differences between primitives and boxed primitives. First, primitives have only their values, whereas boxed primitives have identities distinct from their values. In other words, two boxed primitive instances can have the same value and different identities. Second, primitive types have only fully functional values, whereas each boxed primitive type has one nonfunctional value, which is null, in addition to all of the functional values of its corresponding primitive type. Last, primitives are generally more time- and space-efficient than boxed primitives. All three of these differences can get you into real trouble if you aren't careful.

Consider the following comparator, which is designed to represent ascending numerical order on Integer values. (Recall that a comparator's compare method returns a number that is negative, zero, or positive, depending on whether its first argument is less than, equal to, or greater than its second.) You would not need to write this comparator in practice, as it implements the natural ordering on Integer, which you get without a comparator, but it makes for an interesting example:

```
// Broken comparator - can you spot the flaw?
Comparator<Integer> naturalOrder = new Comparator<Integer>() {
    public int compare(Integer first, Integer second) {
        return first < second ? -1 : (first == second ? 0 : 1);
    }
};
```

This comparator looks good on the face of it, and it will pass many tests. For example, it can be used with Collections.sort to correctly sort a million-element list, whether or not the list contains duplicate elements. But this comparator is deeply flawed. To convince yourself of this, merely print the value of naturalOrder.compare(new Integer(42), new Integer(42)). Both Integer instances represent the same value (42), so the value of this expression should be 0, but it's 1, which indicates that the first Integer value is greater than the second.

So what's the problem? The first test in naturalOrder works fine. Evaluating the expression first < second causes the Integer instances referred to by first and second to be *auto-unboxed*; that is, it extracts their primitive values. The evaluation proceeds to check if the first of the resulting int values is less than the second. But suppose it is not. Then the next test evaluates the expression first == second, which performs an *identity comparison* on the two object references. If first and second refer to distinct Integer instances that represent the same int value, this comparison will return false, and the comparator will incorrectly return 1, indicating that the first Integer value is greater than the second. **Applying the == operator to boxed primitives is almost always wrong.**

The clearest way to fix the problem is to add two local variables, to store the primitive int values corresponding to first and second, and to perform all of the comparisons on these variables. This avoids the erroneous identity comparison:

```
Comparator<Integer> naturalOrder = new Comparator<Integer>() {
    public int compare(Integer first, Integer second) {
        int f = first;   // Auto-unboxing
        int s = second;  // Auto-unboxing
        return f < s ? -1 : (f == s ? 0 : 1); // No unboxing
    }
};
```

Next, consider this little program:

```
public class Unbelievable {
    static Integer i;

    public static void main(String[] args) {
        if (i == 42)
            System.out.println("Unbelievable");
    }
}
```

No, it doesn't print Unbelievable—but what it does is almost as strange. It throws a NullPointerException when evaluating the expression (i == 42). The problem is that i is an Integer, not an int, and like all object reference fields, its initial value is null. When the program evaluates the expression (i == 42), it is comparing an Integer to an int. In nearly every case **when you mix primitives and boxed primitives in a single operation, the boxed primitive is auto-**

unboxed, and this case is no exception. If a null object reference is auto-unboxed, you get a `NullPointerException`. As this program demonstrates, it can happen almost anywhere. Fixing the program is as simple as declaring i to be an `int` instead of an `Integer`.

Finally, consider the program from page 23 (Item 5):

```
// Hideously slow program! Can you spot the object creation?
public static void main(String[] args) {
    Long sum = 0L;
    for (long i = 0; i < Integer.MAX_VALUE; i++) {
        sum += i;
    }
    System.out.println(sum);
}
```

This program is much slower than it should be because it accidentally declares a local variable (sum) to be of the boxed primitive type `Long` instead of the primitive type `long`. The program compiles without error or warning, and the variable is repeatedly boxed and unboxed, causing the observed performance degradation.

In all three of the programs discussed in this item, the problem was the same: the programmer ignored the distinction between primitives and boxed primitives and suffered the consequences. In the first two programs, the consequences were outright failure; in the third, severe performance problems.

So when should you use boxed primitives? They have several legitimate uses. The first is as elements, keys, and values in collections. You can't put primitives in collections, so you're forced to use boxed primitives. This is a special case of a more general one. You must use boxed primitives as type parameters in parameterized types (Chapter 5), because the language does not permit you to use primitives. For example, you cannot declare a variable to be of type `Thread-Local<int>`, so you must use `ThreadLocal<Integer>` instead. Finally, you must use boxed primitives when making reflective method invocations (Item 53).

In summary, use primitives in preference to boxed primitives whenever you have the choice. Primitive types are simpler and faster. If you must use boxed primitives, be careful! **Autoboxing reduces the verbosity, but not the danger, of using boxed primitives.** When your program compares two boxed primitives with the `==` operator, it does an identity comparison, which is almost certainly *not* what you want. When your program does mixed-type computations involving boxed and unboxed primitives, it does unboxing, and **when your program does unboxing, it can throw a `NullPointerException`.** Finally, when your program boxes primitive values, it can result in costly and unnecessary object creations.

Item 50: Avoid strings where other types are more appropriate

Strings are designed to represent text, and they do a fine job of it. Because strings are so common and so well supported by the language, there is a natural tendency to use strings for purposes other than those for which they were designed. This item discusses a few things that you shouldn't do with strings.

Strings are poor substitutes for other value types. When a piece of data comes into a program from a file, from the network, or from keyboard input, it is often in string form. There is a natural tendency to leave it that way, but this tendency is justified only if the data really is textual in nature. If it's numeric, it should be translated into the appropriate numeric type, such as `int`, `float`, or `BigInteger`. If it's the answer to a yes-or-no question, it should be translated into a `boolean`. More generally, if there's an appropriate value type, whether primitive or object reference, you should use it; if there isn't, you should write one. While this advice may seem obvious, it is often violated.

Strings are poor substitutes for enum types. As discussed in Item 30, enums make far better enumerated type constants than strings.

Strings are poor substitutes for aggregate types. If an entity has multiple components, it is usually a bad idea to represent it as a single string. For example, here's a line of code that comes from a real system—identifier names have been changed to protect the guilty:

```
// Inappropriate use of string as aggregate type
String compoundKey = className + "#" + i.next();
```

This approach has many disadvantages. If the character used to separate fields occurs in one of the fields, chaos may result. To access individual fields, you have to parse the string, which is slow, tedious, and error-prone. You can't provide `equals`, `toString`, or `compareTo` methods but are forced to accept the behavior that `String` provides. A better approach is simply to write a class to represent the aggregate, often a private static member class (Item 22).

Strings are poor substitutes for *capabilities*. Occasionally, strings are used to grant access to some functionality. For example, consider the design of a thread-local variable facility. Such a facility provides variables for which each thread has its own value. The Java libraries have had a thread-local variable facility since release 1.2, but prior to that, programmers had to roll their own. When confronted with the task of designing such a facility many years ago, several peo-

ple independently came up with the same design in which client-provided string
keys are used to identify each thread-local variable:

```
// Broken - inappropriate use of string as capability!
public class ThreadLocal {
    private ThreadLocal() { } // Noninstantiable

    // Sets the current thread's value for the named variable.
    public static void set(String key, Object value);

    // Returns the current thread's value for the named variable.
    public static Object get(String key);
}
```

The problem with this approach is that the string keys represent a shared glo-
bal namespace for thread-local variables. In order for the approach to work, the
client-provided string keys have to be unique: if two clients independently decide
to use the same name for their thread-local variable, they unintentionally share a
single variable, which will generally cause both clients to fail. Also, the security is
poor. A malicious client could intentionally use the same string key as another client to gain illicit access to the other client's data.

This API can be fixed by replacing the string with an unforgeable key (sometimes called a *capability*):

```
public class ThreadLocal {
    private ThreadLocal() { }  // Noninstantiable

    public static class Key {  // (Capability)
        Key() { }
    }

    // Generates a unique, unforgeable key
    public static Key getKey() {
        return new Key();
    }

    public static void set(Key key, Object value);
    public static Object get(Key key);
}
```

While this solves both of the problems with the string-based API, you can do
much better. You don't really need the static methods anymore. They can instead
become instance methods on the key, at which point the key is no longer a key for
a thread-local variable: it *is* a thread-local variable. At this point, the noninstantia-

ble top-level class isn't doing anything for you anymore, so you might as well get rid of it and rename the nested class to ThreadLocal:

```
public final class ThreadLocal {
    public ThreadLocal();
    public void set(Object value);
    public Object get();
}
```

This API isn't typesafe, because you have to cast the value from Object to its actual type when you retrieve it from a thread-local variable. It is impossible to make the original String-based API typesafe and difficult to make the Key-based API typesafe, but it is a simple matter to make this API typesafe by generifying the ThreadLocal class (Item 26):

```
public final class ThreadLocal<T> {
    public ThreadLocal();
    public void set(T value);
    public T get();
}
```

This is, roughly speaking, the API that java.lang.ThreadLocal provides. In addition to solving the problems with the string-based API, it is faster and more elegant than either of the key-based APIs.

To summarize, avoid the natural tendency to represent objects as strings when better data types exist or can be written. Used inappropriately, strings are more cumbersome, less flexible, slower, and more error-prone than other types. Types for which strings are commonly misused include primitive types, enums, and aggregate types.

Item 51: Beware the performance of string concatenation

The string concatenation operator (+) is a convenient way to combine a few strings into one. It is fine for generating a single line of output or for constructing the string representation of a small, fixed-size object, but it does not scale. **Using the string concatenation operator repeatedly to concatenate *n* strings requires time quadratic in *n*.** It is an unfortunate consequence of the fact that strings are *immutable* (Item 15). When two strings are concatenated, the contents of both are copied.

For example, consider the following method that constructs a string representation of a billing statement by repeatedly concatenating a line for each item:

```
// Inappropriate use of string concatenation - Performs horribly!
public String statement() {
    String result = "";
    for (int i = 0; i < numItems(); i++)
        result += lineForItem(i);  // String concatenation
    return result;
}
```

This method performs abysmally if the number of items is large. **To achieve acceptable performance, use a `StringBuilder` in place of a `String`** to store the statement under construction. (The `StringBuilder` class, added in release 1.5, is an unsynchronized replacement for `StringBuffer`, which is now obsolete.)

```
public String statement() {
    StringBuilder b = new StringBuilder(numItems() * LINE_WIDTH);
    for (int i = 0; i < numItems(); i++)
        b.append(lineForItem(i));
    return b.toString();
}
```

The difference in performance is dramatic. If `numItems` returns 100 and `lineForItem` returns a constant 80-character string, the second method is eighty-five times faster than the first on my machine. Because the first method is quadratic in the number of items and the second is linear, the performance difference is even more dramatic for larger numbers of items. Note that the second method preallocates a `StringBuilder` large enough to hold the result. Even if it is detuned to use a default-sized `StringBuilder`, it is still fifty times faster.

The moral is simple: don't use the string concatenation operator to combine more than a few strings unless performance is irrelevant. Use `StringBuilder`'s append method instead. Alternatively, use a character array, or process the strings one at a time instead of combining them.

Item 52: Refer to objects by their interfaces

Item 40 contains the advice that you should use interfaces rather than classes as parameter types. More generally, you should favor the use of interfaces rather than classes to refer to objects. **If appropriate interface types exist, then parameters, return values, variables, and fields should all be declared using interface types.** The only time you really need to refer to an object's class is when you're creating it with a constructor. To make this concrete, consider the case of Vector, which is an implementation of the List interface. Get in the habit of typing this:

```
// Good - uses interface as type
List<Subscriber> subscribers = new Vector<Subscriber>();
```

rather than this:

```
// Bad - uses class as type!
Vector<Subscriber> subscribers = new Vector<Subscriber>();
```

If you get into the habit of using interfaces as types, your program will be much more flexible. If you decide that you want to switch implementations, all you have to do is change the class name in the constructor (or use a different static factory). For example, the first declaration could be changed to read

```
List<Subscriber> subscribers = new ArrayList<Subscriber>();
```

and all of the surrounding code would continue to work. The surrounding code was unaware of the old implementation type, so it would be oblivious to the change.

There is one caveat: if the original implementation offered some special functionality not required by the general contract of the interface and the code depended on that functionality, then it is critical that the new implementation provide the same functionality. For example, if the code surrounding the first declaration depended on Vector's synchronization policy, then it would be incorrect to substitute ArrayList for Vector in the declaration. If you depend on any special properties of an implementation, document these requirements where you declare the variable.

So why would you want to change implementations? Because the new implementation offers better performance or because it offers desirable extra functionality. A real-world example concerns the ThreadLocal class. Internally, this class uses a package-private map field in Thread to associate per-thread values with

ThreadLocal instances. In release 1.3, this field was initialized to a HashMap instance. In release 1.4, a new, special-purpose Map implementation, called IdentityHashMap, was added to the platform. By changing a single line of code to initialize the field to an IdentityHashMap instead of a HashMap, the ThreadLocal facility was made faster. The ThreadLocal implementation has since evolved to use a highly optimized store that does not implement the Map interface, but this does nothing to diminish the point.

Had the field been declared as a HashMap instead of a Map, there is no guarantee that a single-line change would have been sufficient. If the client code had used HashMap operations that were not present on the Map interface or passed the map to a method that demanded a HashMap, the code would no longer compile if the field were changed to an IdentityHashMap. Declaring the field with the interface type "keeps you honest."

It is entirely appropriate to refer to an object by a class rather than an interface if no appropriate interface exists. For example, consider *value classes,* such as String and BigInteger. Value classes are rarely written with multiple implementations in mind. They are often final and rarely have corresponding interfaces. It is perfectly appropriate to use such a value class as a parameter, variable, field, or return type. More generally, if a concrete class has no associated interface, then you have no choice but to refer to it by its class whether or not it represents a value. The Random class falls into this category.

A second case in which there is no appropriate interface type is that of objects belonging to a framework whose fundamental types are classes rather than interfaces. If an object belongs to such a *class-based framework*, it is preferable to refer to it by the relevant *base class*, which is typically abstract, rather than by its implementation class. The java.util.TimerTask class falls into this category.

A final case in which there is no appropriate interface type is that of classes that implement an interface but provide extra methods not found in the interface—for example, PriorityQueue. Such a class should be used to refer to its instances only if the program relies on the extra methods. It should rarely be used as a parameter type (Item 40).

These cases are not meant to be exhaustive but merely to convey the flavor of situations where it is appropriate to refer to an object by its class. In practice, it should be apparent whether a given object has an appropriate interface. If it does, your program will be more flexible if you use the interface to refer to the object; if not, just use the least specific class in the class hierarchy that provides the required functionality.

Item 53: Prefer interfaces to reflection

The *core reflection facility*, `java.lang.reflect`, offers programmatic access to information about loaded classes. Given a `Class` object, you can obtain `Constructor`, `Method`, and `Field` instances representing the constructors, methods, and fields of the class represented by the `Class` instance. These objects provide programmatic access to the class's member names, field types, method signatures, and so on.

Moreover, `Constructor`, `Method`, and `Field` instances let you manipulate their underlying counterparts *reflectively*: you can construct instances, invoke methods, and access fields of the underlying class by invoking methods on the `Constructor`, `Method`, and `Field` instances. For example, `Method.invoke` lets you invoke any method on any object of any class (subject to the usual security constraints). Reflection allows one class to use another, even if the latter class did not exist when the former was compiled. This power, however, comes at a price:

- **You lose all the benefits of compile-time type checking,** including exception checking. If a program attempts to invoke a nonexistent or inaccessible method reflectively, it will fail at runtime unless you've taken special precautions.

- **The code required to perform reflective access is clumsy and verbose**. It is tedious to write and difficult to read.

- **Performance suffers**. Reflective method invocation is much slower than normal method invocation. Exactly how much slower is hard to say, because there are so many factors at work. On my machine, the speed difference can be as small as a factor of two or as large as a factor of fifty.

The core reflection facility was originally designed for component-based application builder tools. Such tools generally load classes on demand and use reflection to find out what methods and constructors they support. The tools let their users interactively construct applications that access these classes, but the generated applications access the classes normally, not reflectively. Reflection is used only at *design time*. **As a rule, objects should not be accessed reflectively in normal applications at runtime.**

There are a few sophisticated applications that require reflection. Examples include class browsers, object inspectors, code analysis tools, and interpretive embedded systems. Reflection is also appropriate for use in remote procedure call (RPC) systems to eliminate the need for stub compilers. If you have any doubts as to whether your application falls into one of these categories, it probably doesn't.

You can obtain many of the benefits of reflection while incurring few of its costs by using it only in a very limited form. For many programs that must use a class that is unavailable at compile time, there exists at compile time an appropriate interface or superclass by which to refer to the class (Item 52). If this is the case, you can **create instances reflectively and access them normally via their interface or superclass**. If the appropriate constructor has no parameters, then you don't even need to use java.lang.reflect; the Class.newInstance method provides the required functionality.

For example, here's a program that creates a Set<String> instance whose class is specified by the first command line argument. The program inserts the remaining command line arguments into the set and prints it. Regardless of the first argument, the program prints the remaining arguments with duplicates eliminated. The order in which these arguments are printed, however, depends on the class specified in the first argument. If you specify java.util.HashSet, they're printed in apparently random order; if you specify java.util.TreeSet, they're printed in alphabetical order, as the elements in a TreeSet are sorted:

```
// Reflective instantiation with interface access
public static void main(String[] args) {
    // Translate the class name into a Class object
    Class<?> cl = null;
    try {
        cl = Class.forName(args[0]);
    } catch(ClassNotFoundException e) {
        System.err.println("Class not found.");
        System.exit(1);
    }

    // Instantiate the class
    Set<String> s = null;
    try {
        s = (Set<String>) cl.newInstance();
    } catch(IllegalAccessException e) {
        System.err.println("Class not accessible.");
        System.exit(1);
    } catch(InstantiationException e) {
        System.err.println("Class not instantiable.");
        System.exit(1);
    }

    // Exercise the set
    s.addAll(Arrays.asList(args).subList(1, args.length));
    System.out.println(s);
}
```

While this program is just a toy, the technique it demonstrates is very powerful. The toy program could easily be turned into a generic set tester that validates the specified Set implementation by aggressively manipulating one or more instances and checking that they obey the Set contract. Similarly, it could be turned into a generic set performance analysis tool. In fact, the technique is sufficiently powerful to implement a full-blown *service provider framework* (Item 1). Most of the time, this technique is all that you need in the way of reflection.

This example demonstrates two disadvantages of reflection. First, the example can generate three runtime errors, all of which would have been compile-time errors if reflective instantiation were not used. Second, it takes twenty lines of tedious code to generate an instance of the class from its name, whereas a constructor invocation would fit neatly on a single line. These disadvantages are, however, restricted to the part of the program that instantiates the object. Once instantiated, it is indistinguishable from any other Set instance. In a real program, the great bulk of the code is thus unaffected by this limited use of reflection.

If you try compiling the program, you'll get the following error message:

```
Note: MakeSet.java uses unchecked or unsafe operations.
Note: Recompile with -Xlint:unchecked for details.
```

This warning concerns the program's use of generic types, but it does not indicate a real problem. To learn the best way to suppress the warning, see Item 24.

Another tangential issue that deserves note is this program's use of System.exit. It is rarely appropriate to call this method, which terminates the entire VM. It is, however, appropriate for abnormal termination of a command line utility.

A legitimate, if rare, use of reflection is to manage a class's dependencies on other classes, methods, or fields that may be absent at runtime. This can be useful if you are writing a package that must run against multiple versions of some other package. The technique is to compile your package against the minimal environment required to support it, typically the oldest version, and to access any newer classes or methods reflectively. To make this work, you have to take appropriate action if a newer class or method that you are attempting to access does not exist at runtime. Appropriate action might consist of using some alternate means to accomplish the same goal or operating with reduced functionality.

In summary, reflection is a powerful facility that is required for certain sophisticated system programming tasks, but it has many disadvantages. If you are writing a program that has to work with classes unknown at compile time, you should, if at all possible, use reflection only to instantiate objects, and access the objects using some interface or superclass that is known at compile time.

Item 54: Use native methods judiciously

The Java Native Interface (JNI) allows Java applications to call *native methods*, which are special methods written in *native programming languages* such as C or C++. Native methods can perform arbitrary computation in native languages before returning to the Java programming language.

Historically, native methods have had three main uses. They provided access to platform-specific facilities such as registries and file locks. They provided access to libraries of legacy code, which could in turn provide access to legacy data. Finally, native methods were used to write performance-critical parts of applications in native languages for improved performance.

It is legitimate to use native methods to access platform-specific facilities, but as the Java platform matures, it provides more and more features previously found only in host platforms. For example, `java.util.prefs`, added in release 1.4, offers the functionality of a registry, and `java.awt.SystemTray`, added in release 1.6, offers access to the desktop system tray area. It is also legitimate to use native methods to access legacy code.

It is rarely advisable to use native methods for improved performance. In early releases (prior to 1.3), it was often necessary, but JVM implementations have gotten *much* faster. For most tasks, it is now possible to obtain comparable performance without resorting to native methods. For example, when `java.math` was added to the platform in release 1.1, `BigInteger` was implemented atop a fast multiprecision arithmetic library written in C. At the time, this was necessary for adequate performance. In release 1.3, `BigInteger` was rewritten entirely in Java and carefully tuned. Even then, the new version was faster than the original, and VMs have become much faster in the intervening years.

The use of native methods has serious disadvantages. Because native languages are not *safe* (Item 39), applications using native methods are no longer immune to memory corruption errors. Because native languages are platform dependent, applications using native methods are far less portable. Applications using native code are far more difficult to debug. There is a fixed cost associated with going into and out of native code, so native methods can *decrease* performance if they do only a small amount of work. Finally, native methods require "glue code" that is difficult to read and tedious to write.

In summary, think twice before using native methods. Rarely, if ever, use them for improved performance. If you must use native methods to access low-level resources or legacy libraries, use as little native code as possible and test it thoroughly. A single bug in the native code can corrupt your entire application.

Item 55: Optimize judiciously

There are three aphorisms concerning optimization that everyone should know. They are perhaps beginning to suffer from overexposure, but in case you aren't yet familiar with them, here they are:

> More computing sins are committed in the name of efficiency (without necessarily achieving it) than for any other single reason—including blind stupidity.
> —William A. Wulf [Wulf72]

> We *should* forget about small efficiencies, say about 97% of the time: premature optimization is the root of all evil.
> —Donald E. Knuth [Knuth74]

> We follow two rules in the matter of optimization:
> Rule 1. Don't do it.
> Rule 2 (for experts only). Don't do it yet—that is, not until you have a perfectly clear and unoptimized solution.
> —M. A. Jackson [Jackson75]

All of these aphorisms predate the Java programming language by two decades. They tell a deep truth about optimization: it is easy to do more harm than good, especially if you optimize prematurely. In the process, you may produce software that is neither fast nor correct and cannot easily be fixed.

Don't sacrifice sound architectural principles for performance. **Strive to write good programs rather than fast ones**. If a good program is not fast enough, its architecture will allow it to be optimized. Good programs embody the principle of *information hiding*: where possible, they localize design decisions within individual modules, so individual decisions can be changed without affecting the remainder of the system (Item 13).

This does *not* mean that you can ignore performance concerns until your program is complete. Implementation problems can be fixed by later optimization, but pervasive architectural flaws that limit performance can be impossible to fix without rewriting the system. Changing a fundamental facet of your design after the fact can result in an ill-structured system that is difficult to maintain and evolve. Therefore you must think about performance during the design process.

Strive to avoid design decisions that limit performance. The components of a design that are most difficult to change after the fact are those specifying interactions between modules and with the outside world. Chief among these design components are APIs, wire-level protocols, and persistent data formats. Not only are these design components difficult or impossible to change after the fact, but all of them can place significant limitations on the performance that a system can ever achieve.

Consider the performance consequences of your API design decisions. Making a public type mutable may require a lot of needless defensive copying (Item 39). Similarly, using inheritance in a public class where composition would have been appropriate ties the class forever to its superclass, which can place artificial limits on the performance of the subclass (Item 16). As a final example, using an implementation type rather than an interface in an API ties you to a specific implementation, even though faster implementations may be written in the future (Item 52).

The effects of API design on performance are very real. Consider the getSize method in the java.awt.Component class. The decision that this performance-critical method was to return a Dimension instance, coupled with the decision that Dimension instances are mutable, forces any implementation of this method to allocate a new Dimension instance on every invocation. Even though allocating small objects is inexpensive on a modern VM, allocating millions of objects needlessly can do real harm to performance.

In this case, several alternatives existed. Ideally, Dimension should have been immutable (Item 15); alternatively, the getSize method could have been replaced by two methods returning the individual primitive components of a Dimension object. In fact, two such methods were added to the Component API in the 1.2 release for performance reasons. Preexisting client code, however, still uses the getSize method and still suffers the performance consequences of the original API design decisions.

Luckily, it is generally the case that good API design is consistent with good performance. **It is a very bad idea to warp an API to achieve good performance**. The performance issue that caused you to warp the API may go away in a future release of the platform or other underlying software, but the warped API and the support headaches that come with it will be with you for life.

Once you've carefully designed your program and produced a clear, concise, and well-structured implementation, *then* it may be time to consider optimization, assuming you're not already satisfied with the performance of the program.

Recall that Jackson's two rules of optimization were "Don't do it," and "(for experts only). Don't do it yet." He could have added one more: **measure performance before and after each attempted optimization.** You may be surprised by what you find. Often, attempted optimizations have no measurable effect on performance; sometimes, they make it worse. The main reason is that it's difficult to guess where your program is spending its time. The part of the program that you think is slow may not be at fault, in which case you'd be wasting your time trying to optimize it. Common wisdom says that programs spend 80 percent of their time in 20 percent of their code.

Profiling tools can help you decide where to focus your optimization efforts. Such tools give you runtime information, such as roughly how much time each method is consuming and how many times it is invoked. In addition to focusing your tuning efforts, this can alert you to the need for algorithmic changes. If a quadratic (or worse) algorithm lurks inside your program, no amount of tuning will fix the problem. You must replace the algorithm with one that is more efficient. The more code in the system, the more important it is to use a profiler. It's like looking for a needle in a haystack: the bigger the haystack, the more useful it is to have a metal detector. The JDK comes with a simple profiler and modern IDEs provide more sophisticated profiling tools.

The need to measure the effects of attempted optimization is even greater on the Java platform than on more traditional platforms, because the Java programming language does not have a strong *performance model*. The relative costs of the various primitive operations are not well defined. The "semantic gap" between what the programmer writes and what the CPU executes is far greater than in traditional statically compiled languages, which makes it very difficult to reliably predict the performance consequences of any optimization. There are plenty of performance myths floating around that turn out to be half-truths or outright lies.

Not only is Java's performance model ill-defined, but it varies from JVM implementation to JVM implementation, from release to release, and from processor to processor. If you will be running your program on multiple JVM implementations or multiple hardware platforms, it is important that you measure the effects of your optimization on each. Occasionally you may be forced to make trade-offs between performance on different JVM implementations or hardware platforms.

To summarize, do not strive to write fast programs—strive to write good ones; speed will follow. Do think about performance issues while you're designing systems and especially while you're designing APIs, wire-level protocols, and persistent data formats. When you've finished building the system, measure its performance. If it's fast enough, you're done. If not, locate the source of the problems with the aid of a profiler, and go to work optimizing the relevant parts of the system. The first step is to examine your choice of algorithms: no amount of low-level optimization can make up for a poor choice of algorithm. Repeat this process as necessary, measuring the performance after every change, until you're satisfied.

Item 56: Adhere to generally accepted naming conventions

The Java platform has a well-established set of *naming conventions*, many of which are contained in *The Java Language Specification* [JLS, 6.8]. Loosely speaking, naming conventions fall into two categories: typographical and grammatical.

There are only a handful of typographical naming conventions, covering packages, classes, interfaces, methods, fields, and type variables. You should rarely violate them and never without a very good reason. If an API violates these conventions, it may be difficult to use. If an implementation violates them, it may be difficult to maintain. In both cases, violations have the potential to confuse and irritate other programmers who work with the code and can cause faulty assumptions that lead to errors. The conventions are summarized in this item.

Package names should be hierarchical with the components separated by periods. Components should consist of lowercase alphabetic characters and, rarely, digits. The name of any package that will be used outside your organization should begin with your organization's Internet domain name with the top-level domain first, for example, `edu.cmu`, `com.sun`, `gov.nsa`. The standard libraries and optional packages, whose names begin with `java` and `javax`, are exceptions to this rule. Users must not create packages whose names begin with `java` or `javax`. Detailed rules for converting Internet domain names to package name prefixes can be found in *The Java Language Specification* [JLS, 7.7].

The remainder of a package name should consist of one or more components describing the package. Components should be short, generally eight or fewer characters. Meaningful abbreviations are encouraged, for example, `util` rather than `utilities`. Acronyms are acceptable, for example, `awt`. Components should generally consist of a single word or abbreviation.

Many packages have names with just one component in addition to the Internet domain name. Additional components are appropriate for large facilities whose size demands that they be broken up into an informal hierarchy. For example, the `javax.swing` package has a rich hierarchy of packages with names such as `javax.swing.plaf.metal`. Such packages are known as subpackages, although there is no linguistic support for package hierarchies.

Class and interface names, including enum and annotation type names, should consist of one or more words, with the first letter of each word capitalized, for example, `Timer` or `FutureTask`. Abbreviations are to be avoided, except for acronyms and certain common abbreviations like `max` and `min`. There is little consensus as to whether acronyms should be uppercase or have only their first letter capitalized. While uppercase may be more common, a strong argument can be made in favor of capitalizing only the first letter: even if multiple acronyms occur back-to-back, you can still tell where one word starts and the next word ends. Which class name would you rather see, HTTPURL or HttpUrl?

Method and field names follow the same typographical conventions as class and interface names, except that the first letter of a method or field name should be lowercase, for example, remove or ensureCapacity. If an acronym occurs as the first word of a method or field name, it should be lowercase.

The sole exception to the previous rule concerns "constant fields," whose names should consist of one or more uppercase words separated by the underscore character, for example, VALUES or NEGATIVE_INFINITY. A constant field is a static final field whose value is immutable. If a static final field has a primitive type or an immutable reference type (Item 15), then it is a constant field. For example, enum constants are constant fields. If a static final field has a mutable reference type, it can still be a constant field if the referenced object is immutable. Note that constant fields constitute the *only* recommended use of underscores.

Local variable names have similar typographical naming conventions to member names, except that abbreviations are permitted, as are individual characters and short sequences of characters whose meaning depends on the context in which the local variable occurs, for example, i, xref, houseNumber.

Type parameter names usually consist of a single letter. Most commonly it is one of these five: T for an arbitrary type, E for the element type of a collection, K and V for the key and value types of a map, and X for an exception. A sequence of arbitrary types can be T, U, V or T1, T2, T3.

For quick reference, the following table shows examples of typographical conventions.

Identifier Type	Examples
Package	com.google.inject, org.joda.time.format
Class or Interface	Timer, FutureTask, LinkedHashMap, HttpServlet
Method or Field	remove, ensureCapacity, getCrc
Constant Field	MIN_VALUE, NEGATIVE_INFINITY
Local Variable	i, xref, houseNumber
Type Parameter	T, E, K, V, X, T1, T2

Grammatical naming conventions are more flexible and more controversial than typographical conventions. There are no grammatical naming conventions to speak of for packages. Classes, including enum types, are generally named with a singular noun or noun phrase, for example, `Timer`, `BufferedWriter`, or `ChessPiece`. Interfaces are named like classes, for example, `Collection` or `Comparator`, or with an adjective ending in `able` or `ible`, for example, `Runnable`, `Iterable`, or `Accessible`. Because annotation types have so many uses, no part of speech predominates. Nouns, verbs, prepositions, and adjectives are all common, for example, `BindingAnnotation`, `Inject`, `ImplementedBy`, or `Singleton`.

Methods that perform some action are generally named with a verb or verb phrase (including object), for example, `append` or `drawImage`. Methods that return a `boolean` value usually have names that begin with the word `is` or, less commonly, `has`, followed by a noun, noun phrase, or any word or phrase that functions as an adjective, for example, `isDigit`, `isProbablePrime`, `isEmpty`, `isEnabled`, or `hasSiblings`.

Methods that return a non-`boolean` function or attribute of the object on which they're invoked are usually named with a noun, a noun phrase, or a verb phrase beginning with the verb `get`, for example, `size`, `hashCode`, or `getTime`. There is a vocal contingent that claims that only the third form (beginning with `get`) is acceptable, but there is little basis for this claim. The first two forms usually lead to more readable code, for example:

```
if (car.speed() > 2 * SPEED_LIMIT)
    generateAudibleAlert("Watch out for cops!");
```

The form beginning with `get` is mandatory if the class containing the method is a *Bean* [JavaBeans], and it's advisable if you're considering turning the class into a Bean at a later time. Also, there is strong precedent for this form if the class contains a method to set the same attribute. In this case, the two methods should be named `get`*Attribute* and `set`*Attribute*.

A few method names deserve special mention. Methods that convert the type of an object, returning an independent object of a different type, are often called `to`*Type*, for example, `toString`, `toArray`. Methods that return a *view* (Item 5) whose type differs from that of the receiving object are often called `as`*Type*, for example, `asList`. Methods that return a primitive with the same value as the object on which they're invoked are often called *type*`Value`, for example, `intValue`. Common names for static factories are `valueOf`, `of`, `getInstance`, `newInstance`, `get`*Type*, and `new`*Type* (Item 1, page 10).

Grammatical conventions for field names are less well established and less important than those for class, interface, and method names, as well-designed APIs contain few if any exposed fields. Fields of type `boolean` are often named like `boolean` accessor methods with the initial `is` omitted, for example, `initialized`, `composite`. Fields of other types are usually named with nouns or noun phrases, such as `height`, `digits`, or `bodyStyle`. Grammatical conventions for local variables are similar to those for fields, but even weaker.

To summarize, internalize the standard naming conventions and learn to use them as second nature. The typographical conventions are straightforward and largely unambiguous; the grammatical conventions are more complex and looser. To quote from *The Java Language Specification* [JLS, 6.8], "These conventions should not be followed slavishly if long-held conventional usage dictates otherwise." Use common sense.

CHAPTER 9

Exceptions

WHEN used to best advantage, exceptions can improve a program's readability, reliability, and maintainability. When used improperly, they can have the opposite effect. This chapter provides guidelines for using exceptions effectively.

Item 57: Use exceptions only for exceptional conditions

Someday, if you are unlucky, you may stumble across a piece of code that looks something like this:

```
// Horrible abuse of exceptions. Don't ever do this!
try {
    int i = 0;
    while(true)
        range[i++].climb();
} catch(ArrayIndexOutOfBoundsException e) {
}
```

What does this code do? It's not at all obvious from inspection, and that's reason enough not to use it (Item 55). It turns out to be a horribly ill-conceived idiom for looping through the elements of an array. The infinite loop terminates by throwing, catching, and ignoring an `ArrayIndexOutOfBoundsException` when it attempts to access the first array element outside the bounds of the array. It's supposed to be equivalent to the standard idiom for looping through an array, which is instantly recognizable to any Java programmer:

```
for (Mountain m : range)
    m.climb();
```

So why would anyone use the exception-based loop in preference to the tried and true? It's a misguided attempt to improve performance based on the faulty reasoning that, since the VM checks the bounds of all array accesses, the normal loop termination test—hidden by the compiler but still present in the for-each loop—is redundant and should be avoided. There are three things wrong with this reasoning:

- Because exceptions are designed for exceptional circumstances, there is little incentive for JVM implementors to make them as fast as explicit tests.

- Placing code inside a `try-catch` block inhibits certain optimizations that modern JVM implementations might otherwise perform.

- The standard idiom for looping through an array doesn't necessarily result in redundant checks. Modern JVM implementations optimize them away.

In fact, the exception-based idiom is far slower than the standard one on modern JVM implementations. On my machine, the exception-based idiom is more than twice as slow as the standard one for arrays of one hundred elements.

Not only does the exception-based loop obfuscate the purpose of the code and reduce its performance, but it's not guaranteed to work! In the presence of an unrelated bug, the loop can fail silently and mask the bug, greatly complicating the debugging process. Suppose the computation in the body of the loop invokes a method that performs an out-of-bounds access to some unrelated array. If a reasonable loop idiom were used, the bug would generate an uncaught exception, resulting in immediate thread termination with a full stack trace. If the misguided exception-based loop were used, the bug-related exception would be caught and misinterpreted as a normal loop termination.

The moral of this story is simple: **exceptions are, as their name implies, to be used only for exceptional conditions; they should never be used for ordinary control flow.** More generally, you should use standard, easily recognizable idioms in preference to overly clever techniques that purport to offer better performance. Even if the performance advantage is real, it may not remain in the face of steadily improving platform implementations. The subtle bugs and maintenance headaches that come from overly clever techniques, however, are sure to remain.

This principle also has implications for API design. **A well-designed API must not force its clients to use exceptions for ordinary control flow.** A class with a "state-dependent" method that can be invoked only under certain unpredictable conditions should generally have a separate "state-testing" method indicating whether it is appropriate to invoke the state-dependent method. For example, the `Iterator` interface has the state-dependent method `next` and the corresponding state-testing method `hasNext`. This enables the standard idiom for iterating over a collection with a traditional for loop (as well as the for-each loop, where the has-Next method is used internally):

```
for (Iterator<Foo> i = collection.iterator(); i.hasNext(); ) {
    Foo foo = i.next();
    ...
}
```

If Iterator lacked the hasNext method, clients would be forced to do this instead:

```
// Do not use this hideous code for iteration over a collection!
try {
    Iterator<Foo> i = collection.iterator();
    while(true) {
        Foo foo = i.next();
        ...
    }
} catch (NoSuchElementException e) {
}
```

This should look very familiar after the array iteration example that began this item. In addition to being wordy and misleading, the exception-based loop is likely to perform poorly and can mask bugs in unrelated parts of the system.

An alternative to providing a separate state-testing method is to have the state-dependent method return a distinguished value such as null if it is invoked with the object in an inappropriate state. This technique would not be appropriate for Iterator, as null is a legitimate return value for the next method.

Here are some guidelines to help you choose between a state-testing method and a distinguished return value. If an object is to be accessed concurrently without external synchronization or is subject to externally induced state transitions, you must use a distinguished return value, as the object's state could change in the interval between the invocation of a state-testing method and its state-dependent method. Performance concerns may dictate that a distinguished return value be used if a separate state-testing method would duplicate the work of the state-dependent method. All other things being equal, a state-testing method is mildly preferable to a distinguished return value. It offers slightly better readability, and incorrect use may be easier to detect: if you forget to call a state-testing method, the state-dependent method will throw an exception, making the bug obvious; if you forget to check for a distinguished return value, the bug may be subtle.

In summary, exceptions are designed for use in exceptional conditions. Don't use them for ordinary control flow, and don't write APIs that force others to do so.

Item 58: Use checked exceptions for recoverable conditions and runtime exceptions for programming errors

The Java programming language provides three kinds of throwables: *checked exceptions*, *runtime exceptions*, and *errors*. There is some confusion among programmers as to when it is appropriate to use each kind of throwable. While the decision is not always clear-cut, there are some general rules that provide strong guidance.

The cardinal rule in deciding whether to use a checked or an unchecked exception is this: **use checked exceptions for conditions from which the caller can reasonably be expected to recover.** By throwing a checked exception, you force the caller to handle the exception in a catch clause or to propagate it outward. Each checked exception that a method is declared to throw is therefore a potent indication to the API user that the associated condition is a possible outcome of invoking the method.

By confronting the API user with a checked exception, the API designer presents a mandate to recover from the condition. The user can disregard the mandate by catching the exception and ignoring it, but this is usually a bad idea (Item 65).

There are two kinds of unchecked throwables: runtime exceptions and errors. They are identical in their behavior: both are throwables that needn't, and generally shouldn't, be caught. If a program throws an unchecked exception or an error, it is generally the case that recovery is impossible and continued execution would do more harm than good. If a program does not catch such a throwable, it will cause the current thread to halt with an appropriate error message.

Use runtime exceptions to indicate programming errors. The great majority of runtime exceptions indicate *precondition violations*. A precondition violation is simply a failure by the client of an API to adhere to the contract established by the API specification. For example, the contract for array access specifies that the array index must be between zero and the array length minus one. ArrayIndexOutOfBoundsException indicates that this precondition was violated.

While the Java Language Specification does not require it, there is a strong convention that errors are reserved for use by the JVM to indicate resource deficiencies, invariant failures, or other conditions that make it impossible to continue execution. Given the almost universal acceptance of this convention, it's best not to implement any new Error subclasses. Therefore, **all of the unchecked throwables you implement should subclass RuntimeException** (directly or indirectly).

It is possible to define a throwable that is not a subclass of Exception, RuntimeException, or Error. The JLS does not address such throwables directly but specifies implicitly that they are behaviorally identical to ordinary checked exceptions (which are subclasses of `Exception` but not `RuntimeException`). So when should you use such a beast? In a word, never. It has no benefits over an ordinary checked exception and would merely serve to confuse the user of your API.

To summarize, use checked exceptions for recoverable conditions and runtime exceptions for programming errors. Of course, the situation is not always black and white. For example, consider the case of resource exhaustion, which can be caused by a programming error such as allocating an unreasonably large array or by a genuine shortage of resources. If resource exhaustion is caused by a temporary shortage or by temporarily heightened demand, the condition may well be recoverable. It is a matter of judgment on the part of the API designer whether a given instance of resource exhaustion is likely to allow for recovery. If you believe a condition is likely to allow for recovery, use a checked exception; if not, use a runtime exception. If it isn't clear whether recovery is possible, you're probably better off using an unchecked exception, for reasons discussed in Item 59.

API designers often forget that exceptions are full-fledged objects on which arbitrary methods can be defined. The primary use of such methods is to provide the code that catches the exception with additional information concerning the condition that caused the exception to be thrown. In the absence of such methods, programmers have been known to parse the string representation of an exception to ferret out additional information. This is extremely bad practice (Item 10). Classes seldom specify the details of their string representations, so string representations can differ from implementation to implementation and release to release. Therefore, code that parses the string representation of an exception is likely to be nonportable and fragile.

Because checked exceptions generally indicate recoverable conditions, it's especially important for such exceptions to provide methods that furnish information that could help the caller to recover. For example, suppose a checked exception is thrown when an attempt to make a purchase with a gift card fails because the card doesn't have enough money left on it. The exception should provide an accessor method to query the amount of the shortfall, so the amount can be relayed to the shopper.

Item 59: Avoid unnecessary use of checked exceptions

Checked exceptions are a wonderful feature of the Java programming language. Unlike return codes, they *force* the programmer to deal with exceptional conditions, greatly enhancing reliability. That said, overuse of checked exceptions can make an API far less pleasant to use. If a method throws one or more checked exceptions, the code that invokes the method must handle the exceptions in one or more `catch` blocks, or it must declare that it throws the exceptions and let them propagate outward. Either way, it places a nontrivial burden on the programmer.

The burden is justified if the exceptional condition cannot be prevented by proper use of the API *and* the programmer using the API can take some useful action once confronted with the exception. Unless both of these conditions hold, an unchecked exception is more appropriate. As a litmus test, ask yourself how the programmer will handle the exception. Is this the best that can be done?

```
} catch(TheCheckedException e) {
    throw new AssertionError(); // Can't happen!
}
```

How about this?

```
} catch(TheCheckedException e) {
    e.printStackTrace();        // Oh well, we lose.
    System.exit(1);
}
```

If the programmer using the API can do no better, an unchecked exception would be more appropriate. One example of an exception that fails this test is `CloneNotSupportedException`. It is thrown by `Object.clone`, which should be invoked only on objects that implement `Cloneable` (Item 11). In practice, the `catch` block almost always has the character of an assertion failure. The checked nature of the exception provides no benefit to the programmer, but it requires effort and complicates programs.

The additional burden on the programmer caused by a checked exception is substantially higher if it is the *sole* checked exception thrown by a method. If there are others, the method must already appear in a `try` block, and this exception merely requires another `catch` block. If a method throws a single checked exception, this exception alone is responsible for the fact that the method must appear in a `try` block. Under these circumstances, it pays to ask yourself whether there isn't some way to avoid the checked exception.

One technique for turning a checked exception into an unchecked exception is to break the method that throws the exception into two methods, the first of which returns a `boolean` that indicates whether the exception would be thrown. This API refactoring transforms the calling sequence from this:

```
// Invocation with checked exception
try {
    obj.action(args);
} catch(TheCheckedException e) {
    // Handle exceptional condition
    ...
}
```

to this:

```
// Invocation with state-testing method and unchecked exception
if (obj.actionPermitted(args)) {
    obj.action(args);
} else {
    // Handle exceptional condition
    ...
}
```

This refactoring is not always appropriate, but where it is appropriate, it can make an API more pleasant to use. While the latter calling sequence is no prettier than the former, the resulting API is more flexible. In cases where the programmer knows the call will succeed or is content to let the thread terminate if the call fails, the refactoring also allows this simple calling sequence:

```
obj.action(args);
```

If you suspect that the simple calling sequence will be the norm, then this API refactoring may be appropriate. The API resulting from this refactoring is essentially identical to the state-testing method API in Item 57 and the same caveats apply: if an object is to be accessed concurrently without external synchronization or it is subject to externally induced state transitions, this refactoring is inappropriate, as the object's state may change between the invocations of `actionPermitted` and `action`. If a separate `actionPermitted` method would, of necessity, duplicate the work of the `action` method, the refactoring may be ruled out by performance concerns.

Item 60: Favor the use of standard exceptions

One of the attributes that most strongly distinguishes expert programmers from less experienced ones is that experts strive for and usually achieve a high degree of code reuse. Exceptions are no exception to the general rule that code reuse is good. The Java platform libraries provide a basic set of unchecked exceptions that cover a large fraction of the exception-throwing needs of most APIs. In this item, we'll discuss these commonly reused exceptions.

Reusing preexisting exceptions has several benefits. Chief among these, it makes your API easier to learn and use because it matches established conventions with which programmers are already familiar. A close second is that programs using your API are easier to read because they aren't cluttered with unfamiliar exceptions. Last (and least), fewer exception classes mean a smaller memory footprint and less time spent loading classes.

The most commonly reused exception is `IllegalArgumentException`. This is generally the exception to throw when the caller passes in an argument whose value is inappropriate. For example, this would be the exception to throw if the caller passed a negative number in a parameter representing the number of times some action was to be repeated.

Another commonly reused exception is `IllegalStateException`. This is generally the exception to throw if the invocation is illegal because of the state of the receiving object. For example, this would be the exception to throw if the caller attempted to use some object before it had been properly initialized.

Arguably, all erroneous method invocations boil down to an illegal argument or illegal state, but other exceptions are standardly used for certain kinds of illegal arguments and states. If a caller passes `null` in some parameter for which null values are prohibited, convention dictates that `NullPointerException` be thrown rather than `IllegalArgumentException`. Similarly, if a caller passes an out-of-range value in a parameter representing an index into a sequence, `IndexOutOf-BoundsException` should be thrown rather than `IllegalArgumentException`.

Another general-purpose exception worth knowing about is `ConcurrentMod-ificationException`. This exception should be thrown if an object that was designed for use by a single thread or with external synchronization detects that it is being (or has been) concurrently modified.

A last general-purpose exception worthy of note is `UnsupportedOperation-Exception`. This is the exception to throw if an object does not support an attempted operation. Its use is rare compared to the other exceptions discussed in this item, as most objects support all the methods they implement. This exception is used by implementations that fail to implement one or more optional operations defined by an interface. For example, an append-only `List` implementation would throw this exception if someone tried to delete an element from the list.

This table summarizes the most commonly reused exceptions:

Exception	Occasion for Use
IllegalArgumentException	Non-null parameter value is inappropriate
IllegalStateException	Object state is inappropriate for method invocation
NullPointerException	Parameter value is null where prohibited
IndexOutOfBoundsException	Index parameter value is out of range
ConcurrentModificationException	Concurrent modification of an object has been detected where it is prohibited
UnsupportedOperationException	Object does not support method

While these are by far the most commonly reused exceptions in the Java platform libraries, other exceptions may be reused where circumstances warrant. For example, it would be appropriate to reuse `ArithmeticException` and `NumberFormatException` if you were implementing arithmetic objects such as complex numbers or rational numbers. If an exception fits your needs, go ahead and use it, but only if the conditions under which you would throw it are consistent with the exception's documentation. Reuse must be based on semantics, not just on name. Also, feel free to subclass an existing exception if you want to add a bit more failure-capture information (Item 63).

Finally, be aware that choosing which exception to reuse is not always an exact science, as the occasions for use in the table above are not mutually exclusive. Consider, for example, the case of an object representing a deck of cards. Suppose there were a method to deal a hand from the deck that took as an argument the size of the hand. Suppose the caller passed in this parameter a value that was larger than the number of cards remaining in the deck. This could be construed as an `IllegalArgumentException` (the `handSize` parameter value is too high) or an `IllegalStateException` (the deck object contains too few cards for the request). In this case the `IllegalArgumentException` feels right, but there are no hard-and-fast rules.

Item 61: Throw exceptions appropriate to the abstraction

It is disconcerting when a method throws an exception that has no apparent connection to the task that it performs. This often happens when a method propagates an exception thrown by a lower-level abstraction. Not only is this disconcerting, but it pollutes the API of the higher layer with implementation details. If the implementation of the higher layer changes in a subsequent release, the exceptions that it throws will change too, potentially breaking existing client programs.

To avoid this problem, **higher layers should catch lower-level exceptions and, in their place, throw exceptions that can be explained in terms of the higher-level abstraction.** This idiom is known as *exception translation*:

```
// Exception Translation
try {
    // Use lower-level abstraction to do our bidding
    ...
} catch(LowerLevelException e) {
    throw new HigherLevelException(...);
}
```

Here is an example of exception translation taken from the `AbstractSequentialList` class, which is a *skeletal implementation* (Item 18) of the `List` interface. In this example, exception translation is mandated by the specification of the `get` method in the `List<E>` interface:

```
/**
 * Returns the element at the specified position in this list.
 * @throws IndexOutOfBoundsException if the index is out of range
 *         ({@code index < 0 || index >= size()}).
 */
public E get(int index) {
    ListIterator<E> i = listIterator(index);
    try {
        return i.next();
    } catch(NoSuchElementException e) {
        throw new IndexOutOfBoundsException("Index: " + index);
    }
}
```

A special form of exception translation called *exception chaining* is appropriate in cases where the lower-level exception might be helpful to someone debugging the problem that caused the higher-level exception. The lower-level exception (the *cause*) is passed to the higher-level exception, which provides an accessor method (`Throwable.getCause`) to retrieve the lower-level exception:

```
// Exception Chaining
try {
    ...  // Use lower-level abstraction to do our bidding
} catch (LowerLevelException cause) {
    throw new HigherLevelException(cause);
}
```

The higher-level exception's constructor passes the cause to a *chaining-aware* superclass constructor, so it is ultimately passed to one of `Throwable`'s chaining-aware constructors, such as `Throwable(Throwable)`:

```
// Exception with chaining-aware constructor
class HigherLevelException extends Exception {
    HigherLevelException(Throwable cause) {
        super(cause);
    }
}
```

Most standard exceptions have chaining-aware constructors. For exceptions that don't, you can set the cause using `Throwable`'s `initCause` method. Not only does exception chaining let you access the cause programmatically (with `getCause`), but it integrates the cause's stack trace into that of the higher-level exception.

While exception translation is superior to mindless propagation of exceptions from lower layers, it should not be overused. Where possible, the best way to deal with exceptions from lower layers is to avoid them, by ensuring that lower-level methods succeed. Sometimes you can do this by checking the validity of the higher-level method's parameters before passing them on to lower layers.

If it is impossible to prevent exceptions from lower layers, the next best thing is to have the higher layer silently work around these exceptions, insulating the caller of the higher-level method from lower-level problems. Under these circumstances, it may be appropriate to log the exception using some appropriate logging facility such as `java.util.logging`. This allows an administrator to investigate the problem, while insulating the client code and the end user from it.

In summary, if it isn't feasible to prevent or to handle exceptions from lower layers, use exception translation, unless the lower-level method happens to guarantee that all of its exceptions are appropriate to the higher level. Chaining provides the best of both worlds: it allows you to throw an appropriate higher-level exception, while capturing the underlying cause for failure analysis (Item 63).

Item 62: Document all exceptions thrown by each method

A description of the exceptions thrown by a method is an important part of the documentation required to use the method properly. Therefore, it is critically important that you take the time to carefully document all of the exceptions thrown by each method.

Always declare checked exceptions individually, and document precisely the conditions under which each one is thrown using the Javadoc @throws tag. Don't take the shortcut of declaring that a method throws some superclass of multiple exception classes that it can throw. As an extreme example, never declare that a method "throws Exception" or, worse yet, "throws Throwable." In addition to denying any guidance to the method's user concerning the exceptions that it is capable of throwing, such a declaration greatly hinders the use of the method, as it effectively obscures any other exception that may be thrown in the same context.

While the language does not require programmers to declare the unchecked exceptions that a method is capable of throwing, it is wise to document them as carefully as the checked exceptions. Unchecked exceptions generally represent programming errors (Item 58), and familiarizing programmers with all of the errors they can make helps them avoid making these errors. A well-documented list of the unchecked exceptions that a method can throw effectively describes the *preconditions* for its successful execution. It is essential that each method's documentation describe its preconditions, and documenting its unchecked exceptions is the best way to satisfy this requirement.

It is particularly important that methods in interfaces document the unchecked exceptions they may throw. This documentation forms a part of the interface's *general contract* and enables common behavior among multiple implementations of the interface.

Use the Javadoc @throws tag to document each unchecked exception that a method can throw, but do *not* use the throws keyword to include unchecked exceptions in the method declaration. It is important that the programmers using your API be aware of which exceptions are checked and which are unchecked, as their responsibilities differ in these two cases. The documentation generated by the Javadoc @throws tag in the absence of the method header generated by the throws declaration provides a strong visual cue to help the programmer distinguish checked exceptions from unchecked.

It should be noted that documenting all of the unchecked exceptions that each method can throw is an ideal, not always achievable in the real world. When a class undergoes revision, it is not a violation of source or binary compatibility if an exported method is modified to throw additional unchecked exceptions. Suppose a class invokes a method from another, independently written class. The authors of the former class may carefully document all of the unchecked exceptions that each method throws, but if the latter class is revised to throw additional unchecked exceptions, it is quite likely that the former class (which has not undergone revision) will propagate the new unchecked exceptions even though it does not declare them.

If an exception is thrown by many methods in a class for the same reason, it is acceptable to document the exception in the class's documentation comment rather than documenting it individually for each method. A common example is `NullPointerException`. It is fine for a class's documentation comment to say, "All methods in this class throw a `NullPointerException` if a null object reference is passed in any parameter," or words to that effect.

In summary, document every exception that can be thrown by each method that you write. This is true for unchecked as well as checked exceptions, and for abstract as well as concrete methods. Provide individual `throws` clauses for each checked exception and do not provide `throws` clauses for unchecked exceptions. If you fail to document the exceptions that your methods can throw, it will be difficult or impossible for others to make effective use of your classes and interfaces.

Item 63: Include failure-capture information in detail messages

When a program fails due to an uncaught exception, the system automatically prints out the exception's stack trace. The stack trace contains the exception's *string representation*, the result of invoking its `toString` method. This typically consists of the exception's class name followed by its *detail message*. Frequently this is the only information that programmers or field service personnel will have when investigating a software failure. If the failure is not easily reproducible, it may be difficult or impossible to get any more information. Therefore, it is critically important that the exception's `toString` method return as much information as possible concerning the cause of the failure. In other words, the detail message of an exception should capture the failure for subsequent analysis.

To capture the failure, the detail message of an exception should contain the values of all parameters and fields that "contributed to the exception." For example, the detail message of an `IndexOutOfBoundsException` should contain the lower bound, the upper bound, and the index value that failed to lie between the bounds. This information tells a lot about the failure. Any or all of the three values could be wrong. The actual index could be one less than the lower bound or equal to the upper bound (a "fencepost error"), or it could be a wild value, far too low or high. The lower bound could be greater than the upper bound (a serious internal invariant failure). Each of these situations points to a different problem, and it greatly aids in the diagnosis if the programmer knows what sort of error to look for.

While it is critical to include all of the pertinent "hard data" in the detail message of an exception, it is generally unimportant to include a lot of prose. The stack trace is intended to be analyzed in conjunction with the source files and generally contains the exact file and line number from which the exception was thrown, as well as the files and line numbers of all other method invocations on the stack. Lengthy prose descriptions of the failure are generally superfluous; the information can be gleaned by reading the source code.

The detail message of an exception should not be confused with a user-level error message, which must be intelligible to end users. Unlike a user-level error message, it is primarily for the benefit of programmers or field service personnel for use when analyzing a failure. Therefore, information content is far more important than intelligibility.

One way to ensure that exceptions contain adequate failure-capture information in their detail messages is to require this information in their constructors instead of a string detail message. The detail message can then be generated automatically to include the information. For example, instead of a `String` constructor, `IndexOutOfBoundsException` could have had a constructor that looks like this:

```
/**
 * Construct an IndexOutOfBoundsException.
 *
 * @param lowerBound the lowest legal index value.
 * @param upperBound the highest legal index value plus one.
 * @param index      the actual index value.
 */
public IndexOutOfBoundsException(int lowerBound, int upperBound,
                                 int index) {
    // Generate a detail message that captures the failure
    super("Lower bound: "  + lowerBound +
          ", Upper bound: " + upperBound +
          ", Index: "       + index);

    // Save failure information for programmatic access
    this.lowerBound = lowerBound;
    this.upperBound = upperBound;
    this.index = index;
}
```

Unfortunately, the Java platform libraries do not make heavy use of this idiom, but it is highly recommended. It makes it easy for the programmer throwing an exception to capture the failure. In fact, it makes it hard for the programmer not to capture the failure! In effect, the idiom centralizes the code to generate a high-quality detail message for an exception in the exception class itself, rather than requiring each user of the class to generate the detail message redundantly.

As suggested in Item 58, it may be appropriate for an exception to provide accessor methods for its failure-capture information (`lowerBound`, `upperBound`, and `index` in the above example). It is more important to provide such accessor methods on checked exceptions than on unchecked exceptions, because the failure-capture information could be useful in recovering from the failure. It is rare (although not inconceivable) that a programmer might want programmatic access to the details of an unchecked exception. Even for unchecked exceptions, however, it seems advisable to provide these accessors on general principle (Item 10, page 53).

Item 64: Strive for failure atomicity

After an object throws an exception, it is generally desirable that the object still be in a well-defined, usable state, even if the failure occurred in the midst of performing an operation. This is especially true for checked exceptions, from which the caller is expected to recover. **Generally speaking, a failed method invocation should leave the object in the state that it was in prior to the invocation**. A method with this property is said to be *failure atomic*.

There are several ways to achieve this effect. The simplest is to design immutable objects (Item 15). If an object is immutable, failure atomicity is free. If an operation fails, it may prevent a new object from getting created, but it will never leave an existing object in an inconsistent state, because the state of each object is consistent when it is created and can't be modified thereafter.

For methods that operate on mutable objects, the most common way to achieve failure atomicity is to check parameters for validity before performing the operation (Item 38). This causes any exception to get thrown before object modification commences. For example, consider the `Stack.pop` method in Item 6:

```
public Object pop() {
    if (size == 0)
        throw new EmptyStackException();
    Object result = elements[--size];
    elements[size] = null; // Eliminate obsolete reference
    return result;
}
```

If the initial size check were eliminated, the method would still throw an exception when it attempted to pop an element from an empty stack. It would, however, leave the size field in an inconsistent (negative) state, causing any future method invocations on the object to fail. Additionally, the exception thrown by the pop method would be inappropriate to the abstraction (Item 61).

A closely related approach to achieving failure atomicity is to order the computation so that any part that may fail takes place before any part that modifies the object. This approach is a natural extension of the previous one when arguments cannot be checked without performing a part of the computation. For example, consider the case of TreeMap, whose elements are sorted according to some ordering. In order to add an element to a TreeMap, the element must be of a type that can be compared using the TreeMap's ordering. Attempting to add an incorrectly typed element will naturally fail with a ClassCastException as a result of searching for the element in the tree, before the tree has been modified in any way.

A third and far less common approach to achieving failure atomicity is to write *recovery code* that intercepts a failure that occurs in the midst of an operation and causes the object to roll back its state to the point before the operation began. This approach is used mainly for durable (disk-based) data structures.

A final approach to achieving failure atomicity is to perform the operation on a temporary copy of the object and to replace the contents of the object with the temporary copy once the operation is complete. This approach occurs naturally when the computation can be performed more quickly once the data has been stored in a temporary data structure. For example, `Collections.sort` dumps its input list into an array prior to sorting to reduce the cost of accessing elements in the inner loop of the sort. This is done for performance, but as an added benefit, it ensures that the input list will be untouched if the sort fails.

While failure atomicity is generally desirable, it is not always achievable. For example, if two threads attempt to modify the same object concurrently without proper synchronization, the object may be left in an inconsistent state. It would therefore be wrong to assume that an object was still usable after catching a `ConcurrentModificationException`. As a rule, errors (as opposed to exceptions) are unrecoverable, and methods need not even attempt to preserve failure atomicity when throwing errors.

Even where failure atomicity is possible, it is not always desirable. For some operations, it would significantly increase the cost or complexity. That said, it is often both free and easy to achieve failure atomicity once you're aware of the issue.

As a rule, any generated exception that is part of a method's specification should leave the object in the same state it was in prior to the method invocation. Where this rule is violated, the API documentation should clearly indicate what state the object will be left in. Unfortunately, plenty of existing API documentation fails to live up to this ideal.

Item 65: Don't ignore exceptions

While this advice may seem obvious, it is violated often enough that it bears repeating. When the designers of an API declare a method to throw an exception, they are trying to tell you something. Don't ignore it! It is easy to ignore exceptions by surrounding a method invocation with a `try` statement with an empty `catch` block:

```
// Empty catch block ignores exception - Highly suspect!
try {
    ...
} catch (SomeException e) {
}
```

An empty `catch` block defeats the purpose of exceptions, which is to force you to handle exceptional conditions. Ignoring an exception is analogous to ignoring a fire alarm—and turning it off so no one else gets a chance to see if there's a real fire. You may get away with it, or the results may be disastrous. Whenever you see an empty `catch` block, alarm bells should go off in your head. **At the very least, the `catch` block should contain a comment explaining why it is appropriate to ignore the exception.**

An example of the sort of situation where it might be appropriate to ignore an exception is when closing a `FileInputStream`. You haven't changed the state of the file, so there's no need to perform any recovery action, and you've already read the information that you need from the file, so there's no reason to abort the operation in progress. Even in this case, it is wise to log the exception, so that you can investigate the matter if these exceptions happen often.

The advice in this item applies equally to checked and unchecked exceptions. Whether an exception represents a predictable exceptional condition or a programming error, ignoring it with an empty `catch` block will result in a program that continues silently in the face of error. The program might then fail at an arbitrary time in the future, at a point in the code that bears no apparent relation to the source of the problem. Properly handling an exception can avert failure entirely. Merely letting an exception propagate outward can at least cause the program to fail swiftly, preserving information to aid in debugging the failure.

CHAPTER 10

Concurrency

THREADS allow multiple activities to proceed concurrently. Concurrent programming is harder than single-threaded programming, because more things can go wrong, and failures can be hard to reproduce. But you can't avoid concurrency. It is inherent in much of what we do, and a requirement if you are to obtain good performance from multicore processors, which are now commonplace. This chapter contains advice to help you write clear, correct, well-documented concurrent programs.

Item 66: Synchronize access to shared mutable data

The synchronized keyword ensures that only a single thread can execute a method or block at one time. Many programmers think of synchronization solely as a means of mutual exclusion, to prevent an object from being observed in an inconsistent state while it's being modified by another thread. In this view, an object is created in a consistent state (Item 15) and locked by the methods that access it. These methods observe the state and optionally cause a *state transition*, transforming the object from one consistent state to another. Proper use of synchronization guarantees that no method will ever observe the object in an inconsistent state.

This view is correct, but it's only half the story. Without synchronization, one thread's changes might not be visible to other threads. Not only does synchronization prevent a thread from observing an object in an inconsistent state, but it ensures that each thread entering a synchronized method or block sees the effects of all previous modifications that were guarded by the same lock.

The language specification guarantees that reading or writing a variable is *atomic* unless the variable is of type long or double [JLS, 17.4.7]. In other words, reading a variable other than a long or double is guaranteed to return a value that was stored into that variable by some thread, even if multiple threads modify the variable concurrently and without synchronization.

You may hear it said that to improve performance, you should avoid synchronization when reading or writing atomic data. This advice is dangerously wrong. While the language specification guarantees that a thread will not see an arbitrary value when reading a field, it does not guarantee that a value written by one thread will be visible to another. **Synchronization is required for reliable communication between threads as well as for mutual exclusion.** This is due to a part of the language specification known as the *memory model*, which specifies when and how changes made by one thread become visible to others [JLS, 17; Goetz06, 16].

The consequences of failing to synchronize access to shared mutable data can be dire even if the data is atomically readable and writable. Consider the task of stopping one thread from another. The libraries provide the Thread.stop method, but this method was deprecated long ago because it is inherently *unsafe*—its use can result in data corruption. **Do not use Thread.stop.** A recommended way to stop one thread from another is to have the first thread poll a boolean field that is initially false but can be set to true by the second thread to indicate that the first thread is to stop itself. Because reading and writing a boolean field is atomic, some programmers dispense with synchronization when accessing the field:

```
// Broken! - How long would you expect this program to run?
public class StopThread {
    private static boolean stopRequested;

    public static void main(String[] args)
            throws InterruptedException {
        Thread backgroundThread = new Thread(new Runnable() {
            public void run() {
                int i = 0;
                while (!stopRequested)
                    i++;
            }
        });
        backgroundThread.start();

        TimeUnit.SECONDS.sleep(1);
        stopRequested = true;
    }
}
```

You might expect this program to run for about a second, after which the main thread sets stopRequested to true, causing the background thread's loop to terminate. On my machine, however, the program *never* terminates: the background thread loops forever!

The problem is that in the absence of synchronization, there is no guarantee as to when, if ever, the background thread will see the change in the value of stop-Requested that was made by the main thread. In the absence of synchronization, it's quite acceptable for the virtual machine to transform this code:

```
while (!stopRequested)
    i++;
```

into this code:

```
if (!stopRequested)
    while (true)
        i++;
```

This optimization is known as *hoisting*, and it is precisely what the HotSpot server VM does. The result is a *liveness failure*: the program fails to make progress. One way to fix the problem is to synchronize access to the stopRequested field. This program terminates in about one second, as expected:

```
// Properly synchronized cooperative thread termination
public class StopThread {
    private static boolean stopRequested;
    private static synchronized void requestStop() {
        stopRequested = true;
    }
    private static synchronized boolean stopRequested() {
        return stopRequested;
    }

    public static void main(String[] args)
            throws InterruptedException {
        Thread backgroundThread = new Thread(new Runnable() {
            public void run() {
                int i = 0;
                while (!stopRequested())
                    i++;
            }
        });
        backgroundThread.start();

        TimeUnit.SECONDS.sleep(1);
        requestStop();
    }
}
```

Note that both the write method (requestStop) and the read method (stopRequested) are synchronized. It is *not* sufficient to synchronize only the write method! In fact, **synchronization has no effect unless both read and write operations are synchronized.**

The actions of the synchronized methods in StopThread would be atomic even without synchronization. In other words, the synchronization on these methods is used *solely* for its communication effects, not for mutual exclusion. While the cost of synchronizing on each iteration of the loop is small, there is a correct alternative that is less verbose and whose performance is likely to be better. The locking in the second version of StopThread can be omitted if stopRequested is declared volatile. While the volatile modifier performs no mutual exclusion, it guarantees that any thread that reads the field will see the most recently written value:

```
// Cooperative thread termination with a volatile field
public class StopThread {
    private static volatile boolean stopRequested;

    public static void main(String[] args)
            throws InterruptedException {
        Thread backgroundThread = new Thread(new Runnable() {
            public void run() {
                int i = 0;
                while (!stopRequested)
                    i++;
            }
        });
        backgroundThread.start();

        TimeUnit.SECONDS.sleep(1);
        stopRequested = true;
    }
}
```

You do have to be careful when using volatile. Consider the following method, which is supposed to generate serial numbers:

```
// Broken - requires synchronization!
private static volatile int nextSerialNumber = 0;

public static int generateSerialNumber() {
    return nextSerialNumber++;
}
```

The intent of the method is to guarantee that every invocation returns a different value (so long as there are no more than 2^{32} invocations). The method's state consists of a single atomically accessible field, `nextSerialNumber`, and all possible values of this field are legal. Therefore, no synchronization is necessary to protect its invariants. Still, the method won't work properly without synchronization.

The problem is that the increment operator (++) is not atomic. It performs *two* operations on the `nextSerialNumber` field: first it reads the value, then it writes back a new value, equal to the old value plus one. If a second thread reads the field between the time a thread reads the old value and writes back a new one, the second thread will see the same value as the first and return the same serial number. This is a *safety failure*: the program computes the wrong results.

One way to fix the `generateSerialNumber` method is to add the `synchronized` modifier to its declaration. This ensures that multiple invocations won't be interleaved, and that each invocation will see the effects of all previous invocations. Once you've done that, you can and should remove the `volatile` modifier from `nextSerialNumber`. To bulletproof the method, use `long` instead of `int`, or throw an exception if `nextSerialNumber` is about to wrap.

Better still, follow the advice in Item 47 and use the class `AtomicLong`, which is part of `java.util.concurrent.atomic`. It does exactly what you want and is likely to perform better than the synchronized version of `generateSerialNumber`:

```
private static final AtomicLong nextSerialNum = new AtomicLong();

public static long generateSerialNumber() {
    return nextSerialNum.getAndIncrement();
}
```

The best way to avoid the problems discussed in this item is not to share mutable data. Either share immutable data (Item 15), or don't share at all. In other words, **confine mutable data to a single thread.** If you adopt this policy, it is important to document it, so that it is maintained as your program evolves. It is also important to have a deep understanding of the frameworks and libraries you're using, as they may introduce threads that you are unaware of.

It is acceptable for one thread to modify a data object for a while and then to share it with other threads, synchronizing only the act of sharing the object reference. Other threads can then read the object without further synchronization, so long as it isn't modified again. Such objects are said to be *effectively immutable* [Goetz06, 3.5.4]. Transferring such an object reference from one thread to others is called *safe publication* [Goetz06, 3.5.3]. There are many ways to safely publish an object reference: you can store it in a static field as part of class initialization;

can store it in a volatile field, a final field, or a field that is accessed with normal locking; or you can put it into a concurrent collection (Item 69).

In summary, **when multiple threads share mutable data, each thread that reads or writes the data must perform synchronization.** Without synchronization, there is no guarantee that one thread's changes will be visible to another. The penalties for failing to synchronize shared mutable data are liveness and safety failures. These failures are among the most difficult to debug. They can be intermittent and timing-dependent, and program behavior can vary radically from one VM to another. If you need only inter-thread communication, and not mutual exclusion, the `volatile` modifier is an acceptable form of synchronization, but it can be tricky to use correctly.

Item 67: Avoid excessive synchronization

Item 66 warns of the dangers of insufficient synchronization. This item concerns the opposite problem. Depending on the situation, excessive synchronization can cause reduced performance, deadlock, or even nondeterministic behavior.

To avoid liveness and safety failures, never cede control to the client within a synchronized method or block. In other words, inside a synchronized region, do not invoke a method that is designed to be overridden, or one provided by a client in the form of a function object (Item 21). From the perspective of the class with the synchronized region, such methods are *alien*. The class has no knowledge of what the method does and has no control over it. Depending on what an alien method does, calling it from a synchronized region can cause exceptions, deadlocks, or data corruption.

To make this concrete, consider the following class, which implements an *observable* set wrapper. It allows clients to subscribe to notifications when elements are added to the set. This is the *Observer* pattern [Gamma95, p. 293]. For brevity's sake, the class does not provide notifications when elements are removed from the set, but it would be a simple matter to provide them. This class is implemented atop the reusable `ForwardingSet` from Item 16 (page 84):

```java
// Broken - invokes alien method from synchronized block!
public class ObservableSet<E> extends ForwardingSet<E> {
    public ObservableSet(Set<E> set) { super(set); }

    private final List<SetObserver<E>> observers =
        new ArrayList<SetObserver<E>>();

    public void addObserver(SetObserver<E> observer) {
        synchronized(observers) {
            observers.add(observer);
        }
    }
    public boolean removeObserver(SetObserver<E> observer) {
        synchronized(observers) {
            return observers.remove(observer);
        }
    }
    private void notifyElementAdded(E element) {
        synchronized(observers) {
            for (SetObserver<E> observer : observers)
                observer.added(this, element);
        }
    }
}
```

```java
    @Override public boolean add(E element) {
        boolean added = super.add(element);
        if (added)
            notifyElementAdded(element);
        return added;
    }

    @Override public boolean addAll(Collection<? extends E> c) {
        boolean result = false;
        for (E element : c)
            result |= add(element);   // calls notifyElementAdded
        return result;
    }
}
```

Observers subscribe to notifications by invoking the addObserver method and unsubscribe by invoking the removeObserver method. In both cases, an instance of this *callback* interface is passed to the method:

```java
public interface SetObserver<E> {
    // Invoked when an element is added to the observable set
    void added(ObservableSet<E> set, E element);
}
```

On cursory inspection, ObservableSet appears to work. For example, the following program prints the numbers from 0 through 99:

```java
public static void main(String[] args) {
    ObservableSet<Integer> set =
        new ObservableSet<Integer>(new HashSet<Integer>());

    set.addObserver(new SetObserver<Integer>() {
        public void added(ObservableSet<Integer> s, Integer e) {
            System.out.println(e);
        }
    });

    for (int i = 0; i < 100; i++)
        set.add(i);
}
```

Now let's try something a bit fancier. Suppose we replace the addObserver call with one that passes an observer that prints the Integer value that was added to the set and removes itself if the value is 23:

```
set.addObserver(new SetObserver<Integer>() {
    public void added(ObservableSet<Integer> s, Integer e) {
        System.out.println(e);
        if (e == 23) s.removeObserver(this);
    }
});
```

You might expect the program to print the numbers 0 through 23, after which the observer would unsubscribe and the program complete its work silently. What actually happens is that it prints the numbers 0 through 23, and then throws a ConcurrentModificationException. The problem is that notifyElementAdded is in the process of iterating over the observers list when it invokes the observer's added method. The added method calls the observable set's removeObserver method, which in turn calls observers.remove. Now we are in trouble. We are trying to remove an element from a list in the midst of iterating over it, which is illegal. The iteration in the notifyElementAdded method is in a synchronized block to prevent concurrent modification, but it doesn't prevent the iterating thread itself from calling back into the observable set and modifying its observers list.

Now let's try something odd: let's write an observer that attempts to unsubscribe, but instead of calling removeObserver directly, it engages the services of another thread to do the deed. This observer uses an *executor service* (Item 68):

```
// Observer that uses a background thread needlessly
set.addObserver(new SetObserver<Integer>() {
    public void added(final ObservableSet<Integer> s, Integer e) {
        System.out.println(e);
        if (e == 23) {
            ExecutorService executor =
                Executors.newSingleThreadExecutor();
            final SetObserver<Integer> observer = this;
            try {
                executor.submit(new Runnable() {
                    public void run() {
                        s.removeObserver(observer);
                    }
                }).get();
            } catch (ExecutionException ex) {
                throw new AssertionError(ex.getCause());
            } catch (InterruptedException ex) {
                throw new AssertionError(ex);
            } finally {
                executor.shutdown();
            }
        }
    }
});
```

This time we don't get an exception; we get a deadlock. The background thread calls `s.removeObserver`, which attempts to lock `observers`, but it can't acquire the lock, because the main thread already has the lock. All the while, the main thread is waiting for the background thread to finish removing the observer, which explains the deadlock.

This example is contrived because there is no reason for the observer to use a background thread, but the problem is real. Invoking alien methods from synchronized regions has caused many deadlocks in real systems, such as GUI toolkits.

In both of the previous examples (the exception and the deadlock) we were lucky. The resource that was guarded by the synchronized region (`observers`) was in a consistent state when the alien method (`added`) was invoked. Suppose you were to invoke an alien method from within a synchronized region while the invariant protected by the synchronized region was temporarily invalid. Because locks in the Java programming language are *reentrant*, such calls won't deadlock. As in the first example, which resulted in an exception, the calling thread already holds the lock, so the thread will succeed when it tries to reacquire the lock, even though another conceptually unrelated operation is in progress on the data guarded by the lock. The consequences of such a failure can be catastrophic. In essence, the lock has failed to do its job. Reentrant locks simplify the construction of multithreaded object-oriented programs, but they can turn liveness failures into safety failures.

Luckily, it is usually not too hard to fix this sort of problem by moving alien method invocations out of synchronized blocks. For the `notifyElementAdded` method, this involves taking a "snapshot" of the `observers` list that can then be safely traversed without a lock. With this change, both of the previous examples run without exception or deadlock:

```
// Alien method moved outside of synchronized block - open calls
private void notifyElementAdded(E element) {
    List<SetObserver<E>> snapshot = null;
    synchronized(observers) {
        snapshot = new ArrayList<SetObserver<E>>(observers);
    }
    for (SetObserver<E> observer : snapshot)
        observer.added(this, element);
}
```

In fact, there's a better way to move the alien method invocations out of the synchronized block. Since release 1.5, the Java libraries have provided a *concurrent collection* (Item 69) known as `CopyOnWriteArrayList`, which is tailor-made for this purpose. It is a variant of `ArrayList` in which all write operations are implemented by making a fresh copy of the entire underlying array. Because the internal array is never modified, iteration requires no locking and is very fast. For most uses, the performance of `CopyOnWriteArrayList` would be atrocious, but it's perfect for observer lists, which are rarely modified and often traversed.

The add and `addAll` methods of `ObservableSet` need not be changed if the list is modified to use `CopyOnWriteArrayList`. Here is how the remainder of the class looks. Notice that there is no explicit synchronization whatsoever:

```
// Thread-safe observable set with CopyOnWriteArrayList
private final List<SetObserver<E>> observers =
    new CopyOnWriteArrayList<SetObserver<E>>();

public void addObserver(SetObserver<E> observer) {
    observers.add(observer);
}
public boolean removeObserver(SetObserver<E> observer) {
    return observers.remove(observer);
}
private void notifyElementAdded(E element) {
    for (SetObserver<E> observer : observers)
        observer.added(this, element);
}
```

An alien method invoked outside of a synchronized region is known as an *open call* [Lea00 2.4.1.3]. Besides preventing failures, open calls can greatly increase concurrency. An alien method might run for an arbitrarily long period. If the alien method were invoked from a synchronized region, other threads would be denied access to the protected resource unnecessarily.

As a rule, you should do as little work as possible inside synchronized regions. Obtain the lock, examine the shared data, transform it as necessary, and drop the lock. If you must perform some time-consuming activity, find a way to move the activity out of the synchronized region without violating the guidelines in Item 66.

The first part of this item was about correctness. Now let's take a brief look at performance. While the cost of synchronization has plummeted since the early days of Java, it is more important than ever not to oversynchronize. In a multicore world, the real cost of excessive synchronization is not the CPU time spent obtaining locks; it is the lost opportunities for parallelism and the delays imposed by the need to ensure that every core has a consistent view of memory. Another hidden cost of oversynchronization is that it can limit the VM's ability to optimize code execution.

You should make a mutable class thread-safe (Item 70) if it is intended for concurrent use and you can achieve significantly higher concurrency by synchronizing internally than you could by locking the entire object externally. Otherwise, don't synchronize internally. Let the client synchronize externally where it is appropriate. In the early days of the Java platform, many classes violated these guidelines. For example, `StringBuffer` instances are almost always used by a single thread, yet they perform internal synchronization. It is for this reason that `StringBuffer` was essentially replaced by `StringBuilder`, which is an unsynchronized `StringBuffer`, in release 1.5. When in doubt, do *not* synchronize your class, but document that it is not thread-safe (Item 70).

If you do synchronize your class internally, you can use various techniques to achieve high concurrency, such as lock splitting, lock striping, and nonblocking concurrency control. These techniques are beyond the scope of this book, but they are discussed elsewhere [Goetz06, Lea00].

If a method modifies a static field, you *must* synchronize access to this field, even if the method is typically used only by a single thread. It is not possible for clients to perform external synchronization on such a method because there can be no guarantee that unrelated clients will do likewise. The `generateSerialNumber` method on page 263 exemplifies this situation.

In summary, to avoid deadlock and data corruption, never call an alien method from within a synchronized region. More generally, try to limit the amount of work that you do from within synchronized regions. When you are designing a mutable class, think about whether it should do its own synchronization. In the modern multicore era, it is more important than ever not to synchronize excessively. Synchronize your class internally only if there is a good reason to do so, and document your decision clearly (Item 70).

Item 68: Prefer executors and tasks to threads

The first edition of this book contained code for a simple *work queue* [Bloch01, Item 49]. This class allowed clients to enqueue work items for asynchronous processing by a background thread. When the work queue was no longer needed, the client could invoke a method to ask the background thread to terminate itself gracefully after completing any work that was already on the queue. The implementation was little more than a toy, but even so, it required a full page of subtle, delicate code, of the sort that is prone to safety and liveness failures if you don't get it just right. Luckily, there is no reason to write this sort of code anymore.

In release 1.5, `java.util.concurrent` was added to the Java platform. This package contains an *Executor Framework*, which is a flexible interface-based task execution facility. Creating a work queue that is better in every way than the one in the first edition of this book requires but a single line of code:

```
ExecutorService executor = Executors.newSingleThreadExecutor();
```

Here is how to submit a runnable for execution:

```
executor.execute(runnable);
```

And here is how to tell the executor to terminate gracefully (if you fail to do this, it is likely that your VM will not exit):

```
executor.shutdown();
```

You can do *many* more things with an executor service. For example, you can wait for a particular task to complete (as in the "background thread `SetObserver`" in Item 67, page 267), you can wait for any or all of a collection of tasks to complete (using the `invokeAny` or `invokeAll` methods), you can wait for the executor service's graceful termination to complete (using the `awaitTermination` method), you can retrieve the results of tasks one by one as they complete (using an `ExecutorCompletionService`), and so on.

If you want more than one thread to process requests from the queue, simply call a different static factory that creates a different kind of executor service called a *thread pool*. You can create a thread pool with a fixed or variable number of threads. The `java.util.concurrent.Executors` class contains static factories that provide most of the executors you'll ever need. If, however, you want something out of the ordinary, you can use the `ThreadPoolExecutor` class directly. This class lets you control nearly every aspect of a thread pool's operation.

Choosing the executor service for a particular application can be tricky. If you're writing a small program, or a lightly loaded server, using `Executors.new-CachedThreadPool` is generally a good choice, as it demands no configuration and generally "does the right thing." But a cached thread pool is not a good choice for a heavily loaded production server! In a cached thread pool, submitted tasks are not queued but immediately handed off to a thread for execution. If no threads are available, a new one is created. If a server is so heavily loaded that all of its CPUs are fully utilized, and more tasks arrive, more threads will be created, which will only make matters worse. Therefore, in a heavily loaded production server, you are much better off using `Executors.newFixedThreadPool`, which gives you a pool with a fixed number of threads, or using the `ThreadPoolExecutor` class directly, for maximum control.

Not only should you refrain from writing your own work queues, but you should generally refrain from working directly with threads. The key abstraction is no longer `Thread`, which served as both the unit of work and the mechanism for executing it. Now the unit of work and mechanism are separate. The key abstraction is the unit of work, which is called a *task*. There are two kinds of tasks: Runnable and its close cousin, `Callable` (which is like `Runnable`, except that it returns a value). The general mechanism for executing tasks is the *executor service*. If you think in terms of tasks and let an executor service execute them for you, you gain great flexibility in terms of selecting appropriate execution policies. In essence, the Executor Framework does for execution what the Collections Framework did for aggregation.

The Executor Framework also has a replacement for `java.util.Timer`, which is `ScheduledThreadPoolExecutor`. While it is easier to use a timer, a scheduled thread pool executor is much more flexible. A timer uses only a single thread for task execution, which can hurt timing accuracy in the presence of long-running tasks. If a timer's sole thread throws an uncaught exception, the timer ceases to operate. A scheduled thread pool executor supports multiple threads and recovers gracefully from tasks that throw unchecked exceptions.

A complete treatment of the Executor Framework is beyond the scope of this book, but the interested reader is directed to *Java Concurrency in Practice* [Goetz06].

Item 69: Prefer concurrency utilities to `wait` and `notify`

The first edition of this book devoted an item to the correct use of `wait` and `notify` (Bloch01, Item 50). Its advice is still valid and is summarized at end of this item, but this advice is far less important than it once was. This is because there is far less reason to use `wait` and `notify`. As of release 1.5, the Java platform provides higher-level concurrency utilities that do the sorts of things you formerly had to hand-code atop `wait` and `notify`. **Given the difficulty of using `wait` and `notify` correctly, you should use the higher-level concurrency utilities instead.**

The higher-level utilities in `java.util.concurrent` fall into three categories: the Executor Framework, which was covered only briefly in Item 68; concurrent collections; and synchronizers. Concurrent collections and synchronizers are covered briefly in this item.

The concurrent collections provide high-performance concurrent implementations of standard collection interfaces such as `List`, `Queue`, and `Map`. To provide high concurrency, these implementations manage their own synchronization internally (Item 67). Therefore, **it is impossible to exclude concurrent activity from a concurrent collection; locking it will have no effect** but to slow the program.

This means that clients can't atomically compose method invocations on concurrent collections. Some of the collection interfaces have therefore been extended with *state-dependent modify operations*, which combine several primitives into a single atomic operation. For example, `ConcurrentMap` extends `Map` and adds several methods, including `putIfAbsent(key, value)`, which inserts a mapping for a key if none was present and returns the previous value associated with the key, or `null` if there was none. This makes it easy to implement thread-safe canonicalizing maps. For example, this method simulates the behavior of `String.intern`:

```
// Concurrent canonicalizing map atop ConcurrentMap - not optimal
private static final ConcurrentMap<String, String> map =
    new ConcurrentHashMap<String, String>();

public static String intern(String s) {
    String previousValue = map.putIfAbsent(s, s);
    return previousValue == null ? s : previousValue;
}
```

In fact, you can do even better. `ConcurrentHashMap` is optimized for retrieval operations, such as `get`. Therefore, it is worth invoking `get` initially and calling `putIfAbsent` only if `get` indicates that it is necessary:

```
// Concurrent canonicalizing map atop ConcurrentMap - faster!
public static String intern(String s) {
    String result = map.get(s);
    if (result == null) {
        result = map.putIfAbsent(s, s);
        if (result == null)
            result = s;
    }
    return result;
}
```

Besides offering excellent concurrency, ConcurrentHashMap is very fast. On my machine the optimized intern method above is over six times faster than String.intern (but keep in mind that String.intern must use some sort of weak reference to keep from leaking memory over time). Unless you have a compelling reason to do otherwise, **use ConcurrentHashMap in preference to Collections.synchronizedMap or Hashtable.** Simply replacing old-style synchronized maps with concurrent maps can dramatically increase the performance of concurrent applications. More generally, use concurrent collections in preference to externally synchronized collections.

Some of the collection interfaces have been extended with *blocking operations,* which wait (or *block*) until they can be successfully performed. For example, BlockingQueue extends Queue and adds several methods, including take, which removes and returns the head element from the queue, waiting if the queue is empty. This allows blocking queues to be used for *work queues* (also known as *producer-consumer queues*), to which one or more *producer threads* enqueue work items and from which one or more *consumer threads* dequeue and process items as they become available. As you'd expect, most ExecutorService implementations, including ThreadPoolExecutor, use a BlockingQueue (Item 68).

Synchronizers are objects that enable threads to wait for one another, allowing them to coordinate their activities. The most commonly used synchronizers are CountDownLatch and Semaphore. Less commonly used are CyclicBarrier and Exchanger.

Countdown latches are single-use barriers that allow one or more threads to wait for one or more other threads to do something. The sole constructor for CountDownLatch takes an int that is the number of times the countDown method must be invoked on the latch before all waiting threads are allowed to proceed.

It is surprisingly easy to build useful things atop this simple primitive. For example, suppose you want to build a simple framework for timing the concurrent execution of an action. This framework consists of a single method that takes an executor to execute the action, a concurrency level representing the number of actions to be executed concurrently, and a runnable representing the action. All of the worker threads ready themselves to run the action before the timer thread starts the clock (this is necessary to get an accurate timing). When the last worker thread is ready to run the action, the timer thread "fires the starting gun," allowing the worker threads to perform the action. As soon as the last worker thread finishes performing the action, the timer thread stops the clock. Implementing this logic directly on top of wait and notify would be messy to say the least, but it is surprisingly straightforward on top of CountDownLatch:

```
// Simple framework for timing concurrent execution
public static long time(Executor executor, int concurrency,
        final Runnable action) throws InterruptedException {
    final CountDownLatch ready = new CountDownLatch(concurrency);
    final CountDownLatch start = new CountDownLatch(1);
    final CountDownLatch done  = new CountDownLatch(concurrency);
    for (int i = 0; i < concurrency; i++) {
        executor.execute(new Runnable() {
            public void run() {
                ready.countDown(); // Tell timer we're ready
                try {
                    start.await(); // Wait till peers are ready
                    action.run();
                } catch (InterruptedException e) {
                    Thread.currentThread().interrupt();
                } finally {
                    done.countDown();  // Tell timer we're done
                }
            }
        });
    }
    ready.await();     // Wait for all workers to be ready
    long startNanos = System.nanoTime();
    start.countDown(); // And they're off!
    done.await();      // Wait for all workers to finish
    return System.nanoTime() - startNanos;
}
```

Note that the method uses three countdown latches. The first, ready, is used by worker threads to tell the timer thread when they're ready. The worker threads then wait on the second latch, which is start. When the last worker thread invokes ready.countDown, the timer thread records the start time and invokes start.countDown, allowing all of the worker threads to proceed. Then the timer thread waits on the third latch, done, until the last of the worker threads finishes running the action and calls done.countDown. As soon as this happens, the timer thread awakens and records the end time.

A few more details bear noting. The executor that is passed to the `time` method must allow for the creation of at least as many threads as the given concurrency level, or the test will never complete. This is known as a *thread starvation deadlock* [Goetz06, 8.1.1]. If a worker thread catches an `InterruptedException`, it reasserts the interrupt using the idiom `Thread.currentThread().interrupt()` and returns from its `run` method. This allows the executor to deal with the interrupt as it sees fit, which is as it should be. Finally, note that `System.nanoTime` is used to time the activity rather than `System.currentTimeMillis`. **For interval timing, always use `System.nanoTime` in preference to `System.currentTime-Millis`.** `System.nanoTime` is both more accurate and more precise, and it is not affected by adjustments to the system's real-time clock.

This item only scratches the surface of the concurrency utilities. For example, the three countdown latches in the previous example can be replaced by a single cyclic barrier. The resulting code is even more concise, but it is more difficult to understand. For more information, see *Java Concurrency in Practice* [Goetz06].

While you should always use the concurrency utilities in preference to `wait` and `notify`, you might have to maintain legacy code that uses `wait` and `notify`. The `wait` method is used to make a thread wait for some condition. It must be invoked inside a synchronized region that locks the object on which it is invoked. Here is the standard idiom for using the `wait` method:

```
// The standard idiom for using the wait method
synchronized (obj) {
    while (<condition does not hold>)
        obj.wait(); // (Releases lock, and reacquires on wakeup)

    ... // Perform action appropriate to condition
}
```

Always use the wait loop idiom to invoke the `wait` method; never invoke it outside of a loop. The loop serves to test the condition before and after waiting.

Testing the condition before waiting and skipping the wait if the condition already holds are necessary to ensure liveness. If the condition already holds and the `notify` (or `notifyAll`) method has already been invoked before a thread waits, there is no guarantee that the thread will *ever* wake from the wait.

Testing the condition after waiting and waiting again if the condition does not hold are necessary to ensure safety. If the thread proceeds with the action when the condition does not hold, it can destroy the invariant guarded by the lock. There are several reasons a thread might wake up when the condition does not hold:

- Another thread could have obtained the lock and changed the guarded state between the time a thread invoked `notify` and the time the waiting thread woke.

- Another thread could have invoked `notify` accidentally or maliciously when the condition did not hold. Classes expose themselves to this sort of mischief by waiting on publicly accessible objects. Any `wait` contained in a synchronized method of a publicly accessible object is susceptible to this problem.

- The notifying thread could be overly "generous" in waking waiting threads. For example, the notifying thread might invoke `notifyAll` even if only some of the waiting threads have their condition satisfied.

- The waiting thread could (rarely) wake up in the absence of a notify. This is known as a *spurious wakeup* [Posix, 11.4.3.6.1; JavaSE6].

A related issue is whether you should use `notify` or `notifyAll` to wake waiting threads. (Recall that `notify` wakes a single waiting thread, assuming such a thread exists, and `notifyAll` wakes all waiting threads.) It is often said that you should *always* use `notifyAll`. This is reasonable, conservative advice. It will always yield correct results because it guarantees that you'll wake the threads that need to be awakened. You may wake some other threads, too, but this won't affect the correctness of your program. These threads will check the condition for which they're waiting and, finding it false, will continue waiting.

As an optimization, you may choose to invoke `notify` instead of `notifyAll` if all threads that could be in the wait-set are waiting for the same condition and only one thread at a time can benefit from the condition becoming true.

Even if these conditions appear true, there may be cause to use `notifyAll` in place of `notify`. Just as placing the `wait` invocation in a loop protects against accidental or malicious notifications on a publicly accessible object, using `notifyAll` in place of `notify` protects against accidental or malicious waits by an unrelated thread. Such waits could otherwise "swallow" a critical notification, leaving its intended recipient waiting indefinitely.

In summary, using `wait` and `notify` directly is like programming in "concurrency assembly language," as compared to the higher-level language provided by `java.util.concurrent`. **There is seldom, if ever, a reason to use `wait` and `notify` in new code.** If you maintain code that uses `wait` and `notify`, make sure that it always invokes `wait` from within a `while` loop using the standard idiom. The `notifyAll` method should generally be used in preference to `notify`. If `notify` is used, great care must be taken to ensure liveness.

Item 70: Document thread safety

How a class behaves when its instances or static methods are subjected to concurrent use is an important part of the contract the class makes with its clients. If you don't document this facet of a class's behavior, programmers who use the class will be forced to make assumptions. If those assumptions are wrong, the resulting program may perform insufficient synchronization (Item 66) or excessive synchronization (Item 67). In either case, serious errors can result.

You might hear it said that you can tell if a method is thread-safe by looking for the `synchronized` modifier in its documentation. This is wrong on several counts. In normal operation, Javadoc does not include the `synchronized` modifier in its output, and with good reason. **The presence of the `synchronized` modifier in a method declaration is an implementation detail, not a part of its exported API.** It does not reliably indicate that a method is thread-safe.

Moreover, the claim that the presence of the `synchronized` modifier is sufficient to document thread safety embodies the misconception that thread safety is an all-or-nothing property. In fact, there are several levels of thread safety. **To enable safe concurrent use, a class must clearly document what level of thread safety it supports.**

The following list summarizes levels of thread safety. It is not exhaustive but covers the common cases:

- **immutable**—Instances of this class appear constant. No external synchronization is necessary. Examples include `String`, `Long`, and `BigInteger` (Item 15).

- **unconditionally thread-safe**—Instances of this class are mutable, but the class has sufficient internal synchronization that its instances can be used concurrently without the need for any external synchronization. Examples include `Random` and `ConcurrentHashMap`.

- **conditionally thread-safe**—Like unconditionally thread-safe, except that some methods require external synchronization for safe concurrent use. Examples include the collections returned by the `Collections.synchronized` wrappers, whose iterators require external synchronization.

- **not thread-safe**—Instances of this class are mutable. To use them concurrently, clients must surround each method invocation (or invocation sequence) with external synchronization of the clients' choosing. Examples include the general-purpose collection implementations, such as `ArrayList` and `HashMap`.

- **thread-hostile**—This class is not safe for concurrent use even if all method invocations are surrounded by external synchronization. Thread hostility usually results from modifying static data without synchronization. No one writes a thread-hostile class on purpose; such classes result from the failure to consider concurrency. Luckily, there are very few thread-hostile classes or methods in the Java libraries. The `System.runFinalizersOnExit` method is thread-hostile and has been deprecated.

These categories (apart from thread-hostile) correspond roughly to the *thread safety annotations* in *Java Concurrency in Practice*, which are `Immutable`, `ThreadSafe`, and `NotThreadSafe` [Goetz06, Appendix A]. The unconditionally and conditionally thread-safe categories in the above taxonomy are both covered under the `ThreadSafe` annotation.

Documenting a conditionally thread-safe class requires care. You must indicate which invocation sequences require external synchronization, and which lock (or in rare cases, which locks) must be acquired to execute these sequences. Typically it is the lock on the instance itself, but there are exceptions. If an object represents a *view* on some other object, the client generally must synchronize on the backing object, so as to prevent its direct modification. For example, the documentation for `Collections.synchronizedMap` says this:

> It is imperative that the user manually synchronize on the returned map when iterating over any of its collection views:
>
> ```
> Map<K, V> m = Collections.synchronizedMap(new HashMap<K, V>());
>     ...
> Set<K> s = m.keySet();  // Needn't be in synchronized block
>     ...
> synchronized(m) {  // Synchronizing on m, not s!
>     for (K key : s)
>         key.f();
> }
> ```
>
> Failure to follow this advice may result in non-deterministic behavior.

The description of a class's thread safety generally belongs in its documentation comment, but methods with special thread safety properties should describe these properties in their own documentation comments. It is not necessary to document the immutability of enum types. Unless it is obvious from the return type, static factories must document the thread safety of the returned object, as demonstrated by `Collections.synchronizedMap` (above).

When a class commits to using a publicly accessible lock, it enables clients to execute a sequence of method invocations atomically, but this flexibility comes at a price. It is incompatible with high-performance internal concurrency control, of the sort used by concurrent collections such as `ConcurrentHashMap` and `ConcurrentLinkedQueue`. Also, a client can mount a denial-of-service attack by holding the publicly accessible lock for a prolonged period. This can be done accidentally or intentionally.

To prevent this denial-of-service attack, you can use a *private lock object* instead of using synchronized methods (which imply a publicly accessible lock):

```
// Private lock object idiom - thwarts denial-of-service attack
private final Object lock = new Object();

public void foo() {
    synchronized(lock) {
        ...
    }
}
```

Because the private lock object is inaccessible to clients of the class, it is impossible for them to interfere with the object's synchronization. In effect, we are applying the advice of Item 13 by encapsulating the lock object within the object it synchronizes.

Note that the `lock` field is declared `final`. This prevents you from inadvertently changing its contents, which could result in catastrophic unsynchronized access to the containing object (Item 66). We are applying the advice of Item 15, by minimizing the mutability of the `lock` field.

To reiterate, the private lock object idiom can be used only on *unconditionally* thread-safe classes. Conditionally thread-safe classes can't use this idiom because they must document which lock their clients are to acquire when performing certain method invocation sequences.

The private lock object idiom is particularly well-suited to classes designed for inheritance (Item 17). If such a class were to use its instances for locking, a subclass could easily and unintentionally interfere with the operation of the base class, or vice versa. By using the same lock for different purposes, the subclass and the base class could end up "stepping on each other's toes." This is not just a theoretical problem. For example, it happened with the `Thread` class [Bloch05, Puzzle 77].

To summarize, every class should clearly document its thread safety properties with a carefully worded prose description or a thread safety annotation. The `synchronized` modifier plays no part in this documentation. Conditionally thread-safe classes must document which method invocation sequences require external synchronization, and which lock to acquire when executing these sequences. If you write an unconditionally thread-safe class, consider using a private lock object in place of synchronized methods. This protects you against synchronization interference by clients and subclasses and gives you the flexibility to adopt a more sophisticated approach to concurrency control in a later release.

Item 71: Use lazy initialization judiciously

Lazy initialization is the act of delaying the initialization of a field until its value is needed. If the value is never needed, the field is never initialized. This technique is applicable to both static and instance fields. While lazy initialization is primarily an optimization, it can also be used to break harmful circularities in class and instance initialization [Bloch05, Puzzle 51].

As is the case for most optimizations, the best advice for lazy initialization is "don't do it unless you need to" (Item 55). Lazy initialization is a double-edged sword. It decreases the cost of initializing a class or creating an instance, at the expense of increasing the cost of accessing the lazily initialized field. Depending on what fraction of lazily initialized fields eventually require initialization, how expensive it is to initialize them, and how often each field is accessed, lazy initialization can (like many "optimizations") actually harm performance.

That said, lazy initialization has its uses. If a field is accessed only on a fraction of the instances of a class *and* it is costly to initialize the field, then lazy initialization may be worthwhile. The only way to know for sure is to measure the performance of the class with and without lazy initialization.

In the presence of multiple threads, lazy initialization is tricky. If two or more threads share a lazily initialized field, it is critical that some form of synchronization be employed, or severe bugs can result (Item 66). All of the initialization techniques discussed in this item are thread-safe.

Under most circumstances, normal initialization is preferable to lazy initialization. Here is a typical declaration for a normally initialized instance field. Note the use of the final modifier (Item 15):

```
// Normal initialization of an instance field
private final FieldType field = computeFieldValue();
```

If you use lazy initialization to break an initialization circularity, use a synchronized accessor, as it is the simplest, clearest alternative:

```
// Lazy initialization of instance field - synchronized accessor
private FieldType field;

synchronized FieldType getField() {
    if (field == null)
        field = computeFieldValue();
    return field;
}
```

Both of these idioms (*normal initialization* and *lazy initialization with a synchronized accessor*) are unchanged when applied to static fields, except that you add the `static` modifier to the field and accessor declarations.

If you need to use lazy initialization for performance on a static field, use the *lazy initialization holder class idiom*. This idiom (also known as the *initialize-on-demand holder class idiom*) exploits the guarantee that a class will not be initialized until it is used [JLS, 12.4.1]. Here's how it looks:

```
// Lazy initialization holder class idiom for static fields
private static class FieldHolder {
    static final FieldType field = computeFieldValue();
}
static FieldType getField() { return FieldHolder.field; }
```

When the `getField` method is invoked for the first time, it reads `Field-Holder.field` for the first time, causing the `FieldHolder` class to get initialized. The beauty of this idiom is that the `getField` method is not synchronized and performs only a field access, so lazy initialization adds practically nothing to the cost of access. A modern VM will synchronize field access only to initialize the class. Once the class is initialized, the VM will patch the code so that subsequent access to the field does not involve any testing or synchronization.

If you need to use lazy initialization for performance on an instance field, use the *double-check idiom*. This idiom avoids the cost of locking when accessing the field after it has been initialized (Item 67). The idea behind the idiom is to check the value of the field twice (hence the name *double-check*): once without locking, and then, if the field appears to be uninitialized, a second time with locking. Only if the second check indicates that the field is uninitialized does the call initialize the field. Because there is no locking if the field is already initialized, it is *critical* that the field be declared `volatile` (Item 66). Here is the idiom:

```
// Double-check idiom for lazy initialization of instance fields
private volatile FieldType field;
FieldType getField() {
    FieldType result = field;
    if (result == null) {  // First check (no locking)
        synchronized(this) {
            result = field;
            if (result == null)  // Second check (with locking)
                field = result = computeFieldValue();
        }
    }
    return result;
}
```

This code may appear a bit convoluted. In particular, the need for the local variable `result` may be unclear. What this variable does is to ensure that `field` is read only once in the common case where it's already initialized. While not strictly necessary, this may improve performance and is more elegant by the standards applied to low-level concurrent programming. On my machine, the method above is about 25 percent faster than the obvious version without a local variable.

Prior to release 1.5, the double-check idiom did not work reliably because the semantics of the `volatile` modifier were not strong enough to support it [Pugh01]. The memory model introduced in release 1.5 fixed this problem [JLS, 17; Goetz06, 16]. Today, the double-check idiom is the technique of choice for lazily initializing an instance field. While you can apply the double-check idiom to static fields as well, there is no reason to do so: the lazy initialization holder class idiom is a better choice.

Two variants of the double-check idiom bear noting. Occasionally, you may need to lazily initialize an instance field that can tolerate repeated initialization. If you find yourself in this situation, you can use a variant of the double-check idiom that dispenses with the second check. It is, not surprisingly, known as the *single-check idiom*. Here is how it looks. Note that `field` is still declared `volatile`:

```
// Single-check idiom - can cause repeated initialization!
private volatile FieldType field;

private FieldType getField() {
    FieldType result = field;
    if (result == null)
        field = result = computeFieldValue();
    return result;
}
```

All of the initialization techniques discussed in this item apply to primitive fields as well as object reference fields. When the double-check or single-check idiom is applied to a numerical primitive field, the field's value is checked against 0 (the default value for numerical primitive variables) rather than `null`.

If you don't care whether *every* thread recalculates the value of a field, and the type of the field is a primitive other than `long` or `double`, then you may choose to remove the `volatile` modifier from the field declaration in the single-check idiom. This variant is known as the *racy single-check idiom*. It speeds up field access on some architectures, at the expense of additional initializations (up to one per thread that accesses the field). This is definitely an exotic technique, not for everyday use. It is, however, used by `String` instances to cache their hash codes.

In summary, you should initialize most fields normally, not lazily. If you must initialize a field lazily in order to achieve your performance goals, or to break a harmful initialization circularity, then use the appropriate lazy initialization technique. For instance fields, it is the double-check idiom; for static fields, the lazy initialization holder class idiom. For instance fields that can tolerate repeated initialization, you may also consider the single-check idiom.

Item 72: Don't depend on the thread scheduler

When many threads are runnable, the thread scheduler determines which ones get to run, and for how long. Any reasonable operating system will try to make this determination fairly, but the policy can vary. Therefore, well-written programs shouldn't depend on the details of this policy. **Any program that relies on the thread scheduler for correctness or performance is likely to be nonportable.**

The best way to write a robust, responsive, portable program is to ensure that the average number of *runnable* threads is not significantly greater than the number of processors. This leaves the thread scheduler with little choice: it simply runs the runnable threads till they're no longer runnable. The program's behavior doesn't vary too much, even under radically different thread-scheduling policies. Note that the number of runnable threads isn't the same as the total number of threads, which can be much higher. Threads that are waiting are not runnable.

The main technique for keeping the number of runnable threads down is to have each thread do some useful work and then wait for more. **Threads should not run if they aren't doing useful work.** In terms of the Executor Framework (Item 68), this means sizing your thread pools appropriately [Goetz06, 8.2], and keeping tasks reasonably small and independent of one another. Tasks shouldn't be *too* small, or dispatching overhead will harm performance.

Threads should not *busy-wait*, repeatedly checking a shared object waiting for something to happen. Besides making the program vulnerable to the vagaries of the scheduler, busy-waiting greatly increases the load on the processor, reducing the amount of useful work that others can accomplish. As an extreme example of what *not* to do, consider this perverse reimplementation of CountDownLatch:

```java
// Awful CountDownLatch implementation - busy-waits incessantly!
public class SlowCountDownLatch {
    private int count;
    public SlowCountDownLatch(int count) {
        if (count < 0)
            throw new IllegalArgumentException(count + " < 0");
        this.count = count;
    }

    public void await() {
        while (true) {
            synchronized(this) {
                if (count == 0) return;
            }
        }
    }
}
```

```
    public synchronized void countDown() {
        if (count != 0)
            count--;
    }
}
```

On my machine, SlowCountDownLatch is about 2,000 times slower than CountDownLatch when 1,000 threads wait on a latch. While this example may seem a bit far-fetched, it's not uncommon to see systems with one or more threads that are unnecessarily runnable. The results may not be as dramatic as Slow-CountDownLatch, but performance and portability are likely to suffer.

When faced with a program that barely works because some threads aren't getting enough CPU time relative to others, **resist the temptation to "fix" the program by putting in calls to Thread.yield.** You may succeed in getting the program to work after a fashion, but it will not be portable. The same yield invocations that improve performance on one JVM implementation might make it worse on a second and have no effect on a third. **Thread.yield has no testable semantics.** A better course of action is to restructure the application to reduce the number of concurrently runnable threads.

A related technique, to which similar caveats apply, is adjusting thread priorities. **Thread priorities are among the least portable features of the Java platform.** It is not unreasonable to tune the responsiveness of an application by tweaking a few thread priorities, but it is rarely necessary and is not portable. It is unreasonable to solve a serious liveness problem by adjusting thread priorities. The problem is likely to return until you find and fix the underlying cause.

In the first edition of this book, it was said that the only use most programmers would ever have for Thread.yield was to artificially increase the concurrency for testing. The idea was to shake out bugs by exploring a larger fraction of the program's statespace. This technique was once quite effective, but it was never guaranteed to work. It is within specification for Thread.yield to do nothing at all, simply returning control to its caller. Some modern VMs actually do this. Therefore, you should use Thread.sleep(1) instead of Thread.yield for concurrency testing. Do not use Thread.sleep(0), which can return immediately.

In summary, do not depend on the thread scheduler for the correctness of your program. The resulting program will be neither robust nor portable. As a corollary, do not rely on Thread.yield or thread priorities. These facilities are merely hints to the scheduler. Thread priorities may be used sparingly to improve the quality of service of an already working program, but they should never be used to "fix" a program that barely works.

Item 73: Avoid thread groups

Along with threads, locks, and monitors, a basic abstraction offered by the threading system is *thread groups*. Thread groups were originally envisioned as a mechanism for isolating applets for security purposes. They never really fulfilled this promise, and their security importance has waned to the extent that they aren't even mentioned in the standard work on the Java security model [Gong03].

Given that thread groups don't provide any security functionality to speak of, what functionality do they provide? Not much. They allow you to apply certain Thread primitives to a bunch of threads at once. Several of these primitives have been deprecated, and the remainder are infrequently used.

In an ironic twist, the ThreadGroup API is weak from a thread safety standpoint. To get a list of the active threads in a thread group, you must invoke the enumerate method, which takes as a parameter an array large enough to hold all the active threads. The activeCount method returns the number of active threads in a thread group, but there is no guarantee that this count will still be accurate once an array has been allocated and passed to the enumerate method. If the thread count has increased and the array is too small, the enumerate method silently ignores any threads for which there is no room in the array.

The API that lists the subgroups of a thread group is similarly flawed. While these problems could have been fixed with the addition of new methods, they haven't, because there is no real need: **thread groups are obsolete.**

Prior to release 1.5, there was one small piece of functionality that was available *only* with the ThreadGroup API: the ThreadGroup.uncaughtException method was the only way to gain control when a thread threw an uncaught exception. This functionality is useful, for example, to direct stack traces to an application-specific log. As of release 1.5, however, the same functionality is available with Thread's setUncaughtExceptionHandler method.

To summarize, thread groups don't provide much in the way of useful functionality, and much of the functionality they do provide is flawed. Thread groups are best viewed as an unsuccessful experiment, and you should simply ignore their existence. If you design a class that deals with logical groups of threads, you should probably use thread pool executors (Item 68).

CHAPTER 11

Serialization

THIS chapter concerns the *object serialization* API, which provides a framework for encoding objects as byte streams and reconstructing objects from their byte-stream encodings. Encoding an object as a byte stream is known as *serializing* the object; the reverse process is known as *deserializing* it. Once an object has been serialized, its encoding can be transmitted from one running virtual machine to another or stored on disk for later deserialization. Serialization provides the standard wire-level object representation for remote communication, and the standard persistent data format for the JavaBeans component architecture. A notable feature of this chapter is the *serialization proxy* pattern (Item 78), which can help you avoid many of the pitfalls of object serialization.

Item 74: Implement `Serializable` judiciously

Allowing a class's instances to be serialized can be as simple as adding the words "`implements Serializable`" to its declaration. Because this is so easy to do, there is a common misconception that serialization requires little effort on the part of the programmer. The truth is far more complex. While the immediate cost to make a class serializable can be negligible, the long-term costs are often substantial.

A major cost of implementing `Serializable` is that it decreases the flexibility to change a class's implementation once it has been released. When a class implements `Serializable`, its byte-stream encoding (or *serialized form*) becomes part of its exported API. Once you distribute a class widely, you are generally required to support the serialized form forever, just as you are required to support all other parts of the exported API. If you do not make the effort to design a *custom serialized form*, but merely accept the default, the serialized form will forever be tied to the class's original internal representation. In other words, if you accept the default serialized form, the class's private and package-private instance fields become part of its exported API, and the practice of minimizing access to fields (Item 13) loses its effectiveness as a tool for information hiding.

If you accept the default serialized form and later change the class's internal representation, an incompatible change in the serialized form might result. Clients attempting to serialize an instance using an old version of the class and deserialize it using the new version will experience program failures. It is possible to change the internal representation while maintaining the original serialized form (using `ObjectOutputStream.putFields` and `ObjectInputStream.readFields`), but it can be difficult and leaves visible warts in the source code. Therefore, you should carefully design a high-quality serialized form that you are willing to live with for the long haul (Items 75, 78). Doing so will add to the initial cost of development, but it is worth the effort. Even a well-designed serialized form places constraints on the evolution of a class; an ill-designed serialized form can be crippling.

A simple example of the constraints on evolution that accompany serializability concerns *stream unique identifiers*, more commonly known as *serial version UIDs*. Every serializable class has a unique identification number associated with it. If you do not specify this number explicitly by declaring a static final `long` field named `serialVersionUID`, the system automatically generates it at runtime by applying a complex procedure to the class. The automatically generated value is affected by the class's name, the names of the interfaces it implements, and all of its public and protected members. If you change any of these things in any way, for example, by adding a trivial convenience method, the automatically generated serial version UID changes. If you fail to declare an explicit serial version UID, compatibility will be broken, resulting in an `InvalidClassException` at runtime.

A second cost of implementing `Serializable` is that it increases the likelihood of bugs and security holes. Normally, objects are created using constructors; serialization is an *extralinguistic mechanism* for creating objects. Whether you accept the default behavior or override it, deserialization is a "hidden constructor" with all of the same issues as other constructors. Because there is no explicit constructor associated with deserialization, it is easy to forget that you must ensure that it guarantees all of the invariants established by the constructors and that it does not allow an attacker to gain access to the internals of the object under construction. Relying on the default deserialization mechanism can easily leave objects open to invariant corruption and illegal access (Item 76).

A third cost of implementing `Serializable` is that it increases the testing burden associated with releasing a new version of a class. When a serializable class is revised, it is important to check that it is possible to serialize an instance in the new release and deserialize it in old releases, and vice versa. The amount of testing required is thus proportional to the product of the number of serializable classes and the number of releases, which can be large. These tests cannot be constructed automatically because, in addition to *binary compatibility*, you must test for *semantic compatibility*. In other words, you must ensure both that the serialization-deserialization process succeeds and that it results in a faithful replica of the original object. The greater the change to a serializable class, the greater the need for testing. The need is reduced if a custom serialized form is carefully designed when the class is first written (Items 75, 78), but it does not vanish entirely.

Implementing the `Serializable` interface is not a decision to be undertaken lightly. It offers real benefits. It is essential if a class is to participate in a framework that relies on serialization for object transmission or persistence. Also, it greatly eases the use of a class as a component in another class that must implement `Serializable`. There are, however, many real costs associated with implementing `Serializable`. Each time you design a class, weigh the costs against the benefits. As a rule of thumb, value classes such as `Date` and `BigInteger` should implement `Serializable`, as should most collection classes. Classes representing active entities, such as thread pools, should rarely implement `Serializable`.

Classes designed for inheritance (Item 17) should rarely implement `Serializable`, and interfaces should rarely extend it. Violating this rule places a significant burden on anyone who extends the class or implements the interface. There are times when it is appropriate to violate the rule. For example, if a class or interface exists primarily to participate in a framework that requires all participants to implement `Serializable`, then it makes perfect sense for the class or interface to implement or extend `Serializable`.

Classes designed for inheritance that *do* implement `Serializable` include `Throwable`, `Component`, and `HttpServlet`. `Throwable` implements `Serializable` so exceptions from remote method invocation (RMI) can be passed from server to client. `Component` implements `Serializable` so GUIs can be sent, saved, and restored. `HttpServlet` implements `Serializable` so session state can be cached.

If you implement a class with instance fields that is serializable and extendable, there is a caution you should be aware of. If the class has invariants that would be violated if its instance fields were initialized to their default values (zero for integral types, `false` for `boolean`, and `null` for object reference types), you must add this `readObjectNoData` method to the class:

```
// readObjectNoData for stateful extendable serializable classes
private void readObjectNoData() throws InvalidObjectException {
    throw new InvalidObjectException("Stream data required");
}
```

In case you're curious, the `readObjectNoData` method was added in release 1.4 to cover a corner case involving the addition of a serializable superclass to an existing serializable class. Details can be found in the serialization specification [Serialization, 3.5].

There is one caveat regarding the decision *not* to implement `Serializable`. If a class that is designed for inheritance is not serializable, it may be impossible to write a serializable subclass. Specifically, it will be impossible if the superclass does not provide an accessible parameterless constructor. Therefore, **you should consider providing a parameterless constructor on nonserializable classes designed for inheritance**. Often this requires no effort because many classes designed for inheritance have no state, but this is not always the case.

It is best to create objects with their invariants already established (Item 15). If client-provided data is required to establish these invariants, this precludes the use of a parameterless constructor. Naively adding a parameterless constructor and a separate initialization method to a class whose remaining constructors establish its invariants would complicate the state space, increasing the likelihood of error.

Here is a way to add a parameterless constructor to a nonserializable extendable class that avoids these deficiencies. Suppose the class has one constructor:

```
public AbstractFoo(int x, int y) { ... }
```

The following transformation adds a protected parameterless constructor and an initialization method. The initialization method has the same parameters as the normal constructor and establishes the same invariants. Note that the variables that store the object's state (x and y) can't be final, as they are set by the `initialize` method:

```
// Nonserializable stateful class allowing serializable subclass
public abstract class AbstractFoo {
    private int x, y;  // Our state

    // This enum and field are used to track initialization
    private enum State { NEW, INITIALIZING, INITIALIZED };
    private final AtomicReference<State> init =
        new AtomicReference<State>(State.NEW);

    public AbstractFoo(int x, int y) { initialize(x, y); }

    // This constructor and the following method allow
    // subclass's readObject method to initialize our state.
    protected AbstractFoo() { }
```

```
    protected final void initialize(int x, int y) {
        if (!init.compareAndSet(State.NEW, State.INITIALIZING))
            throw new IllegalStateException(
                "Already initialized");
        this.x = x;
        this.y = y;
        ... // Do anything else the original constructor did
        init.set(State.INITIALIZED);
    }

    // These methods provide access to internal state so it can
    // be manually serialized by subclass's writeObject method.
    protected final int getX() { checkInit(); return x; }
    protected final int getY() { checkInit(); return y; }

    // Must call from all public and protected instance methods
    private void checkInit() {
        if (init.get() != State.INITIALIZED)
            throw new IllegalStateException("Uninitialized");
    }
    ... // Remainder omitted
}
```

All public and protected instance methods in `AbstractFoo` must invoke `checkInit` before doing anything else. This ensures that method invocations fail quickly and cleanly if a poorly written subclass fails to initialize an instance. Note that the `init` field is an *atomic reference*. This ensures object integrity even in the face of a determined adversary. In the absence of this precaution, if one thread invoked `initialize` on an instance while a second thread tried to use it, the second thread might see the instance in an inconsistent state. This pattern, in which `compareAndSet` is used to manipulate an atomic reference to an enum, is a good general-purpose implementation of a *thread-safe state machine*. With this mechanism in place, it is straightforward to implement a serializable subclass:

```
// Serializable subclass of nonserializable stateful class
public class Foo extends AbstractFoo implements Serializable {
    private void readObject(ObjectInputStream s)
            throws IOException, ClassNotFoundException {
        s.defaultReadObject();

        // Manually deserialize and initialize superclass state
        int x = s.readInt();
        int y = s.readInt();
        initialize(x, y);
    }
```

```
    private void writeObject(ObjectOutputStream s)
            throws IOException {
        s.defaultWriteObject();

        // Manually serialize superclass state
        s.writeInt(getX());
        s.writeInt(getY());
    }

    // Constructor does not use the fancy mechanism
    public Foo(int x, int y) { super(x, y); }

    private static final long serialVersionUID = 1856835860954L;
}
```

***Inner classes* (Item 22) should not implement Serializable.** They use compiler-generated *synthetic fields* to store references to *enclosing instances* and to store values of local variables from enclosing scopes. How these fields correspond to the class definition is unspecified, as are the names of anonymous and local classes. Therefore, **the default serialized form of an inner class is ill-defined**. A *static member class* can, however, implement Serializable.

To summarize, the ease of implementing Serializable is specious. Unless a class is to be thrown away after a short period of use, implementing Serializable is a serious commitment that should be made with care. Extra caution is warranted if a class is designed for inheritance. For such classes, an intermediate design point between implementing Serializable and prohibiting it in subclasses is to provide an accessible parameterless constructor. This design point permits, but does not require, subclasses to implement Serializable.

Item 75: Consider using a custom serialized form

When you are producing a class under time pressure, it is generally appropriate to concentrate your efforts on designing the best API. Sometimes this means releasing a "throwaway" implementation that you know you'll replace in a future release. Normally this is not a problem, but if the class implements `Serializable` and uses the default serialized form, you'll never be able to escape completely from the throwaway implementation. It will dictate the serialized form forever. This is not just a theoretical problem. It happened to several classes in the Java platform libraries, including `BigInteger`.

Do not accept the default serialized form without first considering whether it is appropriate. Accepting the default serialized form should be a conscious decision that this encoding is reasonable from the standpoint of flexibility, performance, and correctness. Generally speaking, you should accept the default serialized form only if it is largely identical to the encoding that you would choose if you were designing a custom serialized form.

The default serialized form of an object is a reasonably efficient encoding of the *physical* representation of the object graph rooted at the object. In other words, it describes the data contained in the object and in every object that is reachable from this object. It also describes the topology by which all of these objects are interlinked. The ideal serialized form of an object contains only the *logical* data represented by the object. It is independent of the physical representation.

The default serialized form is likely to be appropriate if an object's physical representation is identical to its logical content. For example, the default serialized form would be reasonable for the following class, which simplistically represents a person's name:

```
// Good candidate for default serialized form
public class Name implements Serializable {
    /**
     * Last name. Must be non-null.
     * @serial
     */
    private final String lastName;

    /**
     * First name. Must be non-null.
     * @serial
     */
    private final String firstName;
```

```
/**
 * Middle name, or null if there is none.
 * @serial
 */
private final String middleName;

... // Remainder omitted
}
```

Logically speaking, a name consists of three strings that represent a last name, a first name, and a middle name. The instance fields in Name precisely mirror this logical content.

Even if you decide that the default serialized form is appropriate, you often must provide a readObject method to ensure invariants and security. In the case of Name, the readObject method must ensure that lastName and first-Name are non-null. This issue is discussed at length in Items 76 and 78.

Note that there are documentation comments on the lastName, firstName, and middleName fields, even though they are private. That is because these private fields define a public API, which is the serialized form of the class, and this public API must be documented. The presence of the @serial tag tells the Javadoc utility to place this documentation on a special page that documents serialized forms.

Near the opposite end of the spectrum from Name, consider the following class, which represents a list of strings (ignoring for the moment that you'd be better off using one of the standard List implementations):

```
// Awful candidate for default serialized form
public final class StringList implements Serializable {
    private int size = 0;
    private Entry head = null;

    private static class Entry implements Serializable {
        String data;
        Entry  next;
        Entry  previous;
    }

    ... // Remainder omitted
}
```

Logically speaking, this class represents a sequence of strings. Physically, it represents the sequence as a doubly linked list. If you accept the default serialized form, the serialized form will painstakingly mirror every entry in the linked list and all the links between the entries, in both directions.

Using the default serialized form when an object's physical representation differs substantially from its logical data content has four disadvantages:

- **It permanently ties the exported API to the current internal representation.** In the above example, the private `StringList.Entry` class becomes part of the public API. If the representation is changed in a future release, the `StringList` class will still need to accept the linked list representation on input and generate it on output. The class will never be rid of all the code dealing with linked list entries, even if it doesn't use them anymore.

- **It can consume excessive space.** In the above example, the serialized form unnecessarily represents each entry in the linked list and all the links. These entries and links are mere implementation details, not worthy of inclusion in the serialized form. Because the serialized form is excessively large, writing it to disk or sending it across the network will be excessively slow.

- **It can consume excessive time.** The serialization logic has no knowledge of the topology of the object graph, so it must go through an expensive graph traversal. In the example above, it would be sufficient simply to follow the `next` references.

- **It can cause stack overflows**. The default serialization procedure performs a recursive traversal of the object graph, which can cause stack overflows even for moderately sized object graphs. Serializing a `StringList` instance with 1,258 elements causes the stack to overflow on my machine. The number of elements required to cause this problem may vary depending on the JVM implementation and command line flags; some implementations may not have this problem at all.

A reasonable serialized form for `StringList` is simply the number of strings in the list, followed by the strings themselves. This constitutes the logical data represented by a `StringList`, stripped of the details of its physical representation. Here is a revised version of `StringList` containing `writeObject` and `readObject` methods implementing this serialized form. As a reminder, the `transient` modifier indicates that an instance field is to be omitted from a class's default serialized form:

```java
// StringList with a reasonable custom serialized form
public final class StringList implements Serializable {
    private transient int size   = 0;
    private transient Entry head = null;

    // No longer Serializable!
    private static class Entry {
        String data;
        Entry  next;
        Entry  previous;
    }

    // Appends the specified string to the list
    public final void add(String s) { ... }

    /**
     * Serialize this {@code StringList} instance.
     *
     * @serialData The size of the list (the number of strings
     * it contains) is emitted ({@code int}), followed by all of
     * its elements (each a {@code String}), in the proper
     * sequence.
     */
    private void writeObject(ObjectOutputStream s)
            throws IOException {
        s.defaultWriteObject();
        s.writeInt(size);

        // Write out all elements in the proper order.
        for (Entry e = head; e != null; e = e.next)
            s.writeObject(e.data);
    }

    private void readObject(ObjectInputStream s)
            throws IOException, ClassNotFoundException {
        s.defaultReadObject();
        int numElements = s.readInt();

        // Read in all elements and insert them in list
        for (int i = 0; i < numElements; i++)
            add((String) s.readObject());
    }

    ... // Remainder omitted
}
```

Note that the first thing `writeObject` does is to invoke `defaultWriteObject`, and the first thing `readObject` does is to invoke `defaultReadObject`, even though all of `StringList`'s fields are transient. **If all instance fields are transient, it is technically permissible to dispense with invoking `defaultWriteObject` and `defaultReadObject`, but it is not recommended.** Even if all instance fields are transient, invoking `defaultWriteObject` affects the serialized form, resulting in greatly enhanced flexibility. The resulting serialized form makes it possible to add nontransient instance fields in a later release while preserving backward and forward compatibility. If an instance is serialized in a later version and deserialized in an earlier version, the added fields will be ignored. Had the earlier version's `readObject` method failed to invoke `defaultReadObject`, the deserialization would fail with a `StreamCorruptedException`.

Note that there is a documentation comment on the `writeObject` method, even though it is private. This is analogous to the documentation comment on the private fields in the `Name` class. This private method defines a public API, which is the serialized form, and that public API should be documented. Like the `@serial` tag for fields, the `@serialData` tag for methods tells the Javadoc utility to place this documentation on the serialized forms page.

To lend some sense of scale to the earlier performance discussion, if the average string length is ten characters, the serialized form of the revised version of `StringList` occupies about half as much space as the serialized form of the original. On my machine, serializing the revised version of `StringList` is over twice as fast as serializing the original version, again with a string length of ten. Finally, there is no stack overflow problem in the revised form, hence no practical upper limit to the size of a `StringList` that can be serialized.

While the default serialized form would be bad for `StringList`, there are classes for which it would be far worse. For `StringList`, the default serialized form is inflexible and performs badly, but it is *correct* in the sense that serializing and deserializing a `StringList` instance yields a faithful copy of the original object with all of its invariants intact. This is not the case for any object whose invariants are tied to implementation-specific details.

For example, consider the case of a hash table. The physical representation is a sequence of hash buckets containing key-value entries. The bucket that an entry resides in is a function of the hash code of its key, which is not, in general, guaranteed to be the same from JVM implementation to JVM implementation. In fact, it isn't even guaranteed to be the same from run to run. Therefore, accepting the default serialized form for a hash table would constitute a serious bug. Serializing and deserializing the hash table could yield an object whose invariants were seriously corrupt.

Whether or not you use the default serialized form, every instance field that is not labeled `transient` will be serialized when the `defaultWriteObject` method is invoked. Therefore, every instance field that can be made transient should be made so. This includes redundant fields, whose values can be computed from "primary data fields," such as a cached hash value. It also includes fields whose values are tied to one particular run of the JVM, such as a `long` field representing a pointer to a native data structure. **Before deciding to make a field nontransient, convince yourself that its value is part of the logical state of the object.** If you use a custom serialized form, most or all of the instance fields should be labeled `transient`, as in the `StringList` example shown above.

If you are using the default serialized form and you have labeled one or more fields `transient`, remember that these fields will be initialized to their *default values* when an instance is deserialized: `null` for object reference fields, zero for numeric primitive fields, and `false` for `boolean` fields [JLS, 4.12.5]. If these values are unacceptable for any transient fields, you must provide a `readObject` method that invokes the `defaultReadObject` method and then restores transient fields to acceptable values (Item 76). Alternatively, these fields can be lazily initialized the first time they are used (Item 71).

Whether or not you use the default serialized form, **you must impose any synchronization on object serialization that you would impose on any other method that reads the entire state of the object.** So, for example, if you have a thread-safe object (Item 70) that achieves its thread safety by synchronizing every method, and you elect to use the default serialized form, use the following `writeObject` method:

```
// writeObject for synchronized class with default serialized form
private synchronized void writeObject(ObjectOutputStream s)
        throws IOException {
    s.defaultWriteObject();
}
```

If you put synchronization in the `writeObject` method, you must ensure that it adheres to the same lock-ordering constraints as other activity, or you risk a resource-ordering deadlock [Goetz06, 10.1.5].

Regardless of what serialized form you choose, declare an explicit serial version UID in every serializable class you write. This eliminates the serial version UID as a potential source of incompatibility (Item 74). There is also a small performance benefit. If no serial version UID is provided, an expensive computation is required to generate one at runtime.

Declaring a serial version UID is simple. Just add this line to your class:

```
private static final long serialVersionUID = randomLongValue ;
```

If you write a new class, it doesn't matter what value you choose for *randomLongValue*. You can generate the value by running the `serialver` utility on the class, but it's also fine to pick a number out of thin air. If you modify an existing class that lacks a serial version UID, and you want the new version to accept existing serialized instances, you must use the value that was automatically generated for the old version. You can get this number by running the `serialver` utility on the old version of the class—the one for which serialized instances exist.

If you ever want to make a new version of a class that is *incompatible* with existing versions, merely change the value in the serial version UID declaration. This will cause attempts to deserialize serialized instances of previous versions to fail with an `InvalidClassException`.

To summarize, when you have decided that a class should be serializable (Item 74), think hard about what the serialized form should be. Use the default serialized form only if it is a reasonable description of the logical state of the object; otherwise design a custom serialized form that aptly describes the object. You should allocate as much time to designing the serialized form of a class as you allocate to designing its exported methods (Item 40). Just as you cannot eliminate exported methods from future versions, you cannot eliminate fields from the serialized form; they must be preserved forever to ensure serialization compatibility. Choosing the wrong serialized form can have a permanent, negative impact on the complexity and performance of a class.

Item 76: Write `readObject` methods defensively

Item 39 contains an immutable date-range class containing mutable private `Date` fields. The class goes to great lengths to preserve its invariants and its immutability by defensively copying `Date` objects in its constructor and accessors. Here is the class:

```
// Immutable class that uses defensive copying
public final class Period {
    private final Date start;
    private final Date end;

    /**
     * @param  start the beginning of the period
     * @param  end the end of the period; must not precede start
     * @throws IllegalArgumentException if start is after end
     * @throws NullPointerException if start or end is null
     */
    public Period(Date start, Date end) {
        this.start = new Date(start.getTime());
        this.end   = new Date(end.getTime());
        if (this.start.compareTo(this.end) > 0)
            throw new IllegalArgumentException(
                        start + " after " + end);
    }

    public Date start () { return new Date(start.getTime()); }

    public Date end ()   { return new Date(end.getTime()); }

    public String toString() { return start + " - " + end; }

    ... // Remainder omitted
}
```

Suppose you decide that you want this class to be serializable. Because the physical representation of a `Period` object exactly mirrors its logical data content, it is not unreasonable to use the default serialized form (Item 75). Therefore, it might seem that all you have to do to make the class serializable is to add the words "`implements Serializable`" to the class declaration. If you did so, however, the class would no longer guarantee its critical invariants.

The problem is that the `readObject` method is effectively another public constructor, and it demands all of the same care as any other constructor. Just as a constructor must check its arguments for validity (Item 38) and make defensive copies of parameters where appropriate (Item 39), so must a readObject method. If a readObject method fails to do either of these things, it is a relatively simple matter for an attacker to violate the class's invariants.

Loosely speaking, readObject is a constructor that takes a byte stream as its sole parameter. In normal use, the byte stream is generated by serializing a normally constructed instance. The problem arises when readObject is presented with a byte stream that is artificially constructed to generate an object that violates the invariants of its class. Assume that we simply added implements Serializable to the class declaration for Period. This ugly program would then generate a Period instance whose end precedes its start:

```
public class BogusPeriod {
    // Byte stream could not have come from real Period instance!
    private static final byte[] serializedForm = new byte[] {
      (byte)0xac, (byte)0xed, 0x00, 0x05, 0x73, 0x72, 0x00, 0x06,
      0x50, 0x65, 0x72, 0x69, 0x6f, 0x64, 0x40, 0x7e, (byte)0xf8,
      0x2b, 0x4f, 0x46, (byte)0xc0, (byte)0xf4, 0x02, 0x00, 0x02,
      0x4c, 0x00, 0x03, 0x65, 0x6e, 0x64, 0x74, 0x00, 0x10, 0x4c,
      0x6a, 0x61, 0x76, 0x61, 0x2f, 0x75, 0x74, 0x69, 0x6c, 0x2f,
      0x44, 0x61, 0x74, 0x65, 0x3b, 0x4c, 0x00, 0x05, 0x73, 0x74,
      0x61, 0x72, 0x74, 0x71, 0x00, 0x7e, 0x00, 0x01, 0x78, 0x70,
      0x73, 0x72, 0x00, 0x0e, 0x6a, 0x61, 0x76, 0x61, 0x2e, 0x75,
      0x74, 0x69, 0x6c, 0x2e, 0x44, 0x61, 0x74, 0x65, 0x68, 0x6a,
      (byte)0x81, 0x01, 0x4b, 0x59, 0x74, 0x19, 0x03, 0x00, 0x00,
      0x78, 0x70, 0x77, 0x08, 0x00, 0x00, 0x00, 0x66, (byte)0xdf,
      0x6e, 0x1e, 0x00, 0x78, 0x73, 0x71, 0x00, 0x7e, 0x00, 0x03,
      0x77, 0x08, 0x00, 0x00, 0x00, (byte)0xd5, 0x17, 0x69, 0x22,
      0x00, 0x78 };

    public static void main(String[] args) {
        Period p = (Period) deserialize(serializedForm);
        System.out.println(p);
    }

    // Returns the object with the specified serialized form
    private static Object deserialize(byte[] sf) {
        try {
            InputStream is = new ByteArrayInputStream(sf);
            ObjectInputStream ois = new ObjectInputStream(is);
            return ois.readObject();
        } catch (Exception e) {
            throw new IllegalArgumentException(e);
        }
    }
}
```

The byte array literal used to initialize serializedForm was generated by serializing a normal Period instance and hand-editing the resulting byte stream. The details of the stream are unimportant to the example, but if you're curious, the serialization byte-stream format is described in the *Java™ Object Serialization Specification* [Serialization, 6]. If you run this program, it prints "Fri Jan 01 12:00:00 PST 1999 - Sun Jan 01 12:00:00 PST 1984." Simply declaring Period serializable enabled us to create an object that violates its class invariants.

To fix this problem, provide a readObject method for Period that calls defaultReadObject and then checks the validity of the deserialized object. If the validity check fails, the readObject method throws an InvalidObjectException, preventing the deserialization from completing:

```
// readObject method with validity checking
private void readObject(ObjectInputStream s)
        throws IOException, ClassNotFoundException {
    s.defaultReadObject();

    // Check that our invariants are satisfied
    if (start.compareTo(end) > 0)
        throw new InvalidObjectException(start +" after "+ end);
}
```

While this fix prevents an attacker from creating an invalid Period instance, there is a more subtle problem still lurking. It is possible to create a mutable Period instance by fabricating a byte stream that begins with a valid Period instance and then appends extra references to the private Date fields internal to the Period instance. The attacker reads the Period instance from the ObjectInput-Stream and then reads the "rogue object references" that were appended to the stream. These references give the attacker access to the objects referenced by the private Date fields within the Period object. By mutating these Date instances, the attacker can mutate the Period instance. The following class demonstrates this attack:

```
public class MutablePeriod {
    // A period instance
    public final Period period;

    // period's start field, to which we shouldn't have access
    public final Date start;

    // period's end field, to which we shouldn't have access
    public final Date end;
```

```
    public MutablePeriod() {
        try {
            ByteArrayOutputStream bos =
                new ByteArrayOutputStream();
            ObjectOutputStream out =
                new ObjectOutputStream(bos);

            // Serialize a valid Period instance
            out.writeObject(new Period(new Date(), new Date()));

            /*
             * Append rogue "previous object refs" for internal
             * Date fields in Period. For details, see "Java
             * Object Serialization Specification," Section 6.4.
             */
            byte[] ref = { 0x71, 0, 0x7e, 0, 5 }; // Ref #5
            bos.write(ref); // The start field
            ref[4] = 4;     // Ref # 4
            bos.write(ref); // The end field

            // Deserialize Period and "stolen" Date references
            ObjectInputStream in = new ObjectInputStream(
                new ByteArrayInputStream(bos.toByteArray()));
            period = (Period) in.readObject();
            start  = (Date)   in.readObject();
            end    = (Date)   in.readObject();
        } catch (Exception e) {
            throw new AssertionError(e);
        }
    }
}
```

To see the attack in action, run the following program:

```
public static void main(String[] args) {
    MutablePeriod mp = new MutablePeriod();
    Period p = mp.period;
    Date pEnd = mp.end;

    // Let's turn back the clock
    pEnd.setYear(78);
    System.out.println(p);

    // Bring back the 60s!
    pEnd.setYear(69);
    System.out.println(p);
}
```

Running this program produces the following output:

```
Wed Apr 02 11:04:26 PDT 2008 - Sun Apr 02 11:04:26 PST 1978
Wed Apr 02 11:04:26 PDT 2008 - Wed Apr 02 11:04:26 PST 1969
```

While the Period instance is created with its invariants intact, it is possible to modify its internal components at will. Once in possession of a mutable Period instance, an attacker might cause great harm by passing the instance on to a class that depends on Period's immutability for its security. This is not so far-fetched: there are classes that depend on String's immutability for their security.

The source of the problem is that Period's readObject method is not doing enough defensive copying. **When an object is deserialized, it is critical to defensively copy any field containing an object reference that a client must not possess.** Therefore, every serializable immutable class containing private mutable components must defensively copy these components in its readObject method. The following readObject method suffices to ensure Period's invariants and to maintain its immutability:

```
// readObject method with defensive copying and validity checking
private void readObject(ObjectInputStream s)
        throws IOException, ClassNotFoundException {
    s.defaultReadObject();

    // Defensively copy our mutable components
    start = new Date(start.getTime());
    end   = new Date(end.getTime());

    // Check that our invariants are satisfied
    if (start.compareTo(end) > 0)
        throw new InvalidObjectException(start +" after "+ end);
}
```

Note that the defensive copy is performed prior to the validity check and that we did not use Date's clone method to perform the defensive copy. Both of these details are required to protect Period against attack (Item 39). Note also that defensive copying is not possible for final fields. To use the readObject method, we must make the start and end fields nonfinal. This is unfortunate, but it is the lesser of two evils. With the new readObject method in place and the final modifier removed from the start and end fields, the MutablePeriod class is rendered ineffective. The above attack program now generates this output:

```
Wed Apr 02 11:05:47 PDT 2008 - Wed Apr 02 11:05:47 PDT 2008
Wed Apr 02 11:05:47 PDT 2008 - Wed Apr 02 11:05:47 PDT 2008
```

In release 1.4, the `writeUnshared` and `readUnshared` methods were added to `ObjectOutputStream` with the goal of thwarting rogue object reference attacks without the cost of defensive copying [Serialization]. Unfortunately, these methods are vulnerable to sophisticated attacks similar in nature to the `ElvisStealer` attack described in Item 77. **Do not use the `writeUnshared` and `readUnshared` methods.** They are typically faster than defensive copying, but they don't provide the necessary safety guarantee.

Here is a simple litmus test for deciding whether the default `readObject` method is acceptable for a class: would you feel comfortable adding a public constructor that took as parameters the values for each nontransient field in the object and stored the values in the fields with no validation whatsoever? If not, you must provide a `readObject` method, and it must perform all the validity checking and defensive copying that would be required of a constructor. Alternatively, you can use the *serialization proxy pattern* (Item 78).

There is one other similarity between `readObject` methods and constructors, concerning nonfinal serializable classes. A `readObject` method must not invoke an overridable method, directly or indirectly (Item 17). If this rule is violated and the method is overridden, the overriding method will run before the subclass's state has been deserialized. A program failure is likely to result [Bloch05, Puzzle 91].

To summarize, anytime you write a `readObject` method, adopt the mind-set that you are writing a public constructor that must produce a valid instance regardless of what byte stream it is given. Do not assume that the byte stream represents an actual serialized instance. While the examples in this item concern a class that uses the default serialized form, all of the issues that were raised apply equally to classes with custom serialized forms. Here, in summary form, are the guidelines for writing a bulletproof `readObject` method:

- For classes with object reference fields that must remain private, defensively copy each object in such a field. Mutable components of immutable classes fall into this category.

- Check any invariants and throw an `InvalidObjectException` if a check fails. The checks should follow any defensive copying.

- If an entire object graph must be validated after it is deserialized, use the `ObjectInputValidation` interface [JavaSE6, Serialization].

- Do not invoke any overridable methods in the class, directly or indirectly.

Item 77:   For instance control, prefer enum types to readResolve

Item 3 describes the *Singleton* pattern and gives the following example of a single-ton class. This class restricts access to its constructor to ensure that only a single instance is ever created:

```
public class Elvis {
    public static final Elvis INSTANCE = new Elvis();
    private Elvis() { ... }

    public void leaveTheBuilding() { ... }
}
```

As noted in Item 3, this class would no longer be a singleton if the words "implements Serializable" were added to its declaration. It doesn't matter whether the class uses the default serialized form or a custom serialized form (Item 75), nor does it matter whether the class provides an explicit readObject method (Item 76). Any readObject method, whether explicit or default, returns a newly created instance, which will not be the same instance that was created at class initialization time.

The readResolve feature allows you to substitute another instance for the one created by readObject [Serialization, 3.7]. If the class of an object being deserial-ized defines a readResolve method with the proper declaration, this method is invoked on the newly created object after it is deserialized. The object reference returned by this method is then returned in place of the newly created object. In most uses of this feature, no reference to the newly created object is retained, so it immediately becomes eligible for garbage collection.

If the Elvis class is made to implement Serializable, the following readResolve method suffices to guarantee the singleton property:

```
// readResolve for instance control - you can do better!
private Object readResolve() {
    // Return the one true Elvis and let the garbage collector
    // take care of the Elvis impersonator.
    return INSTANCE;
}
```

This method ignores the deserialized object, returning the distinguished Elvis instance that was created when the class was initialized. Therefore, the serialized form of an Elvis instance need not contain any real data; all instance fields should be declared transient. In fact, **if you depend on readResolve for instance**

control, all instance fields with object reference types *must* be declared transient. Otherwise, it is possible for a determined attacker to secure a reference to the deserialized object before its readResolve method is run, using a technique that is vaguely similar to the MutablePeriod attack in Item 76.

The attack is a bit complicated, but the underlying idea is simple. If a singleton contains a nontransient object reference field, the contents of this field will be deserialized before the singleton's readResolve method is run. This allows a carefully crafted stream to "steal" a reference to the originally deserialized singleton at the time the contents of the object reference field are deserialized.

Here's how it works in more detail. First, write a "stealer" class that has both a readResolve method and an instance field that refers to the serialized singleton in which the stealer "hides." In the serialization stream, replace the singleton's nontransient field with an instance of the stealer. You now have a circularity: the singleton contains the stealer and the stealer refers to the singleton.

Because the singleton contains the stealer, the stealer's readResolve method runs first when the singleton is deserialized. As a result, when the stealer's readResolve method runs, its instance field still refers to the partially deserialized (and as yet unresolved) singleton.

The stealer's readResolve method copies the reference from its instance field into a static field, so that the reference can be accessed after the readResolve method runs. The method then returns a value of the correct type for the field in which it's hiding. If it didn't do this, the VM would throw a ClassCastException when the serialization system tried to store the stealer reference into this field.

To make this concrete, consider the following broken singleton:

```
// Broken singleton - has nontransient object reference field!
public class Elvis implements Serializable {
    public static final Elvis INSTANCE = new Elvis();
    private Elvis() { }

    private String[] favoriteSongs =
        { "Hound Dog", "Heartbreak Hotel" };
    public void printFavorites() {
        System.out.println(Arrays.toString(favoriteSongs));
    }

    private Object readResolve() {
        return INSTANCE;
    }
}
```

Here is a "stealer" class, constructed as per the description above:

```
public class ElvisStealer implements Serializable {
    static Elvis impersonator;
    private Elvis payload;

    private Object readResolve() {
        // Save a reference to the "unresolved" Elvis instance
        impersonator = payload;

        // Return object of correct type for favoriteSongs field
        return new String[] { "A Fool Such as I" };
    }
    private static final long serialVersionUID = 0;
}
```

Finally, here is an ugly program that deserializes a handcrafted stream to produce two distinct instances of the flawed singleton. The deserialize method is omitted from this program because it's identical to the one on page 303:

```
public class ElvisImpersonator {
    // Byte stream could not have come from real Elvis instance!
    private static final byte[] serializedForm = new byte[] {
      (byte)0xac, (byte)0xed, 0x00, 0x05, 0x73, 0x72, 0x00, 0x05,
      0x45, 0x6c, 0x76, 0x69, 0x73, (byte)0x84, (byte)0xe6,
      (byte)0x93, 0x33, (byte)0xc3, (byte)0xf4, (byte)0x8b,
      0x32, 0x02, 0x00, 0x01, 0x4c, 0x00, 0x0d, 0x66, 0x61, 0x76,
      0x6f, 0x72, 0x69, 0x74, 0x65, 0x53, 0x6f, 0x6e, 0x67, 0x73,
      0x74, 0x00, 0x12, 0x4c, 0x6a, 0x61, 0x76, 0x61, 0x2f, 0x6c,
      0x61, 0x6e, 0x67, 0x2f, 0x4f, 0x62, 0x6a, 0x65, 0x63, 0x74,
      0x3b, 0x78, 0x70, 0x73, 0x72, 0x00, 0x0c, 0x45, 0x6c, 0x76,
      0x69, 0x73, 0x53, 0x74, 0x65, 0x61, 0x6c, 0x65, 0x72, 0x00,
      0x00, 0x00, 0x00, 0x00, 0x00, 0x00, 0x02, 0x00, 0x01,
      0x4c, 0x00, 0x07, 0x70, 0x61, 0x79, 0x6c, 0x6f, 0x61, 0x64,
      0x74, 0x00, 0x07, 0x4c, 0x45, 0x6c, 0x76, 0x69, 0x73, 0x3b,
      0x78, 0x70, 0x71, 0x00, 0x7e, 0x00, 0x02
    };
    public static void main(String[] args) {
        // Initializes ElvisStealer.impersonator and returns
        // the real Elvis (which is Elvis.INSTANCE)
        Elvis elvis = (Elvis) deserialize(serializedForm);
        Elvis impersonator = ElvisStealer.impersonator;

        elvis.printFavorites();
        impersonator.printFavorites();
    }
}
```

Running this program produces the following output, conclusively proving that it's possible to create two distinct Elvis instances (with different tastes in music):

```
[Hound Dog, Heartbreak Hotel]
[A Fool Such as I]
```

You could fix the problem by declaring the favoriteSongs field transient, but you're better off fixing it by making Elvis a single-element enum type (Item 3). Historically, the readResolve method was used for all serializable instance-controlled classes. As of release 1.5, this is no longer the best way to maintain instance control in a serializable class. As demonstrated by the ElvisStealer attack, this technique is fragile and demands great care.

If instead you write your serializable instance-controlled class as an enum, you get an ironclad guarantee that there can be no instances besides the declared constants. The JVM makes this guarantee, and you can depend on it. It requires no special care on your part. Here's how our Elvis example looks as an enum:

```
// Enum singleton - the preferred approach
public enum Elvis {
    INSTANCE;
    private String[] favoriteSongs =
        { "Hound Dog", "Heartbreak Hotel" };
    public void printFavorites() {
        System.out.println(Arrays.toString(favoriteSongs));
    }
}
```

The use of readResolve for instance control is not obsolete. If you have to write a serializable instance-controlled class whose instances are not known at compile time, you will not be able to represent the class as an enum type.

The accessibility of readResolve is significant. If you place a readResolve method on a final class, it should be private. If you place a readResolve method on a nonfinal class, you must carefully consider its accessibility. If it is private, it will not apply to any subclasses. If it is package-private, it will apply only to subclasses in the same package. If it is protected or public, it will apply to all subclasses that do not override it. If a readResolve method is protected or public and a subclass does not override it, deserializing a serialized subclass instance will produce a superclass instance, which is likely to cause a ClassCastException.

To summarize, you should use enum types to enforce instance control invariants wherever possible. If this is not possible and you need a class to be both serializable and instance-controlled, you must provide a readResolve method and ensure that all of the class's instance fields are either primitive or transient.

Item 78: Consider serialization proxies instead of serialized instances

As mentioned in Item 74 and discussed throughout this chapter, the decision to implement Serializable increases the likelihood of bugs and security problems, because it causes instances to be created using an extralinguistic mechanism in place of ordinary constructors. There is, however, a technique that greatly reduces these risks. This technique is known as the *serialization proxy pattern*.

The serialization proxy pattern is reasonably straightforward. First, design a private static nested class of the serializable class that concisely represents the logical state of an instance of the enclosing class. This nested class, known as the *serialization proxy*, should have a single constructor, whose parameter type is the enclosing class. This constructor merely copies the data from its argument: it need not do any consistency checking or defensive copying. By design, the default serialized form of the serialization proxy is the perfect serialized form of the enclosing class. Both the enclosing class and its serialization proxy must be declared to implement Serializable.

For example, consider the immutable Period class written in Item 39 and made serializable in Item 76. Here is a serialization proxy for this class. Period is so simple that its serialization proxy has exactly the same fields as the class:

```java
// Serialization proxy for Period class
private static class SerializationProxy implements Serializable {
    private final Date start;
    private final Date end;

    SerializationProxy(Period p) {
        this.start = p.start;
        this.end = p.end;
    }

    private static final long serialVersionUID =
        234098243823485285L; // Any number will do (Item 75)
}
```

Next, add the following writeReplace method to the enclosing class. This method can be copied verbatim into any class with a serialization proxy:

```java
// writeReplace method for the serialization proxy pattern
private Object writeReplace() {
    return new SerializationProxy(this);
}
```

The presence of this method causes the serialization system to emit a `Serializa-tionProxy` instance instead of an instance of the enclosing class. In other words, the `writeReplace` method translates an instance of the enclosing class to its serialization proxy prior to serialization.

With this `writeReplace` method in place, the serialization system will never generate a serialized instance of the enclosing class, but an attacker might fabricate one in an attempt to violate the class's invariants. To guarantee that such an attack would fail, merely add this `readObject` method to the enclosing class:

```
// readObject method for the serialization proxy pattern
private void readObject(ObjectInputStream stream)
        throws InvalidObjectException {
    throw new InvalidObjectException("Proxy required");
}
```

Finally, provide a `readResolve` method on the `SerializationProxy` class that returns a logically equivalent instance of the enclosing class. The presence of this method causes the serialization system to translate the serialization proxy back into an instance of the enclosing class upon deserialization.

This `readResolve` method creates an instance of the enclosing class using only its public API, and therein lies the beauty of the pattern. It largely eliminates the extralinguistic character of serialization, because the deserialized instance is created using the same constructors, static factories, and methods as any other instance. This frees you from having to separately ensure that deserialized instances obey the class's invariants. If the class's static factories or constructors establish these invariants, and its instance methods maintain them, you've ensured that the invariants will be maintained by serialization as well.

Here is the `readResolve` method for `Period.SerializationProxy` above:

```
// readResolve method for Period.SerializationProxy
private Object readResolve() {
    return new Period(start, end);  // Uses public constructor
}
```

Like the defensive copying approach (page 306), the serialization proxy approach stops the bogus byte-stream attack (page 303) and the internal field theft attack (page 305) dead in their tracks. Unlike the two previous approaches, this one allows the fields of `Period` to be final, which is required in order for the `Period` class to be truly immutable (Item 15). And unlike the two previous approaches, this one doesn't involve a great deal of thought. You don't have to figure out which fields might be compromised by devious serialization attacks, nor do you have to explicitly perform validity checking as part of deserialization.

There is another way in which the serialization proxy pattern is more powerful than defensive copying. The serialization proxy pattern allows the deserialized instance to have a different class from the originally serialized instance. You might not think that this would be useful in practice, but it is.

Consider the case of EnumSet (Item 32). This class has no public constructors, only static factories. From the client's perspective, they return EnumSet instances, but in fact, they return one of two subclasses, depending on the size of the under-lying enum type (Item 1, page 7). If the underlying enum type has sixty-four or fewer elements, the static factories return a RegularEnumSet; otherwise, they return a JumboEnumSet. Now consider what happens if you serialize an enum set whose enum type has sixty elements, then add five more elements to the enum type, and then deserialize the enum set. It was a RegularEnumSet instance when it was serialized, but it had better be a JumboEnumSet instance once it is deserial-ized. In fact that's exactly what happens, because EnumSet uses the serialization proxy pattern. In case you're curious, here is EnumSet's serialization proxy. It really is this simple:

```java
// EnumSet's serialization proxy
private static class SerializationProxy <E extends Enum<E>>
        implements Serializable {
    // The element type of this enum set.
    private final Class<E> elementType;

    // The elements contained in this enum set.
    private final Enum[] elements;

    SerializationProxy(EnumSet<E> set) {
        elementType = set.elementType;
        elements = set.toArray(EMPTY_ENUM_ARRAY);  // (Item 43)
    }

    private Object readResolve() {
        EnumSet<E> result = EnumSet.noneOf(elementType);
        for (Enum e : elements)
            result.add((E)e);
        return result;
    }
    private static final long serialVersionUID =
        362491234563181265L;
}
```

The serialization proxy pattern has two limitations. It is not compatible with classes that are extendable by their clients (Item 17). Also, it is not compatible with some classes whose object graphs contain circularities: if you attempt to invoke a method on an object from within its serialization proxy's `readResolve` method, you'll get a `ClassCastException`, as you don't have the object yet, only its serialization proxy.

Finally, the added power and safety of the serialization proxy pattern are not free. On my machine, it is 14 percent more expensive to serialize and deserialize `Period` instances with serialization proxies than it is with defensive copying.

In summary, consider the serialization proxy pattern whenever you find yourself having to write a `readObject` or `writeObject` method on a class that is not extendable by its clients. This pattern is perhaps the easiest way to robustly serialize objects with nontrivial invariants.

Items Corresponding to First Edition

First Edition Item Number	Second Edition Item Number, Title
1	1, Consider static factory methods instead of constructors
2	3, Enforce the singleton property with a private constructor or an enum type
3	4, Enforce noninstantiability with a private constructor
4	5, Avoid creating unnecessary objects
5	6, Eliminate obsolete object references
6	7, Avoid finalizers
7	8, Obey the general contract when overriding `equals`
8	9, Always override `hashCode` when you override `equals`
9	10, Always override `toString`
10	11, Override `clone` judiciously
11	12, Consider implementing `Comparable`
12	13, Minimize the accessibility of classes and members
13	15, Minimize mutability
14	16, Favor composition over inheritance
15	17, Design and document for inheritance or else prohibit it
16	18, Prefer interfaces to abstract classes
17	19, Use interfaces only to define types

First Edition Item Number	Second Edition Item Number, Title
18	22, Favor static member classes over nonstatic
19	14, In public classes, use accessor methods, not public fields
20	20, Prefer class hierarchies to tagged classes
21	30, Use enums instead of `int` constants
22	21, Use function objects to represent strategies
23	38, Check parameters for validity
24	39, Make defensive copies when needed
25	40, Design method signatures carefully
26	41, Use overloading judiciously
27	43, Return empty arrays or collections, not nulls
28	44, Write doc comments for all exposed API elements
29	45, Minimize the scope of local variables
30	47, Know and use the libraries
31	48, Avoid `float` and `double` if exact answers are required
32	50, Avoid strings where other types are more appropriate
33	51, Beware the performance of string concatenation
34	52, Refer to objects by their interfaces
35	53, Prefer interfaces to reflection
36	54, Use native methods judiciously
37	55, Optimize judiciously
38	56, Adhere to generally accepted naming conventions
39	57, Use exceptions only for exceptional conditions
40	58, Use checked exceptions for recoverable conditions and runtime exceptions for programming errors
41	59, Avoid unnecessary use of checked exceptions

First Edition Item Number	Second Edition Item Number, Title
42	60, Favor the use of standard exceptions
43	61, Throw exceptions appropriate to the abstraction
44	62, Document all exceptions thrown by each method
45	63, Include failure-capture information in detail messages
46	64, Strive for failure atomicity
47	65, Don't ignore exceptions
48	66, Synchronize access to shared mutable data
49	67, Avoid excessive synchronization
50	69, Prefer concurrency utilities to `wait` and `notify`
51	72, Don't depend on the thread scheduler
52	70, Document thread safety
53	73, Avoid thread groups
54	74, Implement `Serializable` judiciously
55	75, Consider using a custom serialized form
56	76, Write `readObject` methods defensively
57	77, For instance control, prefer enum types to `readResolve` 78, Consider serialization proxies instead of serialized instances

References

[Arnold05]   Arnold, Ken, James Gosling, and David Holmes. *The Java*™ *Programming Language, Fourth Edition.* Addison-Wesley, Boston, 2005. ISBN: 0321349806.

[Asserts]   *Programming with Assertions.* Sun Microsystems. 2002. <http://java.sun.com/javase/6/docs/technotes/guides/language/ assert.html>

[Beck99]   Beck, Kent. *Extreme Programming Explained: Embrace Change.* Addison-Wesley, Reading, MA, 1999. ISBN: 0201616416.

[Beck04]   Beck, Kent. *JUnit Pocket Guide.* O'Reilly Media, Inc., Sebastopol, CA, 2004. ISBN: 0596007434.

[Bloch01]   Bloch, Joshua. *Effective Java*™ *Programming Language Guide.* Addison-Wesley, Boston, 2001. ISBN: 0201310058.

[Bloch05]   Bloch, Joshua, and Neal Gafter. *Java*™ *Puzzlers: Traps, Pitfalls, and Corner Cases.* Addison-Wesley, Boston, 2005. ISBN: 032133678X.

[Bloch06]   Bloch, Joshua. Collections. In *The Java*™ *Tutorial: A Short Course on the Basics, Fourth Edition.* Sharon Zakhour et al. Addison-Wesley, Boston, 2006. ISBN: 0321334205. Pages 293–368. Also available as <http://java.sun.com/docs/books/tutorial/collections/index.html>.

[Bracha04]   Bracha, Gilad. *Generics in the Java Programming Language.* 2004. <http://java.sun.com/j2se/1.5/pdf/generics-tutorial.pdf>

[Burn01]   Burn, Oliver. *Checkstyle*. 2001–2007.
                <http://checkstyle.sourceforge.net>

[Collections]   *The Collections Framework*. Sun Microsystems. March 2006.
                <http://java.sun.com/javase/6/docs/technotes/guides/collections/
                index.html>

[Gafter07]   Gafter, Neal. *A Limitation of Super Type Tokens*. 2007.
                <http://gafter.blogspot.com/2007/05/
                limitation-of-super-type-tokens.html>

[Gamma95]   Gamma, Erich, Richard Helm, Ralph Johnson, and John Vlissides.
                Design Patterns: Elements of Reusable Object-Oriented Software.
                Addison-Wesley, Reading, MA, 1995. ISBN: 0201633612.

[Goetz06]   Goetz, Brian, with Tim Peierls et al. *Java Concurrency in Practice*.
                Addison-Wesley, Boston, 2006. ISBN: 0321349601.

[Gong03]   Gong, Li, Gary Ellison, and Mary Dageforde. *Inside Java*™ *2
                Platform Security, Second Edition*. Addison-Wesley, Boston, 2003.
                ISBN: 0201787911.

[HTML401]   *HTML 4.01 Specification*. World Wide Web Consortium.
                December 1999.
                <http://www.w3.org/TR/1999/REC-html401-19991224/>

[Jackson75]   Jackson, M. A. *Principles of Program Design*. Academic Press,
                London, 1975. ISBN: 0123790506.

[Java5-feat]   *New Features and Enhancements J2SE 5.0*. Sun Microsystems.
                2004.
                <http://java.sun.com/j2se/1.5.0/docs/relnotes/features.html>

[Java6-feat]   *Java*™ *SE 6 Release Notes: Features and Enhancements*. Sun
                Microsystems. 2008.
                <http://java.sun.com/javase/6/webnotes/features.html>

[JavaBeans]   *JavaBeans™ Spec.* Sun Microsystems. March 2001.
                <http://java.sun.com/products/javabeans/docs/spec.html>

[Javadoc-5.0]   *What's New in Javadoc 5.0.* Sun Microsystems. 2004.
                <http://java.sun.com/j2se/1.5.0/docs/guide/javadoc/
                whatsnew-1.5.0.html>

[Javadoc-guide] *How to Write Doc Comments for the Javadoc Tool.* Sun
                Microsystems. 2000–2004.
                <http://java.sun.com/j2se/javadoc/writingdoccomments/
                index.html>

[Javadoc-ref]   *Javadoc Reference Guide.* Sun Microsystems. 2002–2006.
                <http://java.sun.com/javase/6/docs/technotes/tools/solaris/
                javadoc.html>
                <http://java.sun.com/javase/6/docs/technotes/tools/windows/
                javadoc.html>

[JavaSE6]   *Java™ Platform, Standard Edition 6 API Specification.* Sun
                Microsystems. March 2006.
                <http://java.sun.com/javase/6/docs/api/>

[JLS]   Gosling, James, Bill Joy, and Guy Steele, and Gilad Bracha. *The
                Java™ Language Specification, Third Edition.* Addison-Wesley,
                Boston, 2005. ISBN: 0321246780.

[Kahan91]   Kahan, William, and J. W. Thomas. *Augmenting a Programming
                Language with Complex Arithmetic.* UCB/CSD-91-667, University
                of California, Berkeley, 1991.

[Knuth74]   Knuth, Donald. Structured Programming with go to Statements. In
                Computing Surveys 6 (1974): 261–301.

[Langer08]   Langer, Angelika. *Java Generics FAQs — Frequently Asked Ques-
                tions.* 2008.
                <http://www.angelikalanger.com/GenericsFAQ/
                JavaGenericsFAQ.html>

[Lea00]   Lea, Doug. *Concurrent Programming in Java*™*: Design Principles and Patterns, Second Edition*, Addison-Wesley, Boston, 2000. ISBN: 0201310090.

[Lieberman86] Lieberman, Henry. Using Prototypical Objects to Implement Shared Behavior in Object-Oriented Systems. In *Proceedings of the First ACM Conference on Object-Oriented Programming Systems, Languages, and Applications*, pages 214–223, Portland, September 1986. ACM Press.

[Liskov87]   Liskov, B. Data Abstraction and Hierarchy. In *Addendum to the Proceedings of OOPSLA '87* and *SIGPLAN Notices,* Vol. 23, No. 5: 17–34, May 1988.

[Meyers98]   Meyers, Scott. *Effective C++, Second Edition: 50 Specific Ways to Improve Your Programs and Designs*. Addison-Wesley, Reading, MA, 1998. ISBN: 0201924889.

[Naftalin07]   Naftalin, Maurice, and Philip Wadler. *Java Generics and Collections*. O'Reilly Media, Inc., Sebastopol, CA, 2007. ISBN: 0596527756.

[Parnas72]   Parnas, D. L. On the Criteria to Be Used in Decomposing Systems into Modules. In *Communications of the ACM* 15 (1972): 1053–1058.

[Posix]   9945-1:1996 (ISO/IEC) [IEEE/ANSI Std. 1003.1 1995 Edition] Information Technology—Portable Operating System Interface (POSIX)—Part 1: System Application: Program Interface (API) C Language] (ANSI), IEEE Standards Press, ISBN: 1559375736.

[Pugh01]   *The "Double-Checked Locking is Broken" Declaration*. Ed. William Pugh. University of Maryland. March 2001. <http://www.cs.umd.edu/~pugh/java/memoryModel/DoubleCheckedLocking.html>

[Serialization]   *Java*™ *Object Serialization Specification.* Sun Microsystems. March 2005. <http://java.sun.com/javase/6/docs/platform/serialization/spec/serialTOC.html>

[Sestoft05]   Sestoft, Peter. *Java Precisely, Second Edition.* The MIT Press, Cambridge, MA, 2005. ISBN: 0262693259.

[Smith62]   Smith, Robert. Algorithm 116 Complex Division. In *Communications of the ACM*, 5.8 (August 1962): 435.

[Snyder86]   Snyder, Alan. Encapsulation and Inheritance in Object-Oriented Programming Languages. In *Object-Oriented Programming Systems, Languages, and Applications Conference Proceedings*, 38–45, 1986. ACM Press.

[Thomas94]   Thomas, Jim, and Jerome T. Coonen. Issues Regarding Imaginary Types for C and C++. In *The Journal of C Language Translation*, 5.3 (March 1994): 134–138.

[ThreadStop]   *Why Are `Thread.stop`, `Thread.suspend`, `Thread.resume` and `Runtime.runFinalizersOnExit` Deprecated?* Sun Microsystems. 1999. <http://java.sun.com/j2se/1.4.2/docs/guide/misc/threadPrimitiveDeprecation.html>

[Viega01]   Viega, John, and Gary McGraw. *Building Secure Software: How to Avoid Security Problems the Right Way.* Addison-Wesley, Boston, 2001. ISBN: 020172152X.

[W3C-validator]   *W3C Markup Validation Service.* World Wide Web Consortium. 2007. <http://validator.w3.org/>

[Wulf72]   Wulf, W. A Case Against the GOTO. In *Proceedings of the 25th ACM National Conference* 2 (1972): 791–797.

Index

Learn What NOT to Do When Programming with Java

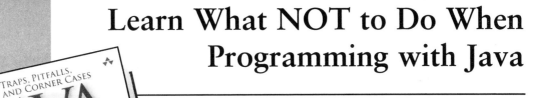

Java™ *Puzzlers*

Joshua Bloch and Neal Gafter

ISBN 978-0-321-33678-1

*"Every programming language has its quirks. This
lively book reveals oddities of the Java programming
language through entertaining and thought provoking
programming puzzles."*

—Guy Steele, Sun Fellow and coauthor of
The Java™ Language Specification

"I laughed, I cried, I threw up (my hands in admiration)."

—Tim Peierls, president, Prior Artisans LLC,
and member of the JSR 166 Expert Group

How well do you really know Java? Are you a code sleuth? Have
you ever spent days chasing a bug caused by a trap or a pitfall in
Java or its libraries? Do you like brainteasers? Then this is the book
for you! In the tradition of *Effective Java*™, Bloch and Gafter dive
deep into the subtleties of the Java programming language and its
core libraries. Illustrated with visually stunning optical illusions,
Java™ *Puzzlers* features 95 diabolical puzzles that educate and
entertain. Anyone with a working knowledge of Java will
understand the puzzles, but even the most seasoned veteran will
find them challenging. Solve these puzzles and you'll never again
fall prey to the counterintuitive or obscure behaviors that can fool
even the most experienced programmers.

Also available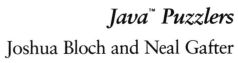

THIS BOOK IS SAFARI ENABLED

INCLUDES FREE 45-DAY ACCESS TO THE ONLINE EDITION

The Safari® Enabled icon on the cover of your favorite technology book means the book is available through Safari Bookshelf. When you buy this book, you get free access to the online edition for 45 days.

Safari Bookshelf is an electronic reference library that lets you easily search thousands of technical books, find code samples, download chapters, and access technical information whenever and wherever you need it.

TO GAIN 45-DAY SAFARI ENABLED ACCESS TO THIS BOOK:

- Go to **informit.com/safarienabled**
- Complete the brief registration form
- Enter the coupon code found in the front of this book on the "Copyright" page

If you have difficulty registering on Safari Bookshelf or accessing the online edition, please e-mail customer-service@safaribooksonline.com.